meet the needs of a pupil, and the headteacher may issue an exclusion, which is the most severe type of punishment. This chapter explains more about suspensions and detentions.

23. Your own welfare

    The famous quote reminds us that we cannot pour from an empty cup; this penultimate chapter encourages us to think of ways we can fill our own cup first to ensure we can keep helping others around us.

24. The importance of a mentor or coach

    This final chapter encourages you to consider mentoring or coaching support on your own pathway or also how you may go forward as a mentor or coach to others in your institution, especially equipped with the guidance you find within this book.

    We hope you enjoy reading this book as much as we enjoyed writing it, and we wish you the very best in supporting your learners on their journeys.

References

Child Poverty Action Group. (2024). *Poverty: Facts and figures | CPAG.* [online] cpag.org.uk. Available at: https://cpag.org.uk/child-poverty/poverty-facts-and-figures.

Department for Education and Skills. (2004). *Every child matters: Change for children in schools.* Nottingham: DES Publications.

NHS. (2022). NHS treating record number of young people for eating disorders. *NHS England.* [online] 7 Mar. Available at: https://www.england.nhs.uk/2022/03/nhs-treating-record-number-of-young-people-for-eating-disorders/.

Marie and Poppy

Thank you to all of the contributors for sharing their reflections and advice:

Dr Sarah Alix, ITT Programme Director, Author and Academic. The Sigma Trust

Leigh Allen, Deputy Headteacher, Edward Jenner School

Professor Jeannette Baxter, Co-Director of A Day of Welcome and Professor of Modern and Contemporary Literature (Anglia Ruskin University, Cambridge).

Emma Bobocea, PhD student, Anglia Ruskin University

Andrew Cowley, Wellbeing author and coach

Sam Crome, Director of Education, Xavier Catholic Education Trust

Dr. Suzie Dick, Lecturer in Education, Queen Margaret University, Edinburgh

Jenny Fogarty, Director of Initial Teacher Training, Anglia Ruskin University

Christina Gabbitas, Author, Coronation Champion, and Honorary Member of the NSPCC Council

Mark Hadley, University of Brighton

Kelsie Lee, Primary Education Graduate, Anglia Ruskin University

Dr Jess Mahdavi-Gladwell, Deputy Head, Robson House

Rachel Olivia O'Brien MSc student at Manchester Metropolitan University

Juliet Oyadoke B.Sc. Childs health, UK

David McBride, Local Education Manager (Novus), HMP Isis

Dr Dave McPartlan University of Cumbria

Paul Portlocksmith, Middle Management Special Education

Nina Preston, BSc(hons), MSc, C.Psychol, CSci, AFBPsS, Clinical Director & Founder of System-isk Psychology Ltd, Consultant Forensic Psychologist

Jocelyn Pryce, Deputy Head, School of Medicine, Anglia Ruskin University

Dr Theresa Redmond, Associate Professor and subject specialist in child sexual abuse and exploitation. The Policing Institute for the Eastern Region, Anglia Ruskin University, UK

Ted Samaras, Instructional Technology Coach, Franklin Township Public Schools, Somerset, NJ, USA

Stephen Scholes, Senior Lecturer in Education, Queen Margaret University, Edinburgh

L.D. Smith, University of Greenwich

It can be a bit like imposter syndrome where I don't feel like I am doing enough or doing the right thing.'

Unpreparedness is linked to stress tolerance (World Health Organisation, 2022). Evidently, my participants demonstrate that teaching is a highly demanding profession which puts the ability to cope with appropriate stress at risk, and according to the Jobs-Demands-Resources model (Bakker and Demerouti, 2007), when demands are high and resources are low, extreme stress is often an outcome and is, therefore, a dependent variable for teacher well-being (Dreer and Gouasé, 2022; Travers, 2017; World Health Organisation, 2022). Despite imposter syndrome not being specifically referred to in Herman et al.'s (2017) study of 121 primary school teachers, my teacher participants' experience with this demonstrates how demands that cause stress through feelings of unpreparedness are linked to lower self-efficacy, job performance, and job satisfaction which Herman et al.'s (2017) study did find.

The participants moved on to explain how their stress inevitably impacts upon the pupils in their classroom:

You rub off their energy and they rub off you.

Specifically, both teachers discussed pupil behaviour as an aspect influenced by their state of well-being. Linking to social contagion theory (Mercer and Gregersen, 2020), one teacher stated that 'if I come in and I am in a good mood and smiling, . . . [the pupils] know that' and, subsequently, agreed that the pupils reflect the same mood they, as the teacher, demonstrates. The teacher also discussed this with another example in a contrasting context:

When I was not very pleased with how they were behaving and I come in grumpy and a bit short with them . . . they . . . [were] very, very quiet. Whereas, usually, they would be asking some questions.
They knew I was not in a good mood.

This might have meant that the pupils were not absorbing the learning as well as they could have been because they refrained from checking their understanding by interacting verbally with their teacher. As a result, misconceptions, if any, would not have been identified by the teacher during their teaching to enable quick correction. Therefore, this shows that when pupils are aware that their teacher is unhappy, they become quieter, supporting the evidence suggesting that teacher enthusiasm fosters a number of pupil outcomes, such as their enjoyment and interest in learning, because when the teacher is unhappy, pupils become more passive during learning (Brigham et al., 1992; Burić, 2019; Frenzel et al., 2009; Patrick et al., 2000). Consequently, a lack of pupil involvement in learning caused by a disengaged teacher could hinder pupils' academic attainment because they refrain from verbally engaging. Therefore, the findings of my study support the fact that pupils respond to their teachers' emotions, proving a reciprocal relationship between teacher well-being and pupil motivation, behaviour, classroom functioning, and educational outcomes (Capone et al., 2019; Field, 2019; Glazzard and Rose, 2020; Madigan and Kim, 2021; Ramberg et al., 2020; Split et al., 2011).

So, how can we promote teacher's well-being at work?

According to the SLT member, a 'reduction of teacher workload to manageable levels is a really big priority in the school'. This explains why both teachers, despite expressing their experiences of stress and overwhelm, mentioned this as an approach that promotes their well-being in school. In particular, the SLT member explains that 'reducing marking' is a way they try to reduce teacher workload. They encourage 'live marking in class as much as possible . . . [and] verbal feedback'. One of the teachers expanded on this strategy with their personal thoughts:

> We . . . have, as teaching staff, a package in terms of we get our PPA time every week which is statutory, we then have some curriculum release time, normally one to two mornings a half-term, which is really good as it is not what other schools necessarily offer.
>
> We also have our PE and music taught for us, so in that time we can use that for whatever we need to, whether that is interventions, or extra PPA, or anything at all – that is our time. Ultimately, you don't actually get to sit down that much because you are normally here, there, and everywhere, but it is extra time for you, which, when I look at my week, that is really nice.

The other teacher participant agreed that 'if I wanted more help . . . the [SLT] would take more of the load for me'. Therefore, support from the SLT appears to be paramount in supporting teacher well-being and, thus, connects with supporting pupil well-being and their educational outcomes (Department for Education, 2021; McCallum and Price, 2016; McCullough, 2015; Rahm and Heise, 2019).

***

Myths

Myth: Talking about our mental health struggles makes things worse.

Truth: There is a misconception that talking about mental health problems exacerbates how we feel. Hopefully, as you have read through this chapter, you have seen the value that comes through us creating inclusive spaces to discuss our mental health and that, in fact, the danger comes when people do not feel able to share how they are feeling with others for fear of judgement.

Myth: The reason we are having a mental health crisis in this country is because we keep encouraging people to talk about their mental health.

Truth: It is correct that we are seeing higher levels of people needing mental health support; however, we do not believe this is a result of speaking up. There are still ripple effects on people's behaviour following the COVID-19 lockdowns during the pandemic, for example, along with issues such as the cost of living crisis in the UK, climate concerns, rising prices, or war and conflict. It may be that as we encourage people to speak up, more people feel able to seek help, and thus, this in itself also contributes to the growing statistics.

Myth:	Children do not understand mental health, and these conversations should be for adults.
Truth:	Children are simply younger people who have not reached adulthood yet. Yes, children have less lived experience and may not be as able to communicate their feelings verbally, but this is perhaps even more reason to help start these conversations earlier in life, to normalise feeling a range of emotions, and develop coping strategies for when we feel sad or angry, or overwhelmed, from an earlier age so that children are better prepared as they navigate their future journeys.

References

Bakker, A.B. and Demerouti, E. (2007). The job demands-resources model: State of the art. *Journal of Managerial Psychology, 22*(3), pp. 309–328. Available at: www.emerald.com/insight/content/doi/10.1108/02683940710733115/full/html

Baumeister, R.F., Campbell, J.D., Krueger, J.I. and Vohs, K.D. (2003). Does high self-esteem cause better performance, interpersonal success, happiness, or healthier lifestyles? *Psychological Science in the Public Interest, 4*(1), pp. 1–44. https://doi.org/10.1111/1529-1006.01431

Berkovich, I. and Eyal, O. (2020). Educational leaders and emotions: An international review of empirical evidence 1992–2019. *Review of Educational Research, 90*(2), pp. 167–210.

Brigham, F.J., Scruggs, T.E. and Mastropieri, M.A. (1992). Teacher enthusiasm in learning disabilities classrooms: Effects on learning and behaviour. *Learning Disabilities Research & Practice, 7*, pp. 68–73.

Burić, I. (2019). The role of emotional labour in explaining teachers' enthusiasm and students' outcomes: A multilevel mediational analysis. *Learning and Individual Differences, 70*, pp. 12–20. https://doi.org/10.1016/j.lindif.2019.01.002

Capone, V., Joshanloo, M. and Park, M.S.A. (2019). Burnout, depression, efficacy beliefs, and work-related variables among school teachers. *International Journal of Educational Research, 95*, pp. 97–108.

Caprara, G.V., Barbaranelli, C., Steca, P. and Malone, P.S. (2006). Teachers' self-efficacy beliefs as determinants of job satisfaction and students' academic achievement: A study at the school level. *Journal of School Psychology, 44*(6), pp. 473–490. https://doi.org/10.1016/j.jsp.2006.09.001

Cherkowski, S. and Walker, K.D. (2018). *Teacher wellbeing: Noticing, nurturing and sustaining flourishing in schools.* Burlington, ON: Word and Deed Publishing.

The Children's Society. (2016). *The good childhood report 2016.* London: The Children's Society. Available at: www.baptist.org.uk/Publisher/File.aspx?ID=178156 [Accessed 7 Dec. 2023].

The Children's Society. (2017). *The good childhood report 2017.* London: The Children's Society. Available at: www.childrenssociety.org.uk/sites/default/files/2023-08/GCR%202017.pdf [Accessed 7 Dec. 2023].

The Children's Society. (2018). *The good childhood report 2018.* London: The Children's Society. Available at: www.researchgate.net/profile/Gwyther-Rees/publication/327338284_The_Good_Childhood_Report_2018/links/5b88f79892851c1e123d4227/The-Good-Childhood-Report-2018.pdf?_tp=eyJjb250ZXh0Ijp7ImZpcnNOUGFnSI6InB1YmxpY2F0aW9uIiwicGFnZSI6InB1YmxpY2F0 aW9uIn19 [Accessed 7 Dec. 2023].

The Children's Society. (2019). *The good childhood report 2019.* London: The Children's Society. Available at: https://saphna.co/wp-content/uploads/2019/11/the_good_childhood_report_2019.pdf [Accessed 7 Dec. 2023].

The Children's Society. (2020). *The good childhood report 2020.* London: The Children's Society. Available at: www.childrenssociety.org.uk/sites/default/files/2020-11/Good-Childhood-Report-2020.pdf [Accessed 7 Dec. 2023].

The Children's Society. (2021). *The good childhood report 2021.* London: The Children's Society. Available at: www.childrenssociety.org.uk/sites/default/files/2021-08/GCR_2021_Full_Report.pdf [Accessed 7 Dec. 2023].

The Children's Society. (2022). *The good childhood report 2022.* London: The Children's Society. Available at: www.childrenssociety.org.uk/sites/default/files/2022-09/GCR-2022-Full-Report.pdf [Accessed 7 Dec. 2023].

Deci, E.L. and Ryan, R.M. (2000). The "what" and "why" of goal pursuits: Human needs and the self-determination of behavior. *Psychological Inquiry,* 11(4), pp. 227–268.

Department for Education. (2021). *The education staff wellbeing Charter.* London: Department for Education. Available at: https://assets.publishing.service.gov.uk/government/uploads/system/uploads/attachment_data/fil e/1034032/DfE_Education_Workforce_Welbeing_Charter_Nov21.pdf [Accessed 1 Dec. 2022].

Department for Education. (2022). *Promoting and supporting mental health and wellbeing in schools and colleges.* London: Department for Education. Available at: www.gov.uk/guidance/mental-health-and-wellbeing-support-in-schools-and-colleges [Accessed 3 Jan. 2024].

Diaz, C.F., Pelletier, C.M. and Provenzo, E.F. (2005). *Touch the future . . . teach!* Boston: Pearson.

Diener, E. and Chan, M.Y. (2011). Happy people live longer: Subjective well-being contributes to health and longevity. *Applied Psychology: Health and Well-Being,* 3(1), pp. 1–43.

Dodd, H.F., Nesbit, R.J. and FitzGibbon, L. (2023). Child's play: Examining the association between time spent playing and child mental health. *Child Psychiatry & Human Development,* 54(6), pp. 1678–1686. Available at: https://link.springer.com/article/10.1007/s10578-022-01363-2

Dreer, B. and Gouasé, N. (2022). Interventions fostering well-being of schoolteachers: A review of research. *Oxford Review of Education,* 48(5), pp. 587–605. https://doi.org/10.1080/03054985.2021.2002290

Duckworth, A.L., Peterson, C., Matthews, M.D. and Kelly, D.R. (2007). Grit: Perseverance and passion for long-term goals. *Journal of Personality and Social Psychology,* 92(6), pp. 1087–1101.

Duckworth, A.L., Quinn, P.D. and Seligman, M.E.P. (2009). Positive predictors of teacher effectiveness. *The Journal of Positive Psychology,* 4(6), pp. 540–547. https://doi.org/10.1080/17439760903157232

Field, J. (2019). *Teacher burnout and student outcomes: Is there a link and are student-teacher relationships a predictor?* Doctoral Thesis. University of Southampton. Available at: https://eprints.soton.ac.uk/437502/ [Accessed 23 Nov. 2022].

Fox, H.B. (2021). *A mixed method item response theory investigation of teacher well-being.* PhD Thesis. The George Washington University. Available at: https://scholarspace.library.gwu.edu/etd/5999n424n

Frenzel, A.C., Goetz, T., Lüdtke, O., Pekrun, R. and Sutton, R.E. (2009). Emotional transmission in the classroom: Exploring the relationship between teacher and student enjoyment. *Journal of Educational Psychology,* 101(3), pp. 705–716. https://doi.org/10.1037/a0014695

Gardner, H.E. and Shulman, L.S. (2005). The professions in America today: Crucial but fragile. *Daedalus,* 134(3), pp. 13–18. https://doi.org/10.1162/0011526054622132

Glazzard, J. and Rose, A. (2020). The impact of teacher well-being and mental health on pupil progress in primary schools. *Journal of Public Mental Health,* 19(4), pp. 349–357. https://doi.org/10.1108/JPMH-02-2019-0023

Goodlad, J. (1990). *Teachers for our nation's schools.* San Francisco: Jossey-Bass.

Goodwin, A.L. (2012). Teaching as a profession: Are we there yet? In C. Day (Ed.), *The Routledge international handbook of teacher and school development* (pp. 44–56). London: Routledge.

GOV.UK. (2023). *Mental health and wellbeing plan: Discussion paper.* Available at: www.gov.uk/government/calls-for-evidence/mental-health-and-wellbeing-plan-discussion-paper-and-call-for-evidence/mental-health-and-wellbeing-plan-discussion-paper#introduction [Accessed 3 Jan. 2024].

Hamre, B.K. and Pianta, R.C. (2004). Self-reported depression in nonfamilial caregivers: Prevalence and associations with caregiver behaviour in child-care settings. *Early Childhood Research Quarterly,* 19(2), pp. 297–318. https://psycnet.apa.org/doi/10.1016/j.ecresq.2004.04.006

Herman, K.C., Hickmon-Rosa, J. and Reinke, W.M. (2017). Empirically derived profiles of teacher stress, burnout, self-efficacy, and coping and associated student outcomes. *Journal of Positive Behaviour Interventions,* 20(2), pp. 90–100. https://doi.org/10.1177/1098300717732066

HM Government. (2021). *Promoting children and young people's mental health and wellbeing: A whole school or college approach.* London: HM Government. Available at: https://assets.publishing.service.gov.uk/government/uploads/system/uploads/attachment_data/file/1020249/Promoting_children_and_young_people_s_mental_health_and_wellbeing.pdf [Accessed 3 Jan. 2024].

Huta, V. and Waterman, A.S. (2014). Eudaimonia and its distinction from hedonia: Developing a classification and terminology for understanding conceptual and operational definitions. *Journal of Happiness Studies,* 15(6), pp. 1426v–1456.

Kristjánsson, K. (2020). Flourishing as the aim of education: Towards a more plausible Aristotelian approach. *Educational Theory*, 70(1), pp. 91–108.

Madigan, D.J. and Kim, L.E. (2021). Does teacher burnout affect students? A systematic review of its association with academic achievement and student-reported outcomes. *International Journal of Educational Research*, 105, pp. 101714.

Malmberg, L.E. and Hagger, H. (2009). Changes in student teachers' agency beliefs during a teacher education year, and relationships with observed classroom quality, and day-to-day experiences. *British Journal of Educational Psychology*, 79(4), pp. 677–694. https://psycnet.apa.org/doi/10.1348/000709909X454814

Martinez, D.M., Desiderio, M.F. and Papakonstantinou, A. (2010). Teaching: A job or a profession? The perceptions of educators. *The Educational Forum*, 74(7), pp. 289–296. https://doi.org/10.1080/00131725.2010.507095

Mazzer, K. and Rickwood, D. (2015). Teachers role breadth and perceived efficacy in supporting student mental health. *Advances in School Mental Health Promotion*, 8(1), pp. 29–41. https://doi.org/10.1080/1754730X.2014.978119

McAdams, D.P. and McLean, K.C. (2013). Narrative identity. *Current Directions in Psychological Science*, 22(3), pp. 233–238.

McCallum, F. (2020). The changing nature of teachers' work and its impact on wellbeing. In M.A. White and F. McCallum (Eds.), *Critical perspectives on teaching, learning and leadership: Enhancing education outcomes* (pp. 17–44). Singapore: Springer.

McCallum, F. and Price, D. (2016). *Nurturing wellbeing development in education: From little things, big things grow.* London: Routledge.

McCullough, M.M. (2015). *Improving elementary teachers' well-being through a strengths-based intervention: A multiple baseline single-case design.* EDS Thesis. University of South Florida. Available at: https://digitalcommons.usf.edu/etd/5990/ [Accessed 17 Nov. 2023].

Mental Health Foundation. (2024). *The most common diagnosed mental health problems: Statistics.* Available at: www.mentalhealth.org.uk/explore-mental-health/statistics/most-common-diagnosed-mental-health-problems-statistics#:~:text=Mixed%20anxiety%20and%20depression%20is,meeting%20the%20criteria%20for%20diagnosis.&text=4%20to%2010%25%20of%20people,experience%20depression%20in%20their%20lifetime

Mercer, S. and Gregersen, T. (2020). *Teacher wellbeing.* Oxford: Oxford University Press.

Miglianico, M., Goyette, N., Dubreuil, P. and Huot, A. (2021). Appreciative inquiry in the classroom: A new model for teacher development. In B. Kutsyuruba, S. Cherkowski and K.D. Walker (Eds.), *Leadership for flourishing in educational contexts* (pp. 243–258). Toronto, Canada: Canadian Scholars.

Mind. (2023). How to improve your mental well-being. *Mind.org.uk.* Available at: www.mind.org.uk/information-support/tips-for-everyday-living/well-being/well-being/

Moberg, J., Skogens, L. and Schön, U.K. (2023). Young people's recovery processes from mental health problems – A scoping review. *Child and Adolescent Mental Health*, 28(3), pp. 393–407. Available at: https://acamh.onlinelibrary.wiley.com/doi/full/10.1111/camh.12594

Moolenaar, N.M. (2010). *Ties with potential: Nature, antecedents, and consequences of social networks in school teams.* PhD Thesis. University of Amsterdam. Available at: https://dare.uva.nl/search?arno.record.id=339484 [Accessed 5 Dec. 2023].

Noddings, N. (2005). *The challenge to care in schools: An alternative approach to education.* New York: Teachers College Press.

Oberle, E. and Schonert-Reichl, K.A. (2016). Stress contagion in the classroom? The link between classroom teacher burnout and morning cortisol in elementary students. *Social Science and Medicine*, 159, pp. 30–37. https://doi.org/10.1016/j.socscimed.2016.04.031

Panchal, U., Salazar de Pablo, G., Franco, M., Moreno, C., Parellada, M., Arango, C. and Fusar-Poli, P. (2023). The impact of COVID-19 lockdown on child and adolescent mental health: Systematic review. *European Child & Adolescent Psychiatry*, 32(7), pp. 1151–1177. Available at: https://link.springer.com/article/10.1007/s00787-021-01856-w

Patrick, B.C., Hisley, J. and Kempler, T. (2000). What's everybody so excited about?: The effects of teacher enthusiasm on student intrinsic motivation and vitality. *The Journal of Experimental Education*, 68(3), pp. 217–236. https://doi.org/10.1080/00220970009600093

Rahm, T. and Heise, E. (2019). Teaching happiness to teachers – Development and evaluation of training in subjective well-being. *Frontiers in Psychology*, 10, p. 2703. https://doi.org/10.3389/fpsyg.2019.02703

Ramberg, J., Låftman, S.B., Åkerstedt, T. and Modin, B. (2020). Teacher stress and students' school well-being: The case of upper secondary schools in Stockholm. *Scandinavian Journal of Educational Research*, 64(6), pp. 816–830.

Roth, G., Assor, A., Kanat-Maymon, Y. and Kaplan, H. (2007). Autonomous motivation for teaching: How self-determined teaching may lead to self-determined learning. *Journal of Educational Psychology*, 99(4), pp. 761–774. https://psycnet.apa.org/doi/10.1037/0022-0663.99.4.761

Seligman, M.E. (2011). *Flourish: A visionary new understanding of happiness and well-being*. New York: Free Press.

Shen, B., McCaughtry, N., Martin, J., Garn, A., Kulik, N. and Fahlman, M. (2015). The relationship between teacher burnout and student motivation. *British Journal of Educational Psychology*, 85(4), pp. 519–532. https://doi.org/10.1111/bjep.12089

Split, J.L., Koomen, H.M.Y. and Thijs, J.T. (2011). Teacher wellbeing: The importance of teacher-student relationships. *Educational Psychology Review*, 23(4), pp. 457–477. https://doi.org/10.1007/s10648-011-9170-y

Tatto, M.T. (2021). Professionalism in teaching and the role of teacher education. *European Journal of Teacher Education*, 44(1), pp. 20–44.

Travers, C. (2017). Current knowledge on the nature, prevalence, sources and potential impact of teacher stress. In T.M. McIntyre, S.E. McIntyre and D.J. Francis (Eds.), *Educator stress: An occupational health perspective* (pp. 23–54). Cham: Springer International Publishing AG.

Waterman, A.S. (2008). Reconsidering happiness: A Eudaimonist's perspective. *The Journal of Positive Psychology*, 3(4), pp. 234–252.

World Health Organisation. (2022). *Constitution*. Available at: www.who.int/about/governance/constitution [Accessed 30 Nov. 2022].

Yeager, D.S. and Dweck, C.S. (2020). What can be learned from growth mindset controversies? *American Psychologist*, 75(9), pp. 1269–1284.

3 Death, loss, and grief

Chapter introduction

This third chapter encourages us to facilitate questions around bereavement, loss and grief sensitively. *How and when should we talk to children about death? What might grief look like, and what strategies can be used to help us when we are grieving?*

This chapter begins with some information around how to talk to children and young people about death and considers how we may feel grief, not just when someone dies, but in the case of the loss of someone in our network through different means such as a change in family situation, adoption, or geographical position, and shares some strategies to support young people who are navigating journeys of grief and loss. The chapter then moves on to include a guest contribution from Jenny Fogarty, Director of Initial Teacher Training, which considers how and when children and young people may encounter death in their environment and why our gentle conversations are vital in supporting them with understanding death and managing any grief they may feel.

How should you talk about death to a child?

The top advice for talking to children and young people about death is just to do it. Do not be afraid to use the word 'died'; say that the animal or person has died. If the child is of primary school age and has a death in their family, ensure you communicate with parents and carers so you know what the child is aware of. When you're talking to a young child about death, the most important thing to consider is your choice of words; language is really important for young children because they don't have full comprehension yet. If you said, 'you've lost someone', a child can literally think that they are lost, like a pet or an object. They might wonder why you don't go and look for them. Explanations such as 'gone to sleep' or 'gone away' may make children frightened to go to sleep or worry that they might not come back when they leave the house.

Use age-appropriate language

When talking about death, a top tip is to focus on the physical body:

> 'When you die you don't need your body anymore. You're not hungry or thirsty, you don't need the toilet, and you don't get cold.'

DOI: 10.4324/9781032697932-3

This can be really reassuring for young children, especially when it comes to explaining a burial or cremation. If a child has not experienced a loss but you want to bring up this topic with them, consider using nature to help – maybe buy a plant or fresh flowers for the classroom. If a child notices that a flower is wilting or changing colour, it's a really great opportunity to explain that the flower has died, and that's what happens to all living things.

Why is it important we talk to them about death?

Talking to a child about death can help them feel better supported and more secure if they do experience a loss. One of the reasons death can be so scary for young children who don't have all of the information is because of their imagination; they might imagine that a person died because of something they said or did or that what happened to that person could also happen to them soon., so even though these conversations will be difficult, especially if you are experiencing a loss yourself, they're really important to have.

What do young children actually understand about death?

It's easy to assume that really young children don't grieve because they don't have a full understanding of what's going on, but even though they don't grieve in the same way that adults do, they can still notice a loss and will have their own way to process that information.

> Universality, the fact that everyone must and will die someday, is usually understood by age six to eight, however other sub-concepts, such as unpredictability – the notion that one can die at any time – and inevitability – that, regardless of what we do to escape death, we can still die – may not come until much later (Mishara, 1999: 105).

Prof Brian L Mishara, PhD, Professor, Psychology Department, Director, Centre for Research and Intervention on Suicide Ethical Issues and End-of-Life Practices (CRISE), University of Quebec at Montreal

Some simple ideas

- The death of a pet or finding a dead animal can be an opportunity to start a conversation about dying. Let the child be there when it is buried, and carry out a ritual like planting flowers.
- Having a class pet (if permissible) can bring this conversation into daily discussion; encourage the children to research not only how to care for the pet but also how long its life span is.
- Memory boxes can be a good way of helping children remember loved ones who have died. These are containers you can create together and fill with photos, letters, and any objects that remind you and your children of the happy times you had with them (or a scrapbook or speak to parents/carers about creating a photobook online at home)

Feelings first aid kit

- One thing I do is talk to children about the idea of a first aid kit. Most children understand the concept of a first aid kit for physical injuries, but we try to create a feelings first aid kit if we are feeling sad at the loss or death of someone. You can talk about feeling sad at loss or death as being called 'grief'. When we are grieving, we can try to find small things to bring us comfort or joy.
- This involves writing a list or putting together a bag of items that help when things are hard after a special person has died.
- A child might choose a bag of sweets and a photograph of the person who has died. Or possibly a teddy bear or some music that can cheer them up. Anything that helps when things are really hard.

Writing a goodbye letter

- Help children and adolescents process their grief using the Goodbye Letter writing exercise. Your pupil will be asked to describe who they are grieving, what their special memories are with that person, and the lessons they have learned from the relationship.
- The goal of this grief activity is to build positive meaning associated with the lost relationship and to begin moving toward closure. This worksheet will be helpful with children and adolescents who have difficulty talking openly about their loss.

Now, Jenny Fogarty shares a deeper dive into why we must not shy away from talking about death with children in the classroom.

Why is death an important topic in the classroom? By Jenny Fogarty, Director of Initial Teacher Training, ARU

To live is to die. It is a fundamental part of the human condition and one of the great mysteries of life that has been pondered on ever since humans have been on the Earth. All the world's major religions make death a rite of passage, marking the loss in some form and providing a space and place for the bereaved to come together to recognise the contribution of the person who has died. Childhood is a time when children learn about all aspects of being human and often question these aspects. They ask puzzling questions to those around them, sometimes in ways that feel unexpected – they have come from nowhere and bear no relation to what is happening at that moment. Often, they become aware of concepts through their peers, television, or other media forms and are naturally inquisitive. As children get older, their experiences change and shape, and they become more aware of the 'right' answers and 'wrong' questions. As teenagers, they are sensitive to taboo subjects and conscious of embarrassment in ways that young children lack awareness of.

The topics of birth, death, and bodily functions appear regularly in the primary classroom. In my own experience as a school leader but primarily a classroom teacher, I would regularly observe conversations with children that their parents might never have heard. Children playing side by side reveal all sorts of insights into their thinking and home life. The types of examples I have observed and overheard include:

> *'My mummy was having a baby, but now she says it's gone away. Where did it go?'*
> *'Nanny is really sick, and she smells funny. I don't like going to see her anymore.'*
> *'Jamie said that when you die, they burn you in a big fire. I don't want that to happen to me!'*

It is a parents', and often teachers', instinct to try and shield children from the unpleasant aspects of life – we want to keep them clean, safe, and away from parts of being human that are upsetting. The topics of death, dying, and loss are often more complex for parents and teachers, depending on their own experiences and responses to them. There is often a broad spectrum of death visibility in the primary classroom that needs to be addressed, varying from the death of a bird on the playground and the fascination attached to seeing it decompose to the profoundly traumatic experiences that, thankfully, a minority of children experience, including parental suicide and violent death. By not having what Dawson et al. (2023) describe as 'sensitive grief education [that] centres on generalised discussions rather than personal experiences' (p2), we are not preparing children with the skills and knowledge to address this in their own life when it happens. The consequences of lack of preparation, acknowledgement, or acceptance of death can be catastrophic (Murray Parkes, 2009), and as teachers, we have a duty to prepare children for all aspects of their adult life, even the challenging ones.

It is necessary to separate discussions of death, dying, and loss with the specialist expertise that is needed to support a child who is recently bereaved effectively. According to the Childhood Bereavement Network (2022) and Parsons (2011), an estimated 1 in 20 children in the UK will experience a significant bereavement during their school years (death of a parent or sibling), and a wide range of specialist bereavement support services are provided by charities and health organisations such as Marie Curie, Cruse, Winston's Wish, and local hospices (Monroe and Krause, 2005). These voluntary support services are crucial, and their resources and expertise provide much-needed guidance at times of family crisis; however, this is separate and distinct from the conversations around loss that teachers need to be able to navigate every day.

The COVID-19 outbreak brought into sharp focus a national conversation around death, with daily death tolls being reported in the news for everyone to discuss, including children and young people, and, although fortunately, most children and young people in England do not experience significant bereavement at a young age, the Coronavirus pandemic resulted in an estimated 139,000 excess deaths in England and Wales between March 2020 and July 2022 (Kings Fund, 2022). As the important bridge between home and school, teachers will inevitably find themselves in the space where questions on this topic are asked, and this can provoke anxiety about knowing what to say.

Gordon (2023) explores the importance of dialogue and communication when discussing bereavement in the classroom, and her assertion to 'just say something' reflects the importance of talking to children and acknowledging the importance of their questions. Fear of not giving the right answer, upsetting the child or parents, or showing their own emotions, often paralyses teachers who decide to move the conversation on. But practising likely questions and possible answers, sharing experiences with other colleagues, and recognising how our own experiences of loss may impact on our ability to respond to children, teachers can begin to break down this taboo in their classrooms.

With an increased focus on loss as part of primary school well-being curriculum, there are more resources available now to support teachers with the teaching of this subject, but the unexpected question relies on teachers using the most fundamental of tools in their toolbox, the strength of the relationship with the child they know well. Acknowledging the question, recognising it may be tricky to answer, thinking aloud together about the answer, and appreciating our own uncertainty on one of life's 'big questions' are all ways of addressing this subject in an age-appropriate way.

Death is around children as they grow up, and with sensitive training to begin initial discussions and support to signpost to the wide variety of specialist services available, teachers can begin to provide meaningful life education on this important subject. As a bereaved child myself, this is an area of education that is scarcely addressed but with huge opportunities for positive impact as loss affects us all.

***

Myths

Myth: We should not talk to children about death as it will upset them.

Truth: If we do not help prepare children to understand death, even if, at an age-appropriate way in the early years, by looking at the death of plants and animals initially, then we are doing them a disservice. Death is the most natural part of life and something that will happen to every single one of us. Avoiding talking about it will not mean it won't happen.

Myth: Grief gets better over time.

Truth: It is true that time can be a great healer, and for some people, grief may improve vastly over time. However, grief is totally subjective, and for some people, it will not improve over time; they may just find ways to distract themselves or develop coping strategies. We must not assume grief is the same for everyone, and this is part of why we should talk to children and young people about death so they see it is alright to speak up about the sadness around grief and loss.

Myth: Talking about death and grief is morbid and dark.

Truth: We should not see talking about death as a dark concept; in fact, helping share ideas for memorials, writing letters to loved ones, or sharing how we keep their memories alive, such as through visiting their favourite places, can be, in fact, a joyful experience that can bring some solace following the death of a person in our lives.

References

Childhood Bereavement Network. (2022). *Key statistics.* Available at: https://childhoodbereavementnetwork.org.uk/about-1/what-we-do/research-evidence/key-statistics [Accessed Feb. 2024].

Dawson, L., Hare, R., Selman, L., Boseley, T., Penny, A. and Adams, J. (2023). *PolicyBristol: Let's talk about death: All children should receive grief education at school.* Available at: www.bristol.ac.uk/policybristol/policy-briefings/grief-education-schools/ [Accessed Feb. 2024].

Gordon, A.L. (2023). Just say something. *BERA Blog.* Available at: www.bera.ac.uk/blog/just-say-something [Accessed Feb. 2024].

Kings Fund. (2022). *Deaths from Covid-19 (coronavirus): How are they counted and what do they show.* Available at: www.kingsfund.org.uk/publications/deaths-covid-19 [Accessed Feb. 2024].

Monroe, B. and Krause, F. (Eds.). (2005). *Brief interventions with bereaved children.* Oxford: Oxford University Press.

Mishara, B.L. (1999). Conceptions of death and suicide in children aged 6-12 and their implications for suicide prevention. *Suicide and Life Threatening Behavior,* 29(2), 105-118.

Murray Parkes, C. (2009). *Love and loss: The roots of grief and its complications* London: Routledge.

Parsons, S. (2011). *Long-term impact of childhood bereavement: Preliminary analysis of the 1970 British Cohort Study (BCS70).* London: Child Well-being Research Centre.

Create a calming atmosphere

Introduce elements that promote relaxation. This could include items like a cozy blanket, a comfortable pillow, or even a photo that brings back happy memories. The goal is to create a safe space within the box.

Write a crisis plan

Include a crisis plan or list of coping strategies for difficult moments. This could be a reminder of alternative activities to try or contact information for support services, friends, or family members.

Regularly update and review

Periodically review the contents of your self-soothe box and update it as needed. As your preferences and needs evolve, the box can evolve with you. Consider adding new items or removing those that no longer bring comfort.

Store in an accessible location

Keep the self-soothe box in an easily accessible location. This ensures that it's readily available during times of distress. Consider having a smaller portable version for when you're on the go.

The ripple effect

Much like the ripple effect I will speak about in the suicide prevention chapter, it is essential to consider the wider impact when someone is self-harming. You may have a few young people in your class going through this, at risk of going through it or recovering. There is evidence that friends and peers offer a source of support, and there is some indication that support from peers can help to delay the act of self-harm or avoid it entirely (Exploring the helpful and unhelpful aspects of online peer support for self harm, n.d.).

However, in my experience, although peers are extremely understanding of each other, we are often told that seeing or hearing about others' self-harm can be 'triggering'. We often speak to young people about keeping wounds covered. You may also need to have some sensitive conversations about who they go to for support if one of their peers is finding it too much.

Harmless ran a study with young people on the benefits and risks of internet support groups and found that the benefits of internet use discussed by participants were:

- Reduced isolation
- Promotion of recovery
- Sense of belonging
- Reduced self-harm

- Reduced distress
- Reduced thoughts of self-harm

However, the most common risks reported were:

- Increased distress
- Increased self-harm
- Increased thoughts of self-harm
- Introduction to new methods of self-harm

(Exploring the helpful and unhelpful aspects of online peer support for self-harm, n.d.)

Accessing support

Various professionals can offer assistance to young individuals who engage in self-harm, including their GP, school nurse, and counselling support. Additionally, helplines are available to provide further support. I have provided a list of helpful resources and sources of support at the end of this chapter.

Digital self-harm

Digital self-harm, also known as self-trolling, self-cyberbullying, or cyber self-harm (2013), can be defined as the act of anonymously posting, sending, or sharing hurtful content about oneself online (Patchin, 2017). Digital self-harm is 'the online communication and activity that leads to, supports, or exacerbates, non-suicidal yet intentional harm or impairment of an individual's physical wellbeing' (Pater and Mynatt, 2017).

It gained global attention in August 2013 when 14-year-old Hannah Smith tragically died by suicide after enduring months of online harassment. Her grieving father called for an investigation into the cyberbullying that may have contributed to her suicide. Shockingly, investigators discovered that Hannah herself had posted the hurtful messages on social media (AIPC, 2019).

One of the most pressing questions surrounding this is the motivation behind it. Why would anyone, particularly a vulnerable teenager with fragile self-esteem, create 'ghost' accounts and secretly direct hurtful comments towards themselves?

Three primary motivations have been identified:

A cry for help: Individuals who already feel lonely, misunderstood, or exhibit symptoms of depression are more inclined to engage in digital self-harm. This is especially true for girls, who often engage in self-trolling as a manifestation of their depression (AIPC, 2019). Some of these teens expressed their reasons as follows: 'Because I already felt bad and just wanted to feel worse' or 'Because I feel sad and wanted attention from others'.

To look cool: Boys sometimes engage in self-bullying online as a form of humour, jokingly making self-deprecating comments. They might say, 'I don't like hurting others, but it's easy to make fun of myself. I was bored and did it to maybe make others laugh as a joke' (AIPC, 2019). It's also suggested that some teens may seek to enhance their social status by portraying themselves as popular enough to attract negative comments from 'haters'.

Triggering compliments: Individuals with low self-esteem or self-doubt may insult themselves anonymously in an attempt to 'fish' for compliments. They hope that their friends will respond with kind words to counteract the negative comments.

Helping someone dealing with digital self-harm is a complex task, as, like other forms of self-harm, it often involves feelings of shame and embarrassment. Support should always be non-judgmental and safe, with an emphasis on building a support network and seeking professional help when necessary.

Myth: Self-harm is just attention-seeking behaviour.

Truth: Self-harming is an extremely personal and private matter, and people who self-harm often make significant efforts to conceal their injuries. The shame associated with self-harm and the difficulty in discussing it often leads to further isolation for individuals, intensifying their challenges in opening up about their experiences.

Myth: Only teenage girls self-harm.

Truth: Although the reported number of boys self-harming is lower than girls, this could be because boys are less likely to seek help. The signs can also present differently, and boys may explain them with reasons associated with macho male culture, such as:

- I got in a fight
- That's from football practice
- We were messing with our pocketknives, and I accidentally got cut
- I wrecked my bike
- I fell off my skateboard

There's no such thing as a typical person who self-harms. It can affect anyone of any gender, age, background, or race.

Myth: It's just a phase.

Truth: Some people self-harm regularly, while others do it sporadically or just once. For some, it's a way of coping with a specific issue, and they discontinue it once that problem is resolved. Others may engage in self-harm for years or in response to particular pressures and challenges.

Resources

Mind's helplines provide information and support by phone and email.

Side by Side is Mind's supportive online community for anyone experiencing a mental health problem.

British Association for Behavioural and Cognitive Psychotherapies (BABCP) babcp.com
gives information about cognitive behavioural therapy and related treatments, including details of accredited therapists.

British Association for Counselling and Psychotherapy (BACP) bacp.co.uk
Professional body for talking therapy and counselling. Provides information and a list of accredited therapists.

Harmless harmless.org.uk
User-led organisation that supports people who self-harm and their friends and family.

Hub of Hope hubofhope.co.uk
UK-wide mental health service database. Lets you search for local, national, peer, community, charity, private, and NHS mental health support. You can filter results to find specific kinds of support.

LifeSIGNS lifesigns.org.uk
User-led self-harm guidance and support network.

The Mix
0808 808 4994
85258 (crisis messenger service, text THEMIX)
themix.org.uk
Support and advice for under 25s, including a helpline, crisis messenger service, and webchat.

National Self Harm Network (NSHN)
nshn.co.uk
Survivor-led online support forum for people who self-harm, their friends and families.

Patient Advice and Liaison Services (PALS)
nhs.uk/common-health-questions/nhs-services-and-treatments/what-is-pals-patient-advice-and-liaison-service
Offers confidential advice, support, and information on health-related matters. You can find services by searching on NHS UK or asking a doctor or healthcare professional for their details.

Samaritans
116 123 (freephone)
jo@samaritans.org
Freepost SAMARITANS LETTERS
samaritans.org
Samaritans are open 24/7 for anyone who needs to talk. You can visit some Samaritans branches in person. Samaritans also have a Welsh Language Line on 0808 164 0123 (7 pm–11 pm every day).

Sane
0300 304 7000
sane.org.uk
Offers emotional support and information for anyone affected by mental health problems, including a helpline.

Self-injury Support
(formerly BCSW – Bristol Crisis Service for Women)
0808 800 8088
0780 047 2908 (text support)
selfinjurysupport.org.uk
Information and support for women and girls affected by self-harm, trauma, and abuse.

UK Council for Psychotherapy (UKCP)
psychotherapy.org.uk
Professional body for the education, training, and accreditation of psychotherapists and psychotherapeutic counsellors. Provides an online register of psychotherapists offering different talking treatments privately.

YoungMinds
0808 802 5544 (Parents Helpline)
85258 (text the word 'shout')
youngminds.org.uk
Provides advice and support to young people for their mental health, as well as supporting parents and carers.

- Concealing or being secretive about their eating habits
- Engaging in excessive physical activity
- Experiencing dizziness or faintness
- Opting for baggy clothing to conceal their body shape
- Feeling consistently cold
- Isolating themselves from social interactions

Orthorexia

Dr. Steven Bratman, MD, introduced the term 'Orthorexia' in 1997, defining it as an unhealthy fixation with consuming 'pure' food. In fact, people restrict their diet based not on the quantity of food they consume but based on its quality. Bratman coined the term 'orthorexia nervosa' to describe people whose extreme diets – intended for health reasons are conversely leading to malnutrition and impairment of daily functioning (Dunn and Bratman, 2016).

Orthorexia involves an obsession with consuming foods deemed 'pure', though perceptions of what constitutes purity can vary among individuals. It's essential to note that adhering to a healthy eating regimen or diet does not necessarily indicate orthorexia. Similar to other eating disorders, such as anorexia, fixating on 'clean' or 'healthy' eating serves as a coping mechanism for managing negative emotions or asserting control. Individuals employing food in this manner may experience significant anxiety or guilt when consuming foods they consider unhealthy.

Orthorexia can lead to physical complications when individuals adhere strictly to their beliefs about what qualifies as healthy, potentially resulting in the exclusion of essential nutrients or entire food groups from their diet. As with all eating disorders, orthorexia is a severe mental illness requiring prompt treatment to optimise the chances of full recovery.

Orthorexia shares similarities with anorexia, and individuals exhibiting symptoms of orthorexia may receive a diagnosis of anorexia if their symptoms align with those of the latter disorder.

Orthorexia can be more difficult to spot as, on a surface level, it may present as a conscientious effort to eat healthy foods. But some of the signs are:

Behavioural indicators

- Eliminating specific foods or food groups from their diet in an attempt to enhance their healthfulness, often progressively restricting more items over time.
- Adapting an existing theory of healthy eating by incorporating additional personal beliefs.
- Experiencing difficulties with concentration.
- Passing judgement on others' eating habits.
- Displaying an obsession with maintaining a healthy or purportedly healthy diet.
- Heightened preoccupation with food choices that may encroach upon other aspects of their life, such as relationships or work.
- Feeling unable to put aside 'rules' about what they can and can't eat, even if they want to.
- Feelings of anxiety, guilt, or uncleanliness if they eat food they regard as unhealthy; in fact, their mood and well-being become dependent on eating the 'right' food.

Bulimia nervosa

People with bulimia might engage in binge-eating episodes, followed by vomiting, excessive exercise, or using laxatives. This behaviour is termed purging and often stems from feelings of guilt about their food intake, concerns about bingeing, or the discomfort in their stomach. Many people with bulimia maintain a 'normal' weight, making it challenging to detect.

Identifiable signs may involve:

- Fluctuations in weight
- Secrecy regarding food consumption
- An increase in exercise beyond typical levels
- Visits to the restroom after meals
- Social isolation
- Skin-related issues
- Scarring on fingers, knuckles, or the back of hands, accompanied by unpleasant breath due to vomiting
- Negative emotions about their body image

Often, when people start vomiting, it may have been an occasional occurrence aimed at regaining control over breaking a diet or exceeding planned food intake. Over time, it likely evolves into a perceived 'safety net' that they can rely on whenever they eat the 'wrong foods' or consume more than intended.

They might have believed that vomiting immediately after eating allows them to eliminate the calories ingested, and this notion might have led them to eat more than they usually would. The habit may then have developed further as they found it easier to vomit with a full stomach. Perhaps they started thinking that even after eating anything, not just during a binge, vomiting could contribute to weight loss, creating a sense of safety in eating.

At this stage, vomiting becomes a habit and integrates into a harmful cycle of (binge) eating and purging.

Dangers of Chronic Vomiting:

Erosion of Tooth Enamel: Chronic vomiting can lead to the erosion of tooth enamel, sometimes requiring tooth replacement.

Swelling of Salivary Glands: The parotid glands may swell, resulting in a 'chipmunk face'.

Damage to the Oesophagus: Tearing and bleeding of the oesophagus can occur.

Electrolyte Imbalance: Serious consequences such as seizures, cardiac arrest, and even death may result from electrolyte imbalance.

Digestive System Disruption: Chronic vomiting can disrupt the digestive system, causing discomfort and triggering the urge to vomit even with small food amounts in the stomach.

Psychological Consequences: Beyond encouraging overeating and distorting hunger cues, vomiting leads to feelings of guilt, shame, anxiety, and depression, contributing to a vicious cycle of binge eating and purging.

Binge eating disorder

People with binge eating disorder frequently engage in regular episodes of excessive food consumption. Bingeing in this context isn't merely consuming slightly more than usual; it often involves consuming several days' worth of food in a single sitting, typically consisting of what is commonly deemed 'unhealthy' food. These binges are frequently premeditated and carried out discreetly. While someone might experience a temporary sense of relief during the binge, feelings of guilt and anxiety usually follow. Coping with these emotions may involve planning the next binge.

Signs

- Secret eating
- Concealing food packaging
- Weight gain
- Significant expenditure on food
- Feeling self-conscious about eating in the presence of others
- Experiencing a decline in confidence and self-esteem
- Voluntarily withdrawing from social interactions
- ARFID (Avoidant/Restrictive Food Intake Disorder)

Avoidant/Restrictive Food Intake Disorder, commonly known as ARFID, is characterised by individuals avoiding certain foods or types of food, restricting their overall food intake, or a combination of both (Priory, 2023).

There are various reasons why someone may avoid or restrict their food intake:

Sensory sensitivity

Some individuals may be highly sensitive to the taste, texture, smell, or appearance of certain foods, or they may only tolerate foods at specific temperatures. This sensitivity can lead to avoidance or restriction of certain foods based on sensory factors.

Research has shown that ARFID and autism frequently coexist, and people with ARFID are more likely to have autism than those who don't struggle with this eating disorder. The BioPsychoSocial Medicine journal estimates that between 12.5% and 33.3% of people with ARFID are also on the autism spectrum, although research in this area is still ongoing (Priory, 2023).

Traumatic experience

Others may have had distressing experiences with food, such as choking, vomiting, or experiencing significant abdominal pain. These experiences can instil fear and anxiety around food, leading to avoidance of specific foods or textures. Some individuals may have general worries about the consequences of eating, which are difficult to articulate and may restrict their intake to what they perceive as 'safe' foods.

Lack of hunger recognition

In some cases, individuals may not recognise hunger cues in the same way as others, or they may have a generally poor appetite. Eating may feel like a chore rather than an enjoyable activity, leading to difficulties in consuming enough food. These individuals may restrict their intake due to a lack of interest in eating.

It's important to note that individuals with ARFID may have one or more of these reasons behind their avoidance or restriction of food intake at any given time. These factors are not mutually exclusive, and ARFID may manifest differently in different individuals, making it an umbrella term that encompasses various difficulties related to food intake.

Other significant aspects of ARFID include its potential negative impact on physical health and psychological well-being. Inadequate food intake can lead to weight loss, failure to thrive in children and young people, and nutritional deficiencies that affect overall health, development, and daily functioning. In severe cases, individuals may require treatment for serious weight loss or nutritional deficiencies, including prescription of nutritional supplements or, in extreme cases, tube feeding.

ARFID can also pose challenges in various aspects of life, including at home, school or college, work, and social settings. It can affect mood, daily functioning, social interactions, and the ability to engage in activities such as going out or going on holiday.

OSFED (Other specified feeding or eating disorder)

Diagnosing anorexia, bulimia, and binge eating disorder involves identifying anticipated behavioural, psychological, and physical symptoms. Occasionally, individuals exhibit symptoms that do not precisely align with any of these specific disorders. In such cases, they might receive a diagnosis of 'other specified feeding or eating disorder' (OSFED).

OSFED constitutes the highest percentage of eating disorders. It can affect individuals of any age, gender, ethnicity, or background and is as severe as anorexia, bulimia, or binge eating disorder. OSFED can either stem from or evolve into another diagnosis, emphasising the importance of providing treatment to those grappling with it, just like individuals facing other eating disorders.

Given that OSFED is an overarching term, those diagnosed may exhibit a diverse array of symptoms. Examples of OSFED include:

- Atypical anorexia: Where all anorexia symptoms are present except for maintaining a 'normal' weight.
- Bulimia nervosa (of low frequency and/or limited duration): Displaying bulimia symptoms with less frequent or shorter binge/purge cycles.
- Binge eating disorder (of low frequency and/or limited duration): Having binge eating disorder symptoms but with less frequent or shorter binging episodes.
- Purging disorder: Engaging in purging behaviours without the typical binge/purge cycles.
- Night eating syndrome: Consuming food excessively at night, either after waking from sleep or after the evening meal.

Similar to other eating disorders, OSFED is a serious mental illness connected not only to food behaviour but also to underlying thoughts and emotions. It may serve as a coping mechanism or a way for individuals to feel in control.

Those with OSFED may conceal their illness, and physical symptoms may not manifest for a considerable time, if at all. Symptoms associated with bulimia, anorexia, or binge eating disorder can be part of OSFED, carrying comparable short-term and long-term risks. Changes in behaviour and emotions are typically the initial signs observed by others, preceding any physical indicators.

Signs of OSFED include

- Excessive focus on or secretive behaviour regarding food
- Self-consciousness while eating in front of others
- Low confidence and self-esteem
- Poor body image
- Irritability and mood swings
- Fatigue
- Social withdrawal
- Feelings of shame, guilt, and anxiety
- Difficulty concentrating

PICA

PICA refers to Pica, the consumption of non-food items devoid of nutritional value, such as paper, soap, paint, chalk, or ice. To receive a diagnosis of pica, the behaviour must persist for at least one month, be unrelated to cultural practices, and be developmentally inappropriate. Typically, it is not diagnosed in children under two years old, as mouthing objects during infancy is common and may inadvertently lead to ingesting non-food substances. Often, PICA remains undetected until medical complications arise, such as metal toxicity, dental damage, or infections.

PICA can affect individuals of any gender or age, although it is more prevalent among children initially. It may coexist with other conditions, including various eating disorders. When PICA behaviour stems from another underlying illness, a separate PICA diagnosis is warranted only if the behaviour necessitates additional clinical attention beyond that provided for the primary illness.

Individuals with PICA usually do not avoid conventional food, potentially receiving adequate nutrients. However, ingestion of certain non-food items can pose significant risks, particularly in large quantities.

The precise etiology of PICA remains unclear, though some researchers have linked it to the nervous system, considering it a learned behaviour or coping mechanism. While deficiencies in specific minerals or vitamins have been observed in some cases, this is not consistently present.

Certain conditions are associated with an increased likelihood of PICA, including:

- Pregnancy
- Iron deficiency anaemia

- Autism
- Intellectual developmental disorders
- Depression
- Obsessive-compulsive disorder and related conditions such as trichotillomania (hair-pulling) and excoriation disorder (skin-picking)
- Schizophrenia

Some substances craved by individuals with PICA can be highly harmful. If ingestion of non-food items occurs, immediate medical assistance should be sought, potentially requiring emergency services.

Possible signs of PICA

- Strong cravings for non-food items
- Consumption of non-food substances
- Physical illness resulting from ingesting harmful substances

Support

This isn't to suggest that you as a teacher or educator will be establishing this with your pupils, but knowing the advice is helpful and the reasons why.

Establishing consistent eating patterns is a crucial aspect of overcoming an eating disorder. Regular eating serves as the cornerstone for fostering positive changes in dietary habits.

Why is regular eating Important?

Adhering to a regular eating routine aids in overcoming an eating disorder by:

Providing structure: Regular eating introduces a sense of structure to your dietary habits, making eating a routine part of daily life.

Facilitating meal and snack consumption: Establishing a routine enables the incorporation of meals and snacks, allowing for modification in food content and portion sizes.

Combating delayed or infrequent eating: Regular eating helps counteract delayed or irregular meal patterns.

Addressing unstructured eating: It mitigates unstructured eating behaviours like grazing.

Preventing binge eating: By avoiding prolonged periods without food, regular eating helps prevent extreme hunger that often leads to binge eating.

Maintaining blood sugar levels: Consistent eating helps stabilise blood sugar levels, reducing feelings of tiredness, dizziness, and irritability.

Sustaining metabolism: Leaving extended gaps between meals can trigger the body's 'starvation mode', slowing metabolism. Regular eating prevents this metabolic slowdown.

Tips for establishing regular eating: To implement a healthier routine, good advice is to try and:

Plan meals: Schedule and plan meals and snacks.

Prioritise eating: Make eating a significant part of the day, potentially taking precedence over other activities.

Avoid skipping meals: Do not skip any meals or snacks.

Limit gaps: Keep intervals between meals/snacks to no more than four hours.

Resist unplanned eating: Refrain from eating between scheduled meals and snacks. Overcoming such urges is possible with awareness and time.

No purging: Choose what to eat but refrain from purging (vomiting or using laxatives).

Carry Snacks.

Drink water: Water is vital for the body's functions, such as nutrient absorption, waste removal, and temperature regulation. Adults are recommended to drink 1.5–2 litres of water daily. Inadequate water intake may lead to dehydration, affecting physical and mental performance, salivary gland function, and increasing the risk of various health issues, including urinary tract and colon cancers.

Treatment information

The Access and Waiting Time Standard for Children and Young People with an Eating Disorder was published in 2015 and applies to children and young people up to the age of 19. The standard states that by 2020, 95% of those referred for assessment or treatment for an eating disorder should receive NICE-approved treatment within one week in urgent cases and four weeks in routine/non-urgent cases. The ability of services to meet this standard has been monitored since 2016 (Shamim, 2015).

Myth: Eating disorders only affect young, white females.

Truth: Eating disorders can affect individuals of any age, gender, race, ethnicity, socio-economic background, and body size. While they are more commonly diagnosed in young females, they can also impact males, older adults, and individuals from diverse cultural backgrounds.

Myth: Eating disorders are primarily about food and weight.

Truth: While food and weight may be outward manifestations of eating disorders, these conditions are complex mental health issues with underlying psychological, emotional, and social factors. Eating disorders often involve distorted body image, low self-esteem, perfectionism, control issues, trauma, and other co-occurring mental health conditions.

Myth: Eating disorders are a choice or a lifestyle.

Truth: Eating disorders are serious mental illnesses with biological, psychological, and environmental factors contributing to their development. They are not simply lifestyle choices, phases, or fads. Eating disorders have severe physical and emotional consequences and require professional treatment, including therapy, medical care, and nutritional support, to address underlying issues and promote recovery.

Resources

(NHS): The NHS provides medical and psychological treatment for eating disorders through specialised services such as Community Eating Disorder Services (CEDS) and Adult Eating Disorder Services (AEDS). Patients can access these services through their GP referral.

Beat: Beat is the UK's leading charity supporting those affected by eating disorders. They offer a Helpline, online support groups, and one-to-one webchat support for individuals with eating disorders, as well as their families and friends. Beat also provides information and resources on its website, including guidance on seeking treatment and recovery.

Eating disorder charities: Various charities in the UK focus on providing support and resources for individuals with eating disorders, such as Anorexia & Bulimia Care (ABC), SEED Eating Disorder Support Services, and Men Get Eating Disorders Too (MGEDT). These organisations offer helplines, support groups, online forums, and educational resources.

Therapy and Counselling Services: Individuals with eating disorders can access therapy and counselling services through private therapists, psychologists, and counsellors specialising in eating disorder treatment. Therapy modalities may include cognitive behavioural therapy (CBT), dialectical behaviour therapy (DBT), interpersonal therapy (IPT), and family therapy.

Community Mental Health Teams (CMHTs): CMHTs provide mental health support in local communities across the UK. They may offer assessments, therapy, and support for individuals with eating disorders, in addition to coordinating care with other healthcare providers.

Online Resources: Several online platforms provide information, resources, and support for individuals with eating disorders, including websites like Mind, Rethink Mental Illness, and NHS Choices. These websites offer articles, self-help tools, and directories to help individuals find local support services.

Support Groups: Peer-led support groups for individuals with eating disorders, such as Overeaters Anonymous (OA) and Anorexics and Bulimics Anonymous (ABA), provide a safe space for sharing experiences, receiving support, and connecting with others on a similar journey.

Recovery Apps: There are various mobile applications available to support individuals in their eating disorder recovery journey, offering tools for self-monitoring, coping strategies, mindfulness exercises, and peer support.

References

Beat. (2021). Statistics for journalists. *Beat*. [online] Available at: www.beateatingdisorders.org.uk/media-centre/eating-disorder-statistics/

Bernie. (2023). Body image: The GEC and THO young people survey. *Innovative Enterprise*. [online] Available at: https://innovativeenterprise.co.uk/2023/10/05/body-image-the-gec-and-tho-young-people-survey/ [Accessed 14 Feb. 2024].

Dunn, T.M. and Bratman, S. (2016). On orthorexia nervosa: A review of the literature and proposed diagnostic criteria. *Eating Behaviors*, 21, pp. 11–17. https://doi.org/10.1016/j.eatbeh.2015.12.006

Pelc, A., Winiarska, M., Polak, E., Godula, J. and Stępień, A.E. (2023). Low self-esteem and life satisfaction as a significant risk factor for eating disorders among adolescents. *Nutrients*, 15(7), pp. 1603–1603. https://doi.org/10.3390/nu15071603

Priory. (2023). *ARFID and autism*. [online] Available at: www.priorygroup.com/blog/arfid-and-autism

Shamim, S. (2015). *Access and waiting time standard for children and young people with an eating disorder commissioning guide*. [online] Available at: www.england.nhs.uk/wp-content/uploads/2015/07/cyp-eating-disorders-access-waiting-time-standard-comm-guid.pdf

6 Suicide prevention and awareness

Quote: 'I just don't see the point anymore'.
'Stigma is vicious and the primary enemy of suicide prevention'.

Suicide is the biggest killer of males and females under 35 in the UK. Read that again. The biggest killer. Recent shocking statistics equate to 4 children aged 10 and above dying a week from suicide. Yet, it isn't on our curriculum. PSHE education became compulsory for all schools in September 2020. This covers Relationships Education at key stages 1 and 2, Relationships and Sex Education (RSE) at key stages 3 and 4, and Health Education from key stages 1 to 4. We talk about sex; we talk about healthy relationships. We talk about safety, including online, drugs, alcohol, and gambling. But at present, there is no statutory obligation to educate our pupils on suicide and suicide prevention. There are discussions underway to include this on the curriculum, so it is my hope that this will change soon.

The Policy Paper: Suicide prevention strategy for England: 2023 to 2028 was published on 11 September 2023 and outlines the visions and aims to prevent self-harm and suicide, including the actions the government and other organisations will take to save lives (Department of Health and Social Care, 2023).

The aim of this cross-government strategy is to bring everybody together around common priorities and set out actions that can be taken to:

- Reduce the suicide rate over the next five years – with initial reductions seen within half this time or sooner
- Improve support for people who have self-harmed
- Improve support for people bereaved by suicide

Priority groups have been identified as those that may need tailored support:

- Children and young people
- Middle-aged men
- People who have self-harmed
- People in contact with mental health services
- People in contact with the justice system

DOI: 10.4324/9781032697932-6

- Autistic people
- Pregnant women and new mothers

One study of deaths by suicide in those under the age of 20 found that 25% had been bereaved (including by suicide), 15% had a mental illness, and 30% had a physical health condition, 6% reported being LGBT or uncertain, and 8% had experience of the care system. People with experience in the care system have been found to be four to five times more likely to attempt suicide in adulthood than their peers (Office for National Statistics, 2023).

Autistic children and young people may be at a higher risk of dying by suicide compared with those who are not autistic. Specific factors that increase the risk of suicide among autistic people include traumatic, painful life experiences, barriers to accessing support, masking and feelings of not belonging. Autistic people also report difficulties in accessing mental health support (Pelton et al., 2020).

Social isolation and loneliness have also been linked to suicidal ideation and behaviour. Studies have found that social isolation was experienced by 15% of under-20-year-olds and 11% of 20-to-24-year-olds who died by suicide, and qualitative research undertaken by the Samaritans found loneliness played a significant role in young people's suicidal thoughts or feelings (Samaritans, n.d.).

Two-thirds of people who die by suicide have not been in contact with mental health services within the previous year.

As part of my work in raising awareness of suicide prevention, I spoke to Tim from 3 Dads Walking. If you haven't heard of 3 Dads Walking, please look them up. The work they do raising awareness is incredible and simply humbling. Their background is that all three, Andy, Tim, and Mike, lost their girls to suicide, and they now campaign to raise awareness and to have it included in the curriculum. Some of the key points that Tim made in our conversation are:

- Suicide doesn't discriminate
- There is a lack of awareness about support
- Too often, suicide support is reactive, for example, brought in after someone has died
- You can have these conversations in gentle, age-appropriate ways
- If you embed help-seeking behaviours in children and young people early, they will grow up knowing it is ok to talk and where to get support
- If we don't teach our pupils and talk to them, they will find information themselves online, and this might not be safe

(*Marie in conversation with Tim from 3 Dads walking*, available on YouTube).

Students are more likely to approach their teacher for support with their mental health than any other professional. Conversely, a survey by Young Minds has shown that 77% of secondary school teachers do not believe they have had sufficient training on children and young people's mental health (YoungMinds, n.d.).

As daunting as it sounds, you are one of the best people to talk to your pupils about this difficult subject. Education professionals see children's emotions and behaviours day-to-day and have an ongoing relationship with them, making them ideally placed to educate, support and respond to concerns. It is more common to speak to a teacher than to seek support from family or friends. Ground-breaking research by the Centre for Economic Performance (CEP) has shown that the influence of individual teachers on pupils' mental health is as significant as their influence on academic test scores. Longitudinal research shows that teachers significantly affect the long-term physical and mental health of their pupils. Children's sense of being valued by their teachers and peers, known as school connectedness, affects rates of substance misuse, early sexual initiation, violence, injury, emotional distress, disordered eating, and suicide. School connectedness is particularly important for vulnerable children as it can compensate for low connectedness in other areas of life (Lowry et al., 2022).

How can we educate and support our pupils and students?

Suicide is everyone's business. This is the key message, and everyone should feel they have the confidence and skills to play their part in this.

Talking about suicide can be difficult for both the student and the educator. It might be that they struggle to put into words how they are feeling, or they might be scared to say. An approach I have used before is to pitch it differently, to focus on 'a friend'. Taking the personal 'I, you' out of it can make it less intense, and pupils may be more likely to talk. As well as this, we often see that pupils with low self-esteem and mental health needs may not listen to advice for themselves, believing they are not worthy of it but will listen on behalf of others.

The next thing to think about is the language we are using. Suicide and suicidal thoughts have historically been shrouded with shame and surrounded by stigma. The phrase 'committed suicide' has been widely used for years, but this suggests a crime has been committed. Suicide hasn't been a crime since 1961. Using the word 'commit' suggests that it is still a crime which perpetuates stigma or the sense that it's a sin.

Sally Spencer-Thomas, Ph.D., one of the premier psychologists working in suicide prevention today, states,

> the litmus test for talking about suicide is to substitute the word 'cancer' for the word 'suicide' to see if the sentence still makes sense or if it has a negative connotation. We wouldn't say 'committed cancer' or 'successful cancer' – we would simply say 'cancer death' or 'died of cancer.' Thus, when it comes to suicide, we should say 'suicide death' or 'died of suicide.'
>
> (Suicide Prevention Alliance, n.d.)

It is recognised that language can help as well as harm. Papyrus talks about 'using sensitive and appropriate language' to 'help build awareness and understanding to increase empathy and support'. Their website holds useful resources which can be downloaded to help start conversations about suicide. However, the Table 6.1 shows unhelpful and helpful language which might be helpful to be aware of:

Table 6.1 Helpful and unhelpful language

Unhelpful language	Why it is unhelpful	Language to use instead (using Papyrus guidance)
Successful suicide	If someone dies by suicide it cannot ever be a success.	Died by suicide Ended their life Took their own life Killed themselves
Commit suicide	Suicide hasn't been a crime since 1961. Using the word 'commit' suggests that it is still a crime which perpetuates stigma or the sense that it's a sin.	Died by suicide Ended their life Took their own life Killed themselves
You're not thinking of doing something stupid/silly, are you?	This suggests that the person's thoughts of suicide is stupid or silly, and/or that the person is him/herself stupid or silly. If asked this question, people are most likely to deny their true feelings for fear of being viewed negatively.	Are you telling me you want to kill yourself/end your life/die/die by suicide? Sometimes, when people are feeling the way you are, they think about suicide. Is that what you're thinking about? It sounds like you're thinking about suicide; is that right?
'Unsuccessful suicide attempt'	This attributes feelings of achievement or failure.	'Suicide attempt'

(CONVERSATION STARTERS, n.d.)

It is important to use careful and accurate language when talking about suicide. When we swap problematic words for neutral and respectful ones, we contribute to changing how society responds to and understands suicide. This helps make discussions about suicide safer.

Know the signs

There can be some signs and indicators that someone is feeling suicidal. The most obvious one is talking about suicide, about killing themselves or wanting to die, even in a jokey way.

However, it may not be as straightforward as this. There are also lots of subtle signs and indicators:

- Talking about feelings of hopelessness, of people being better off without them, or feeling numb
- Sleeping a lot or not sleeping
- Reluctant or evasive about plans for the future or not wanting to commit to things
- Giving their things away, including prized possessions
- Increasing alcohol and drug use

- Taking risks with their own health and safety can also be referred to as indirect suicide
- Suddenly seeming lighter and calmer, this could be due to making a plan or a decision to act on their suicidal thoughts

One of the most important points I can make in this chapter is that **_talking about suicide will not cause someone to act on it_**. Having these important conversations or teaching classes how to recognise possible signs of suicidal thoughts will not cause someone to make a suicide attempt. It will not put ideas into people's heads. But asking, 'Have you been thinking about suicide? Have you made a plan?' are crucial questions to ask when someone is suffering and just needs someone to listen.

Teaching suicide prevention and awareness is crucial, and engaging activities can help ease meaningful discussions and promote understanding. Here are some activity ideas:

Interactive workshops

Conduct interactive workshops that cover the warning signs of suicide, how to speak to someone in crisis, and where to seek help.

Guest speakers

Invite mental health professionals, counsellors, or individuals with personal experiences to share their insights on suicide prevention. This provides students with diverse perspectives and real-world knowledge.

Film or documentary screening

Show films or documentaries that address mental health and suicide prevention. Follow up with discussions to explore the emotions and themes portrayed, allowing students to reflect on the topic.

Art and expression

Encourage artistic expression through activities like creating posters, poetry, or artwork that promotes mental health awareness and resilience. This allows students to express their emotions creatively.

Guest panel discussion

Arrange a panel discussion with mental health experts, survivors, and advocates. This provides an opportunity for students to ask questions and gain deeper insights into the complexities of mental health issues.

Anonymous Q&A sessions

Create a safe space for students to submit questions related to mental health and suicide prevention anonymously. Address these questions during a dedicated session, promoting open and honest dialogue.

Mindfulness and relaxation techniques

Introduce mindfulness and relaxation techniques to help students manage stress and promote mental well-being. Activities such as deep breathing exercises and guided meditation can be beneficial.

Resource scavenger hunt

Organise a resource scavenger hunt where students explore and gather information about local mental health resources, helplines, and support services. This encourages awareness of available help.

Community outreach projects

Engage students in community outreach projects related to mental health. This could involve collaborating with local organisations, taking part in awareness campaigns, or organising events to reduce stigma.

Create a mental health wall

Establish a wall where students can post positive affirmations, messages of support, and resources related to mental health. This serves as a visual reminder of the importance of collective well-being.

Journaling exercises

Introduce journaling exercises that encourage self-reflection on personal well-being. Students can express their feelings, set goals for mental health, and track their emotional journey over time.

Peer support training

Provide training for students to become peer supporters or ambassadors for mental health. Equip them with the skills to offer a listening ear and guide peers toward appropriate resources.

Remember to approach these activities with sensitivity and ensure that students have access to support services if needed. Always be mindful of the potential emotional impact and create a safe and supportive environment for discussions. Remember to reiterate the message: talking about suicide will not put the idea into someone's head.

Individual support and disclosures

If you have concerns that someone might be contemplating suicide, approach the matter directly by asking them openly if they are thinking about suicide. Use clear and specific terms like 'suicide', 'ending your life', or 'taking your own life', avoiding vague expressions such as 'dark thoughts' or 'thoughts of harming yourself'.

Initiating the conversation in a gentle manner with open-ended questions and phrases like 'I'm curious about how you're feeling right now' or 'I've observed that . . .' can help ease into the discussion for both of you.

Addressing the topic directly communicates that talking about it is acceptable, that you're open to hearing them, and that you are a trustworthy person for them to confide in. To prepare for the conversation, you might find it beneficial to practise saying the words aloud on your own.

If you're uncertain about how to approach the conversation, you can refer to the conversation starters provided by Prevention of Young Suicide (Papyrus). Additionally, you can reach out to their Hopeline for assistance, information, and guidance over the phone. They can support you with aspects like preparing for the conversation, processing the discussion afterward, and planning the next steps.

What if your pupil tells you they are thinking about suicide?

The first thing is not to panic.

Give them time and a quiet space to talk to you.

Reassure them. They are not in trouble, and they have not done anything wrong in telling you this or feeling this way.

Contact your DSL and safeguarding team.

Seek support for yourself. I cannot emphasise this step enough.

Postvention and prevention plans

Suicides are tragic and deeply distressing. Suicides are also the leading cause of death in young people (males and females), with around 200 children and young people in the UK dying by suicide each year (Office for National Statistics).

When there is a death by (suspected) suicide, there is likely to be a ripple effect; it is estimated that after a death by suicide, around 135 people are exposed to the suicide (Cerel et al., 2018). People bereaved by suicide can be up to 65% more likely to attempt suicide themselves and are particularly vulnerable. It is therefore important to prevent suicides and the impact of a suicide.

Potential clusters of suicides should be identified at the earliest opportunity, and an early intervention response and effective support for those affected should be put in place. Implementation of this protocol is important in delivering this objective. Other aspects of this work include early identification and data sharing on suicide. When a death by suicide (or suspected suicide) occurs of someone connected to a school/college (student, member of staff, parent, for example), the ripple effect is likely to be even wider. In some parts of the country, this has translated into a cluster or contagion effect where several young people have taken their lives following the death of a friend. This clustering can relate to geography, gender, age grouping, ethnic grouping, and social connections. Exposure to suicide may be a strong predictor of suicidality (Swanson and Colman, 2013). Schools and communities should be aware of an increased risk for at least two years following a suicide event.

The purpose of a policy is to provide guidance and support in effectively responding to and managing the aftermath of a suicide or other traumatic event within the community. The policy aims to promote the emotional well-being of students, staff, parents, and the wider organisation community, while also preventing further harm and promoting resilience. You may be reading this as a member of SLT, in which case, please take this to your team if you don't already have a policy. If you are not SLT, you may wish to raise this with your line manager. Having a clear and cohesive policy in preparation for a devastating event such as this can provide a framework for action at a time when people will be in shock and processing.

Myth:	Talking about suicide will give people ideas to try it.
Truth:	Suicide is a difficult topic to talk about, but evidence shows that asking someone if they're suicidal can, in fact, protect them.
Myth:	If someone self-harms, they are suicidal.
Truth:	Although there is a correlation between self-harm and suicide, it's important to note that engaging in self-harm does not automatically indicate a subsequent suicide attempt.

Studies indicate that individuals who die by suicide often have a history of self-harm. However, self-harm can serve as a coping mechanism rather than a manifestation of suicidal intentions. Consequently, certain individuals may resort to self-harm without undergoing suicidal ideation.

Myth:	People who are suicidal want to die.
Truth:	The majority of people who feel suicidal do not actually want to die; they just want the situation they're in or the way they're feeling to stop and often can't see any other way out. The distinction may seem small, but it is very important. That's why talking through other options and getting support at the right time is so vital.

Resources

There are some excellent resources to support you to identify and work with someone who is, or who may be, feeling suicidal. These are available here:

1.   Papyrus website
2.   MIND website
3.   Samaritans website
4.   Rethink website

Useful contacts and support

Urgent/crisis situation

Help is at Hand
http://supportaftersuicide.org.uk/support-guides/help-is-at-hand/

Help is at Hand provides people affected by suicide with both emotional and practical support. The guide is designed to be given out by bereavement support organisations and by those who are likely to be first on the scene after a suspected suicide, including police and ambulance staff. It will also be widely promoted online through partnerships with coroners, funeral directors, police, doctors, and bereavement counselling and support organisations. Samaritans

www.samaritans.org.uk

Confidential listening ear available 24/7, 365 days a year, via phone, text, email, or face-to-face, for all ages. You don't have to be suicidal to make contact.

MIND

www.mind.org.uk

YoungMinds Crisis Messenger

Provides free, 24/7 crisis support across the UK if you are experiencing a mental health crisis.

- If you need urgent help, text YM to 85258
- All texts are answered by trained volunteers, with support from experienced clinical supervisors
- Texts are free from EE, O2, Vodafone, 3, Virgin Mobile, BT Mobile, GiffGaff, Tesco Mobile and Telecom Plus

Papyrus

www.papyrus-uk.org

National charity for the prevention of young suicides. HOPELineUK is a specialist telephone service staffed by trained professionals who give non-judgemental support, practical advice, and information to:

- Children, teenagers, and young people up to the age of 35 who are worried about how they are feeling
- Anyone who is concerned about a young person

Call: 0800 068 41 41

Email: pat@papyrus-uk.org

SMS: 07786 209697

CALM (Campaign Against Living Miserably)

www.thecalmzone.net

- Offers support to young men in the UK who are down or in a crisis.
- Helpline: 0800 58 58 58 (Daily 17:00-midnight)
- Webchat

Longer-term/follow-up support

Child and Adolescent Mental Health Service (CAMHS)

Children and adolescent mental health services (CAMHS) are made up of specialist teams offering assessment and treatment to children and young people up to age 18 who have emotional, behavioural, or mental health problems.

MindOut Lesbian, Gay, Bisexual, Trans & Queer Mental Health Service

- Offers support, information, and advocacy, including suicide prevention support, to LGBTQ communities.

- 01273 234839
- info@mindout.org.uk

Childline

www.childline.org.uk

If you're under 19, you can confidentially call, email, or chat online about any problem, big or small.

Freephone 24-hour helpline: 0800 1111

Sign up for a ChildLine account on the website to message a counsellor anytime without using your email address.

Chat 1:1 with an online advisor

The Mix

www.themix.org.uk

- If you're under 25, you can talk to The Mix for free on the phone, by email or on their webchat. You can also use their phone counselling service or get more information on the support services you might need.
- Freephone: 0808 808 4994 (13:00–23:00 daily)

Bereavement (by suicide) services/agencies

Survivors of Bereavement by Suicide (SoBS)

http://uk-sobs.org.uk/

Red Lipstick Foundation

As a foundation built from personal experience, Red Lipstick is dedicated to supporting families bereaved by suicide. This is structured, linked, telephone support, and the possibility of one-to-one (depending on location) with other families from all walks of life, at different stages in their journey, who are also experiencing suicide or a sudden young person's bereavement.

Email: theredlipstickfoundation@gmail.com

Cruse Bereavement Care

www.crusebereavementcare.org.uk

References

Cerel, J., Brown, M.M., Maple, M., Singleton, M., van de Venne, J., Moore, M. and Flaherty, C. (2018). How many people are exposed to suicide? Not six. *Suicide Life Threat Behavior*, Apr. 49(2) pp. 529–534. https://doi.org/10.1111/sltb.12450. Epub 2018 Mar 7. PMID: 29512876.

CONVERSATION STARTERS. (n.d.). Available at: https://www.papyrus-uk.org/wp-content/uploads/2018/09/PAPYRUS-Conversation-Starters-2023-DIGITAL.pdf [Accessed 29 Jun. 2024].

Department of Health and Social Care. (2023). Suicide prevention strategy for England: 2023 to 2028. *GOV.UK*. [online] Available at: www.gov.uk/government/publications/suicide-prevention-strategy-for-england-2023-to-2028

Lowry, C., Leonard-Kane, R., Gibbs, B., Muller, L.-M., Peacock, A. and Jani, A. (2022). Teachers: The forgotten health workforce. *Journal of the Royal Society of Medicine*, [online] 115(4), pp. 133–137. https://doi.org/10.1177/01410768221085692

Office for National Statistics. (2023). Suicides in England and Wales – Office for national statistics. www.ons.gov.uk. [online] Available at: www.ons.gov.uk/peoplepopulationandcommunity/birthsdeathsandmarriages/deaths/bulletins/suicidesintheunitedkingdom/2022registrations

Pelton, M.K., Crawford, H., Robertson, A.E., Rodgers, J., Baron-Cohen, S. and Cassidy, S. (2020). Understanding suicide risk in autistic adults: Comparing the interpersonal theory of suicide in autistic and non-autistic samples. *Journal of Autism and Developmental Disorders.*https://doi.org/10.1007/s10803-020-04393-8

Samaritans. (n.d.). *Young people and suicide*. [online] Available at: www.samaritans.org/about-samaritans/research-policy/young-people-suicide/

Suicide Prevention Alliance. (n.d.). *Suicide language*. [online] Available at: www.suicidepreventionalliance.org/about-suicide/suicide-language/#:~:text=According%20to%20Sally%20Spencer%2DThomas [Accessed 14 Feb. 2024].

Swanson, S.A. and Colman, I. (2013). Association between exposure to suicide and suicidality outcomes in youth. *CMAJ*, 9 Jul. 185(10) pp. 870–877. https://doi.org/10.1503/cmaj.121377. Epub 2013 May 21. PMID: 23695600; PMCID: PMC3707992.

www.youtube.com. (n.d.). *Marie in conversation with Tim from 3 Dads walking*. [online] Available at: https://youtu.be/UReJfoYpxow?si=daHFPsVq3fDcsF1_ [Accessed 14 Feb. 2024].

YoungMinds. (n.d.). *New survey finds huge gaps in early mental health support*. [online] Available at: www.youngminds.org.uk/about-us/media-centre/press-releases/huge-gaps-in-early-support-for-young-people-with-mental-health-problems/

7 Bullying

Chapter introduction

Bullying can be loosely defined as behaviour designed to harm, upset, or threaten another, often through verbal or physical abuse. This seventh chapter explores some of the research and literature on the effects of bullying and encourages you to consider ways we can continue to develop inclusive and supportive environments to help combat bullying. Bullying can look different in different contexts and can also include online bullying and cyberbullying, so to help give a fuller picture of how we must work together to foster these safe environments for young people, our staff, several experienced educators, practitioners, and psychologists share their perspectives within this chapter. Thank you to Leigh Allen, Mark Hadley, Dr Dave McPartlan, Nina Preston, Dr Jess Mahdavi-Gladwell, and Rachel O'Brien for telling their stories.

We begin with this overview from Rachel Olivia O'Brien, which helps us understand more about why bullying may happen and what bullying may look like in terms of behaviours and dynamics. Rachel shares how it is through fostering a culture of inclusivity and respect that we can help to reduce bullying behaviours, and Rachel highlights the need to empower bystanders to become allies for the victims of bullying instead.

Understanding and addressing bullying in schools: a guide for educators, by Rachel Olivia O'Brien

Introduction

Bullying persists as a significant challenge in schools, resulting in negative health and educational consequences for students across primary and secondary levels, persisting into adulthood (Armitage, 2021). There is substantial evidence that being bullied as a child or adolescent has a causal relationship to the development of mental health issues, including depression, anxiety, and suicidality, extending into adulthood (Copeland et al., 2013). As educators in critical development stages, primary and secondary school teachers and trainees play a vital role in fostering safe and inclusive learning environments and in the management of classroom bullying (Yoon and Bauman, 2014). Therefore, fostering an understanding and knowledge of bullying within teachers and trainee teachers is highly important (De Luca et al., 2019). Henceforth, this reflection aims to equip teachers and trainee teachers within

DOI: 10.4324/9781032697932-7

primary and secondary education levels with insights into and strategies to combat bullying, enabling educators to address bullying effectively and support their students.

Understanding the dynamics of bullying

On a daily basis, teachers stand at the frontline, dealing with complex behavioural issues amongst children and adolescents, including bullying. In order to effectively identify, intervene, prevent, and combat bullying, it is essential for educators to have considerable knowledge of bullying and its nuanced dynamics and manifestations across primary and secondary school levels (Shamsi et al., 2019). Characterised by repeated victimisation within a power-imbalanced relationship, bullying manifests in various forms, frequencies, and aggression levels, ranging from teasing and name-calling to physical, verbal, and social abuse (Armitage, 2021). Traditional bullying involves typical characteristics such as direct, overt physical, and verbal abuse, including pushing, teasing, and taunting. However, indirect, covert abuse that damages the self-esteem or social status of the victim, such as passing nasty notes and exclusion, is also characteristic of traditional bullying (Rivers and Smith, 1994). While traditional bullying is widely recognised, cyberbullying represents a relatively new phenomenon in which bullying now takes place through digital modalities (Armitage, 2021), specifically mobile phones, the internet, and social media, for instance, the spreading of false stories about a victim online (Slonje and Smith, 2008). Due to the increased potential for larger audiences and anonymous attacks, couples with decreased adult supervision, it is feared that cyberbullying may pose a greater threat to child and adolescent mental health than traditional bullying modalities (Sticca and Perren, 2013). Research findings indicate that more than half of young people have experienced some form of peer victimisation in their lives, with approximately two in five young people reporting a form of bullying in the previous year. Experiences of bullying differ across social groups, with ethnic minority pupils facing significantly more bullying than their majority group peers (Vitoroulis and Vaillancourt, 2015), and pupils with special educational needs and disabilities, as well as LGBTQ plus pupils facing similar bullying disparities (Chatzitheochari et al., 2016; Mitchell et al., 2014). By understanding these dynamics, teachers can identify bullying behaviour and intervene proactively, creating a culture of respect and empathy within their classrooms and schools.

Fostering a culture of inclusivity and respect

Creating a positive classroom climate begins with fostering a culture of inclusivity and respect. Primary and secondary educators must model positive behaviour, promote empathy, and celebrate diversity to cultivate environments where every student feels respected, valued, and supported (Dewsbury and Brame, 2019). By integrating these practices into their classrooms and teaching methods, teachers can empower students to embrace differences, preventing bullying. Research has demonstrated that classroom climate influences the prevalence of bullying behaviours (Bokhove et al., 2022), with one study finding that a positive school climate was related to lower rates of bullying (Cornell et al., 2013).

Integrating social-emotional learning

Social-emotional learning holds significance in addressing bullying at both primary and secondary levels, with studies showing that social-emotional learning prevents and reduces school bullying behaviour (Song and Kim, 2022). Educators can embed social-emotional learning principles into their lessons, teaching students essential skills such as empathy, emotional regulation, and conflict resolution. By nurturing students' social and emotional competencies, teachers equip them with the tools important for social and emotional competence, allowing them to foster increased positive peer interactions and respond resiliently to bullying situations (Husaj, 2016).

Embracing restorative practices

Restorative practices offer a constructive approach to addressing bullying, pivoting on principles of accountability, empathy, and healing (Lodi et al., 2022). At its core, restorative practices aim to repair the harm caused by bullying incidents and restore relationships within the school (Patrizi, 2019). This approach involves restorative circles, or mediation, where all parties affected by the bullying, including the victim and the perpetrator, are given the opportunity to share their perspectives, express their feelings, and collectively determine how to move forward. The process emphasises understanding the impact of one's actions, taking responsibility for harm caused, and collaboratively developing solutions to prevent future bullying occurrences. Through restorative practices, educators create a space for healing, learning, and growth, enabling students to develop empathy, build positive relationships, and contribute to a culture of respect and accountability within the school community. Restorative practices within school settings have been successfully adopted to prevent and manage bullying (Lodi et al., 2022).

Providing individualised support

It is important to recognise that each bullying situation is unique, and teachers must provide personalised support which best meets the need of the pupil/s involved (Department of Education, 2022). Primary and secondary educators can actively monitor for signs of bullying and offer targeted interventions and resources, collaborating with school counsellors and support staff as needed. This support may involve referral to external support services based on the unique needs and circumstances of the student. By taking a proactive and individualised approach, teachers empower students to navigate challenging situations and access the support that they need to thrive.

Empowering bystanders as allies

Bullying involves bystanders, who observe bullying and can assume a range of roles, including 'reinforcers', who provide support to bullies, 'outsiders', who remain uninvolved, and 'defenders', who help or support the bullying victim (Salmivalli et al., 1996). Bystanders possess the potential to intervene and provide an effective transformative change in bullying scenarios, overall having important effects on their peers (Thornberg et al., 2012). Increased 'defender' bystander behaviours have been found to reduce the occurrence of bullying within schools (Polanin et al., 2012). Primary and secondary educators can equip students to become active 'defender' bystanders by imparting strategies for safe intervention and seeking assistance, as well as by providing students with an empathetic classroom environment and teaching students empathy skills via social-emotional learning. By fostering a culture that champions bystander intervention, teachers cultivate the confidence and skills requisite for students to stand up against bullying, as demonstrated by Thornberg et al. (2012), who found that the belief that teachers want bystanders to intervene was reported as a moral reason which motivates bystander intervention.

Adopting a whole-school approach

Addressing bullying necessitates a comprehensive and collaborative effort across the entirety of the school system (Francis et al., 2022). Primary and secondary educators can champion a whole-school approach by advocating for clear anti-bullying policies, engaging in professional development initiatives focused on prevention and intervention, and forging partnerships with families and community stakeholders (Mawila et al., 2023). Through collective action and alignment of efforts, schools can craft a unified strategy to combat bullying effectively, ensuring the holistic well-being and success of all students.

Conclusion

The influence which primary and secondary educators have on their students is profound. Teachers play an important role in their students' lives, shaping their educational landscape and nurturing their growth and development. The influence of teachers is not limited to the space of education but extends into personal life (Malureanu and Enachi-Vasluianu, 2021). By confronting bullying and embracing appropriate, effective support strategies, teachers and trainees play a critical role in managing bullying and cultivating environments where all learners thrive (Shamsi et al., 2019).

***

Next, in this second contribution, Nina Preston, Consultant Forensic Psychologist, BSc(hons), MSc, CPsychol, CSci, AFBPsS, Clinical Director of Systemisk Psychology Ltd, shares a perspective on bullying from a psychological point of view.

Bullying, by Nina Preston

Bullying; an experience of social rejection, intimidation, marginalisation, and humiliation. The impact of which can be as devastating as loss of life or a life lived in a chronic state of fear (complex PTSD). Mental Health practitioners train for many years to be able to manage the complexities of risk to self and others. They have 'safety scaffolding' measures such as supervision, training, policy, and their own well-being counselling to support the 'holding' of such a responsibility in the preservation of life. Is this a responsibility teachers should be expected to have every single day of their careers? No. Teachers, at all levels, do the best job they can possibly do with the level of knowledge and resources available to them in taking action against bullying, but this should not be a burden they carry. It should be the school's culture that holds the responsibility of safety for all. Urgent systemic changes are needed to support pupils, teachers, and schools in creating 'classrooms of community' where the environment and the culture take ownership of every individual's welfare. Here are some insights into why and some hope as to potentially how.

Why does bullying occur in schools?

There are many hypothesises around why bullying occurs. Here is where I land, given it can be applied across many contexts, not just schools. Within an evolutionary context, our very survival as a species is dependent on our sense of belonging to a social group. In early years, this comes from our connection to family through the provision of our attachment needs: feeling safe, being soothed in moments of distress, a sense of security that comes with our caregivers' predictable response to attending to our survival needs, and being seen as an important member of the group to be looked after. If we did not have this sense of belonging to our caregivers, we simply would not survive.

Within adolescence, our attachment survival needs shift from family to peers to support the development of important social and emotional skills that are key to navigating adulthood. Belonging to a peer social group at this age and stage is critical, and within an evolutionary context, it is experienced as extreme as life or death. If you don't find your tribe, you have limited opportunities to access resources or chances to reproduce. Within adulthood, we continue to seek out certainty and security in our social groups in work, at home, and with friends.

Social acceptance, social hierarchy, and a sense of belonging, therefore, matter a great deal to humans. They are factors that are the foundations of our very survival. Social rejection, abandonment, or marginalisation hurts, but at its worst, it results in death, be it from reduced access to resources for survival or, increasingly in modern society, from suicide because the pain connected to these experiences is so intolerable.

Therefore, based on how we are designed, it would make sense for us to create environments that support social inclusion, acceptance, and status for all, particularly at critical ages and stages of development such as childhood and adolescence. Yet often, school systems are designed around competition and hierarchy, which serves to create a culture polar opposite to what we need to feel safe. Some examples include rewards systems that often favour those with existing ability and, therefore, existing status. Negative systems often penalise areas the individual already knows they are struggling in, fostering shame and withdrawal. Public status markers such as head pupils, leadership positions, or sports team selections enhance hierarchy. Detention as a consequence of disruptive behaviour, not recognising these as attempts to self-regulate within an environment that feels unsafe. All innocent decisions to support pupil progress, talent, and learning but inadvertently, along the way, strengthening the hierarchy, and therefore social competition, that exists within the culture of the school. The strong are elevated, supported, and their sense of belonging is cemented within the social group (school community), whilst the remainder is indirectly marginalised, their own strengths and skill-set unrewarded or unrecognised given the structure and intention of schools and the curriculum.

Bullying does not sit within the fault of an individual, be it that teacher or pupil. Children and young people do not want to be mean; no baby is born with the intention to want to cause harm to others. Bullying takes place as a form of communication around the degree of safety felt within the social group in which the bullying is taking place. Without a systemic change to address the inadvertent competitive and hierarchical culture in schools, when it comes to bullying, we are only ever going to be treating the symptom, not the cause.

How can bullying be reduced in schools?

A social group with a collective understanding of each other's strengths and the part each person plays in strengthening the social group has a flattened hierarchy with transient opportunities to step into leadership roles. This is where responsibility for bullying should be held via the culture that everyone creates. Everyone is accountable. Everyone has a part to play in maintaining the safety of the group through compassionate curiosity and active rupture-repair.

We have three flows of compassion: a flow that gives compassion to another, a flow that receives compassion from others, and a flow of compassion inward toward the self. A culture that supports the unblocking of these flows through meaningful rupture-repair processes, over time, enhances the sense of safety and social connectedness of a group, minimising the likelihood of bullying based on the presented hypothesis.

A community rupture-repair (RR) model

The Community RR model is a threat system responsive approach to enhancing the experience of safety states in schools by targeting the blocked flows of compassion. Activities detailed within the Community RR Model should be encouraged following the young person returning to a more regulated state. This is important because the 'thinking brain' goes offline in heightened states of arousal – when a child has tipped out of their window of tolerance – therefore, engagement in the tasks detailed within Table 7.1, should not be expected prior to co-regulation and collaborative grounding occurring in the first instance.

Some co-regulation and grounding techniques to get the young person to return to a more regulated state could include:

- Butterfly hugs
- Soothing rhythm breathing (mirrored by the adult)
- Taking a sip of water and mindfully noticing how it feels in the mouth and when swallowed
- Star-jumps, running on the spot, take a short walk, general movement
- Validating and reassuring statements that big feelings show up sometimes and take us all by surprise
- 5, 4, 3, 2, 1 senses (5 things you can see, 4 things you can hear, 3 things you can touch, 2 things you can smell, 1 thing you can taste)

Table 7.1 Community RR Model: Repair actions that unblock compassionate flows

Flow of compassion	Behavioural response when flow is blocked	Function	Ways to unblock	Ideas
Self to Self: Providing self-compassion to oneself	Self-sabotaging behaviours	To communicate – I am not ok ('I do not feel safe with my own value') Rejecting themselves	Agree to an act that supports compassion inwards towards themselves to support self-worth and reduce experiences of shame.	Write a therapeutic letter to the self-referencing strengths, talents, and positive attributes. Repeat positive affirmations of achievement/effort and then reattempt the task that they 'failed at'/didn't do as expected. 5:1 rule – for every one critical thought/belief, think of five supportive thoughts/beliefs and say to self, 'How would I speak to a friend in this situation?' Write a supportive letter to yourself sharing guidance and understanding of current difficulties.
Self to Others: Providing compassion to others	Disengagement behaviours	To communicate – The world is not ok ('I do not feel safe here') Rejecting the school community	Agree to an action that supports giving compassion towards someone else to repair behavioural responses linked to hurting/disrespecting another and enhance connectivity to the community.	Undertake a task that contributes to the school environment (tidy a classroom cupboard, noticeboard, etc.). Support a teacher or a pupil with a task that relates to the strength of the person experiencing difficulties. Engage in a mediation process. Engage in a mentor role. Engage in a team task – either with other pupils or teachers.
Others to Self: Receiving compassion from others	Disruptive behaviours	To communicate – You are not ok ('I do not feel safe with you') Rejecting the relationship	Agree to an act that supports receiving compassion from someone to assist the child in accepting and experiencing a person's help and kindness.	Engage with someone assisting with homework or classwork (have a mentor help/support). Engage in a team task – either with other pupils or teachers. Engage in activities that are playful or nurturing.

If we work to enhance compassionate cultures in school by unblocking compassion flows, we create 'classrooms of community' where everyone is 'held in mind' and valued within the social group, be that a friendship group, class, or whole school. This model helps facilitate meaningful repairs where there is a responsibility taken by each and every person in the school community to maintain the sense of safety of the group. This is when children will reach their full potential. This is when bullying stops.

***

Thirdly, we have a reflection from a leadership position, with this short, thoughtful contribution from Leigh Allen, Deputy Headteacher, Edward Jenner School.

Bullying in school, by Leigh Allen

It is inevitable that at some point in your career, you will be faced with a conversation about bullying. It may be from a parent directly, or it may be from a middle or senior leader who has been tasked with investigating the said set of circumstances. Bullying is a continued and repeated pattern of behaviours that are unkind, threatening, and intrusive. Experiences of this in today's society are presented as problematic because of the use of social media platforms. Especially a problem in secondary education. But as a whole, young people are so exposed to the internet and all that it has to 'offer'.

It is normal to hear the following set of circumstances:

Said perpetrator/s sent a message, and said victim responds; it is rarely to say, 'please stop'.

Remember, you're managing a teenage brain here. There is a stigma attached to 'blocking' or 'leaving the group chat'. Then said victim becomes distressed, withdrawn, anxious, or one of the many other behaviours associated with not managing conflict. Parents discover messages, memes, images, and the school gets a call. School! Whilst your school will undoubtedly share essential messages and provide parents with tools to support their young people to understand and manage bullying, you will be the person who is so-called 'in charge' of the situation.

So, here it is. Prove it. The best advice is to know your school policy and, as with all of them, follow them to the letter. Log even the smallest detail you might overhear or witness. The tiny things build the bigger picture. Even better advice for today's society is to know where you stand on cyberbullying, where you as a teacher, and where the school that you work in sits in terms of responsibility. You'd be surprised what the DFE states about incidents that happen outside of school hours. A parent will cite all of the previous to you, so always be aware of its context.

There is a thin line between teaching and parental responsibility when it comes to this. It's much easier for a worried parent to seek blame and resolve.

I can assure you that as a parent myself, it is not unusual that all my professional knowledge and rationale disappear when my own child is suffering. The advantage parents have over teachers (who have to cross every metaphorical 't' and dot the same metaphorical 'i' in a tiny window of opportunity) is time to manage a situation without the black cloud of getting it wrong or not meeting the need hanging over them. A teacher doesn't have this. Use this to support the parent you are managing. Help them come up with a plan to build the picture. Use them to guide you and allow you to understand what you might need to be vigilant for in your setting. When, where, who, how, and why. It is the most important thing that a parent/carer feels listened to.

Promote resilience and self-love. Promote and reassure that friends come and go and help young people realise what a friend is. Promote the power to control how others make us feel.

Mostly, look after you and use your support network. Never be afraid to seek more advice. There is so much wealth and experience available. Always.

***

Next, Mark Hadley, Innovation Advisor on the Knowledge Exchange Team from the University of Brighton, shares some teaching experiences on this topic.

The effects of bullying, by Mark Hadley

When we consider the effects of bullying as teachers, I find that sometimes it is rather restricted to a specific child being identified as a bully, and then this label tends to get attached to them throughout their school life. However, there are many instances of bullying, not just one child on another. When I was working in a primary school a few years ago, in the Year 7 class I was looking after, a group of girls all acted collectively to bully some of the other girls who were not part of their group. I often found the child who was bullied crying during playtime, as the collective effect of the group was very traumatic. When I was teaching in a secondary school, there were often a few children who would pick on the children they didn't like, and often this was because they were fat, had a mental health condition, or were not English, and the bullying took many forms, such as stealing their pens, hiding their bag, writing nasty things on their exercise books. We must not leave out some of the practices that teachers and, indeed, schools, because of their management systems, inflict a type of subtle bullying. For example, I was told repeatedly in the secondary school not to allow any children to go to the toilets during a class. Is this right? Should they sit there until they pee themselves, or maybe a girl is menstruating? This is a type of indirect bullying, and I always let the children go to the toilet if they need it; how are they going to concentrate otherwise on their learning process?

The effect of bullying hits the emotional well-being of the children, whoever it may be; they struggle with their feeling of self-worth and feel unaccepted, quite often isolated – leading to them becoming either angry or withdrawing from the class. Sometimes, groups of bullies hang around during breaks, pre- or post-school day, and pick on children. The children subjected to this have huge anxiety and a constant feeling of insecurity, which makes attending school fearful. The effects of individual or group bullying lead to social isolation for the subject child; they may withdraw from any friendships they had and avoid social engagements or after-school events or activities. The effect leads to depression and huge loneliness for some children, who really despair about their school life – the long-term effects lay down emotional scars that persist throughout life for some children. Bullied children will experience other effects, such as loss of appetite or poor sleep at night; the impact of the stress on them leads to other acute healthcare problems the longer it lasts, affecting not just their mental health but their physical well-being. Also, the long-term effects impact the bullied children's learning; they are fearful, so they do not concentrate on the learning process, as they always feel vulnerable. Where the effects are severe, children will not want to go to school and will do anything they can to avoid attendance.

I recall one child who was just like this. He was a pal with one of my boys, but he was so fearful of school attendance that, in the end, his mother had to homeschool the poor boy. Bullied children will miss as much of the school interactions as they can, they will find ways to skip school or truant, and when it's overbearing, they just drop out of school, having huge consequences for the rest of their educational development. Lastly, what are the long-term effects? Bullied children are twice as likely to use mental health services as adults, which is a shocking outcome. We also know that fearful, bullied children will also seek to protect themselves by carrying knives, which can lead to severe consequences if used in any situation and have huge impacts on their lives thereafter. Parents and friends of bullied children need to pick up on the effects that children experience from bullying at an early stage; they need to speak to the school about the negative aspects and get this information to the teachers, which may be able to change things and keep close tabs on those children who are involved in the bullying. How do I know this? Well, at seven years old, I moved from the West Midlands down to Sussex. My accent in schools thereafter made me stand out from the other children, and I was bullied frequently because it didn't sound like them. By the time I went to secondary school, I had adopted a Sussex accent to try and blend in. This did help, but it's not so easy to lose your Brummie accent. Listen to children and let them discuss their fears and concerns – this is essential to deal with this from the bullied perspective.

***

Next, Dr Dave McPartlan, Honorary Researcher at the University of Cumbria, considers the complexity of bullying and questions the 'types' of bullies and bullying and the relationship with identity.

The complexities of bullying in schools, by Dr Dave McPartlan

My 35 years as a teacher saw me follow the pastoral route. During the formative years of my career, I was a form tutor. I then became a Head of Year, followed by what we called a Director of Learning. I finished my teaching career with 12 years as the pastoral assistant headteacher in a large comprehensive academy. Throughout my time in schools, bullying was always high on the list of priorities, and school initiatives were often introduced with the aim of developing strategies to reduce the problems associated with it.

To my mind, there seemed to be three very different categories of bullying in secondary schools. The first and possibly most serious were the clear incidents of victimisation of one individual by another(s). Often random in nature, it could be systematic and frequently traumatic for the victim. Then there were the incidents which were less clear-cut and often resulted from relationship breakdowns. After a fallout, there would be name-calling, peer groups getting involved, and a chaotic situation of accusation and counter-accusation, something which was rarely easy to solve. The final type was where, over a period of time, a young person would come to report bullying incidents from different peers on multiple occasions.

All the different bullying 'types' had their challenges, but the one which caused me the greatest consternation was the final one. I found it difficult to understand how one individual could be the victim of many other young people. These cases had nothing to do with the domino effect of a young person being 'passed on' from one peer group member to another, as sometimes did happen. These were incidents reported by the same person but allegedly committed by different and unconnected individuals, sometimes over several months. Whilst thinking it was strange that one young person could be targeted by unconnected individuals, I confess to wondering whether reports had been made up. How does someone return repeatedly, suggesting they were a victim of others' unpleasantness? At the time, we always took complaints seriously; we often arranged meetings with parents. Despite my uncertainty regarding the legitimacy of the accusations, I would never dismiss them and always try to support the 'victim'.

Many years later, having just completed a PhD investigating the efficacy of a whole school mental health strategy, I am starting to piece together the possible reasons behind the behaviour described in the previous paragraph. My research took place in the school where I taught. Because we believed my previous position may compromise the integrity of the research, the approach we chose was a participative one. I developed an action research project where I collaborated with self-selecting 6th formers who collected data with the younger participants who were volunteers from the Pupil Premium (PP) cohort. This took place during a weekly cycle of meetings over a four-month period.

Also, during this time, my reading drew me to research young people's identity and sense of self and how this can impact their agency to act and their epistemic agency. Epistemic agency is the *ability and motivation to refine and alter one's belief-forming methods and practices* (McPartlan, 2023). As a teacher, I saw this on a daily basis. Young people, often from the PP cohort, did not seem to fit in and were uncomfortable in secondary school. It seemed that the vast majority of them would find the environment challenging. Sometimes, they would rebel and be excluded, but more often than not, they would merge into the background, becoming invisible and often going on to underachieve. Many strategies were attempted to get them to engage, but they rarely worked. I now see they had neither the *'ability nor motivation to alter their belief-forming methods and practices'*.

Agency is also a complex issue; it is not something one possesses (Horgan et al., 2017; Oswell, 2013) but exists in the context of an individual's relationship with others (Oswell, 2013). Agency is created through several factors, including family circumstances, upbringing, and interactions within social institutions such as schools. Young people do not choose their family (Archer, 1995); moreover, 'they are context-dependant relational beings' (Horgan et al., 2017, p.276) who are impacted by the environments in which they live.

Agency, particularly epistemic agency, is linked with a sense of self (Houlders et al., 2021). The following elements are some of those that make up a sense of self and include memory, relationships, bodily awareness, and affect (Houlders et al., 2021). As someone who spent his entire working life teaching young people, I saw first-hand how a sense of self can be enhanced or diminished due to circumstances that have been thrust upon them. Relationships with primary caregivers or friends, personal events, and traumatic life events are just a few examples of how young people's sense of self can be influenced by outside agents (Houlders et al., 2021). In addition, there is also consensus in research that autobiographical narratives are linked to feelings of selfhood (Dennett, 1992; Huttunen and Kakkori, 2002; Stenberg, 2011). Throughout my career, I saw how individuals from diverse backgrounds experienced life differently, impacting their sense of self. This was often communicated through a personal narrative that was also affected by sociological structures, such as schools and interpersonal relationships, and these events and interactions often framed their lives (Houlders et al., 2021). Those young people who live in stable family units and have enough money for food, clothes, heating, and leisure activities are likely to have a more stable sense of self than less advantaged young people.

The young people I write about, who reported multiple incidences of bullying, came from a similar profile to the PP participants in my study. They came from economically disadvantaged backgrounds and the associated challenges that come with this. As I suggested previously, living in poverty is likely to impact these young people, and I am now starting to consider whether their underdeveloped epistemic agency and a weak sense of self may have contributed to their patterns of behaviour around bullying. It was often the case that when we investigated the bullying, it was extremely difficult to come to a conclusion about what had taken place. I would suggest there is a cohort of vulnerable young people who find many aspects of school challenging. They have a poor sense of self and, as such, find the environment difficult to navigate. This can include both how they develop and interpret relationships with their peers. It can often lead to misunderstandings with the possibility that they struggle to decipher social situations and, thus, occasionally, misconstrue signals sent by others.

If there were one thing I could take back to my earlier teaching career, from my PhD, it would be what I have learnt in regards to the development of epistemic agency and how it can impact the sense of self and the performance of young people, particularly those from a disadvantaged background. With the new knowledge I have acquired during my research, I believe that approaches could have been modified to ensure interventions for this cohort could have been more effective. If only I knew then what I know now!

***

Moving on, we must not forget that bullying can take place in online spaces as well as offline. In this final contribution, Dr Jess Mahdavi-Gladwell, CPsychol AFBPsS CTeach MCCT FHEA, shares some strategies for reducing cyberbullying.

Cyberbullying, by Dr Jess Mahdavi-Gladwell

Bullying has been researched and discussed for decades. Prior to becoming a teacher, I did my doctorate in the area of bullying before completing some post-doctoral research looking at cyberbullying, which was a newly emerging phenomenon at the time. Despite being involved in the very earliest days of research in this area, there are things I have learned from being in the classroom.

Taking away phones doesn't solve the problem

Most adults don't want to navigate their working week or social life without access to technology, and neither do our young people. If reports of cyberbullying are met with a removal of technology, then the outcome will be that adults don't find out about our young people's experiences of cyberbullying.

Even if access to phones or devices is prevented, someone can experience the negative impact of cyberbullying even if they don't have access to a device. Though initially, this may sound ridiculous, if unkind messages are being shared about someone, the individual's inability to access them doesn't mean that the messages don't exist or that they have no impact. Knowing others in a group are seeing and discussing negative posts impacts the child both directly in terms of how they feel and also in terms of their interactions with other members of the group.

Things change faster than it's possible to keep up

Smith et al. (2008) identified seven types of cyberbullying. By 2010, Rivers and Noret had identified ten subtypes of text messages which were described as abusive. At the time both these studies were written, Social Media did not exist in the form we currently know it. Though some of the types identified by Smith and colleagues are unlikely to be within the cultural reference of young people today (e.g., chatroom bullying), platforms such as TikTok weren't yet thought of. Whatever pre-emptive or responsive measures schools put in place, however thorough and well-considered anti-bullying policies are, the rapid developments in technology mean there will regularly be times when policy and practice are playing catch up.

The newness impacts adults' ability to teach the social use of technology

The fast pace of technology development means that adults are learning at the same time as (or perhaps after) the young people we serve. None of us learned to access the platforms available today as adolescents. When we access these platforms as adults, we don't have the same experiences as young people, and this can make it difficult to empathise with their feelings and experience, particularly when something which seems trivial to adults is of vital importance to children and young people. It is difficult for those we teach to have a sense of adults having subject-specific expertise in this area, and so would they give us the same credence as when listening to us explain (for example) the process of mummification, learning which hasn't developed in our lifetimes?

It's really difficult not to be able to 'fix' something instantly

Anti-bullying work is a long game. Research into programmes to address and reduce bullying began in the 1980s and continues, adapting in response to increased understanding and knowledge (e.g. Olweus, 2013; Chicote-Beato et al., 2024). As teachers, the desire to teach, to remove barriers to learning, and to respond to needs means that not being able to find a quick fix can be challenging. This challenge can leave us feeling deskilled and frustrated at the impact that cyberbullying might have on academic performance and, indeed, the future of those we teach. Aside from the potential impact on academic progress and attainment, it's difficult to see children and young people distressed, whether that is as a result of direct experience of cyberbullying, from seeing a friend or peer experience cyberbullying, or seeing a young person experiencing levels of distress which mean that their response is to engage in cyberbullying others. The need to sit alongside a young person who is distressed, knowing that there isn't an immediate solution to that distress, and still doing our best to support, mitigate, and care is a professional challenge faced by teachers every day.

***

Myth: Bullying will often stop on its own.

Truth: Bullying often does not stop on its own without intervention, and as a result, bullying can continue over an extended period of time and sometimes escalate as the bully feels more powerful over the victim as time passes without any consequence and lack of support in tackling the underlying needs of the behaviours.

Myth: The best thing for a victim of bullying to do is to just ignore the bully.

Truth: Ignoring bullies may work in some situations, but the best thing is to encourage both victims and bystanders to speak up and speak out when they witness – or are subject to – unfair and unkind behaviours. This can reduce the power of the bully within the bullying relationship and can mean that interventions can be sought, as well as help and support for the bully who may be exhibiting these behaviours due to their own neglect or abuse in their home environment, for example.

Myth: Bullying usually involves verbal teasing or physical harm.

Truth: Bullying can look like a range of behaviours, and with the injection and integration of technology into our lives, children and young people now have to navigate online spaces where they may be bullied or 'trolled'. Bullying can also involve threats and blackmail, especially in these online spaces where images may be sent.

References

Archer, M. (1995). *Realist social theory; the morphogenetic approach.* Cambridge: Cambridge University Press.

Armitage, R. (2021). Bullying in children: Impact on child health. *BMJ Paediatrics Open,* 5(1). http://doi.org/10.1136/bmjpo-2020-000939

Bokhove, C., Muijs, D. and Downey, C. (2022). The influence of school climate and achievement on bullying: Comparative evidence from international large-scale assessment data. *Educational Research,* 64(1), pp. 18–40. https://doi.org/10.1080/00131881.2021.1992294

Chatzitheochari, S., Parsons, S. and Platt, L. (2016). Doubly disadvantages? Bullying experiences among disabled children and young people in England. *Sociology,* 50(4), pp. 695–713. https://doi.org/10.1177/0038038515574813

Chicote-Beato, M., González-Víllora, S., Bodoque-Osma, A.R. and Olivas, R.N. (2024). Cyberbullying intervention and prevention programmes in primary education (6 to 12 years): A systematic review. *Aggression and Violent Behavior,* p. 101938.

Copeland, W.E., Wolke, D. and Angold, A. (2013). Adult psychiatric outcomes of bullying and being bullied by peers in childhood and adolescence. *JAMA Psychiatry,* 70(4), pp. 419–426. http://doi.org/10.1001/jamapsychiatry.2013.504

Cornell, D., Gregory, A., Huang, F. and Fan, X. (2013). Perceived prevalence of teasing and bullying predicts high school dropout rates. *Journal of Educational Psychology,* 105(1), pp. 138–149. https://psycnet.apa.org/doi/10.1037/a0030416

De Luca, L., Nocentini, A. and Menesini, E. (2019). The teacher's role in preventing bullying. *Frontiers in Educational Psychology,* 10. https://doi.org/10.3389%2Ffpsyg.2019.01830

Dennett, D.C. (1992). The self as a centre of narrative gravity. In D. Kessel, F. Cole and P. Johnson (Eds.), *Self and consciousness: Multiple perspectives* (pp. 67–83). https://doi.org/10.5209/rev-ASEM.2013.v46.42862

Department of Education. (2022). *Effective responses to bullying behaviour.*http://niopa.qub.ac.uk/handle/NIOPA/14739

Dewsbury, B. and Brame, C.J. (2019). Inclusive teaching. *CBE Life Sciences Education,* 18(2). https://doi.org/10.1187/cbe.19-01-0021

Francis, J., Trapp, G., Pearce, N., Burns, S. and Cross, D. (2022). School built environments and bullying behaviour: A conceptual model based on qualitative interviews. *International Journal of Environmental Research and Public Health,* 19(23). http://doi.org/10.3390/ijerph192315955

Horgan, D., Forde, C., Martin, S. and Parkes, A. (2017). Children's participation: Moving from the performative to the social. *Children's Geographies,* 15, pp. 274–288.

Houlders, J.W., Bortolotti, L. and Broome, M.R. (2021). Threats to epistemic agency in young people with unusual experiences and beliefs. *Synthese.* https://doi.org/10.1007/s11229-021-03133-4

Husaj, S. (2016). Social Emotional Learning (SEL). *European Journal of Multidisciplinary Studies,* 1(3). https://doi.org/10.26417/ejms.v1i3.p168-171

Huttunen, R. and Kakkori, L. (2002). The hermeneutics of truth and selfhood – Heidegger's, Gadamer's and Ricouer's significance in the autobiographical research. (Dec. 2016). https://doi.org/10.1080/14733285.2016.1219022

Lodi, E., Perrella, L., Lepri, G.L., Scarpa, M.L. and Patrizi, P. (2022). Use of restorative justice and restorative practices at school: A systematic literature review. *International Journal of Environmental Research and Public Health,* 19(1). https://doi.org/10.3390/ijerph19010096

Malureanu, F. and Enachi-Vasluianu, L. (2021). Teachers' influence on students in their lifelong development. *Society Integration Education Proceedings of the International Scientific Conference,* 2, pp. 340–347. http://doi.org/10.17770/sie2021vol2.6213

Mawila, D., Munongi, L. and Mabaso, N. (2023). Student teachers' preparedness to raise awareness about bullying among grade R learners. *South African Journal of Childhood Education,* 13(1). Johannesburg, South Africa. https://doi.org/10.4102/sajce.v13i1.1230

McPartlan, D. (2023). *Young researchers in schools: A participative action research study into the efficacy of a whole school mental health strategy.* University of Cumbria. Available at: https://insight.cumbria.ac.uk/id/eprint/7274

Mitchell, M., Gray, M. and Beninger, K. (2014). Tackling homophobic, biphobic and transphobic bullying among school-age children and young people. *Evidence Review and Typology of Initiatives.* London: NatCen.

Olweus, D. (2013). Bully/victim problems among schoolchildren: Basic facts and effects of a school based intervention program. In *The development and treatment of childhood aggression* (pp. 411–448). Toronto, Canada: Psychology Press.

Oswell, D. (2013). *The agency of children: From family to global human rights.* Cambridge: Cambridge University Press.

Patrizi, P. (2019). La giustizia riparativa. In *Psicologia e Diritto per il Benessere di Persone e Comunità.* Rome: Carocci.

Polanin, J.R., Espelage, D.L. and Pigott, T.D. (2012). A meta-analysis of school-based bullying prevention programs' effects on bystander intervention behavior. *School Psychology Review,* 41(1), pp. 47–65. https://doi.org/10.1080/02796015.2012.12087375

Rivers, I. and Noret, N. (2010). 'I h8 u': Findings from a five-year study of text and email bullying, *British Educational Research Journal,* 36(4), pp. 643–671.

Rivers, I. and Smith, P.K. (1994). Types of bullying behaviour and their correlates. *Aggressive Behavior,* 20(5), pp. 359–368. https://doi.org/10.1002/1098-2337(1994)20:5%3C359::AID-AB2480200503%3E3.0.CO;2-J

Salmivalli, C., Lagerspetz, K., Björkqvist, K., Österman, K. and Kaukiainen, A. (1996). Bullying as a group process: Participant roles and their relations to social status within the group. *Aggressive Behavior,* 22(1), pp. 1–15. https://doi.org/10.1002/(SICI)1098-2337(1996)22:1%3C1::AID-AB1%3E3.0.CO;2-T

Shamsi, N.I., Andrades, M. and Ashraf, H. (2019). Bullying in school children: How much do teachers know? *Journal of Family Medicine and Primary Care,* 8(7), pp. 2395–2400. https://doi.org/10.4103%2Fjfmpc.jfmpc_370_19

Slonje, R. and Smith, P.K. (2008). Cyberbullying: Another main type of bullying? *Scandinavian Journal of Psychology,* 49(2), pp. 147–154. https://doi.org/10.1111/j.1467-9450.2007.00611.x

Smith, P.K. et al. (2008). Cyberbullying: Its nature and impact in secondary school pupils, *Journal of Child Psychology and Psychiatry, and Allied Disciplines,* 49(4), pp. 376–385.

Song, Y.-M. and Kim, S. (2022). Effects of a social and emotional competence enhancement program for adolescents who bully: A quasi-experimental design. *International Journal of Environmental Research and Public Health,* 19(12). https://doi.org/10.3390/ijerph19127339

Stenberg, K. (2011). *Working with identities – Promoting student teachers' professional development.* Available at: https://helda.helsinki.fi/bitstream/handle/10138/24379/Workingw.pdf?sequence=1

Sticca, F. and Perren, S. (2013). Is cyberbullying worse than traditional bullying? Examining the differential roles of medium, publicity, and anonymity for the perceived severity of bullying. *Journal of Youth and Adolescence,* 42(5), pp. 739–750. https://doi.org/10.1007/s10964-012-9867-3

Thornberg, R., Tenenbaum, L., Varjas, K., Meyers, J., Jungert, T. and Vanegas, G. (2012). Bystander motivation in bullying incidents: To intervene or not to intervene? *The Western Journal of Emergency Medicine,* 13(3), pp. 247–252. https://doi.org/10.5811%2Fwestjem.2012.3.11792

Vitoroulis, I. and Vaillancourt, T. (2015). Meta-analytic results of ethnic group differences in peer victimization. *Aggressive Behavior,* 41(2), pp. 149–170. https://doi.org/10.1002/ab.21564

Yoon, J. and Bauman, S. (2014). Teachers: A critical but overlooked component of bullying prevention and intervention. *Theory into Practice,* 53(4), pp. 308–314. http://doi.org/10.1080/00405841.2014.947226

8 Special educational needs and disabilities (SEND)

Quote: 'It's frustrating when a teacher just doesn't get why I'm struggling in class, like I'm speaking a different language and they're not even trying to learn it'.

Special educational needs and disabilities (SEND) can affect a child or young person's ability to learn. They can affect their:

- Behaviour or ability to socialise
- Reading and writing
- Ability to understand things
- Concentration levels
- Physical ability

(GOV.UK, 2012)

I have been privileged to work with pupils with SEND for the entirety of my career, over 20 years now. I am passionate about the foundational principles upon which education should be based: recognition of diversity, acknowledgment of students' rights, and the understanding that effective teaching can enable all students to learn. Every student is entitled to receive quality teaching and actively participate in the school community, as outlined in international agreements such as the UN Convention on the Rights of the Child (1989) and education legislation in the UK, including the Equality Act (2010) and the Children and Families Act (2014). I also believe strongly in ambition for each and every student, regardless of need, with the accommodations and adjustments that allow this to be realised.

The Government's SEND and AP plan is based on the principles that:

- Needs should be met in mainstream education
- Needs should be met earlier
- This will result in reduced requirements for EHCPs

(Department for Education, 2023)

The SEND Code of Practice 0–25 is explicit in stating that the quality of teaching for students with Special Educational Needs (SEN) and their progress should be integral to the school's

DOI: 10.4324/9781032697932-8

performance management processes and its approach to professional development for all teaching and support staff (Department for Education, 2014).

Equality: This means offering the same rights and opportunities to all people.

Equity: This means offering those rights and opportunities fairly, which means catering to people's differences so they are given fair access to the opportunities.

Diversity: This is understanding that each person is unique. It means embracing the range of human differences, including people's beliefs, abilities, preferences, backgrounds, values, and identities.

Inclusion is an extension of all these things. It means that all people, without exception, have the right to be included, respected, and appreciated as valuable members of the community.

To put this into an educational context:

Picture a school where a teacher sends out a school-wide announcement and invites all students to participate in a club meeting. This is inclusion because everyone in the school community is given the opportunity to join.

Several students accept the invitation, and during the meeting, the teacher asks each student, in turn, to share their thoughts on the upcoming project. This reflects equality since every student is given the same chance to contribute to the discussion.

Now, imagine a student in the group who has a learning disability and requires additional support to engage in the discussion fully. In this case, the teacher demonstrates equity by providing the student with the necessary resources or accommodations, such as extra time or specific learning materials, ensuring they have equal access to participate. Individualised support options are valuable tools when they bridge access gaps for students, and lessons designed to anticipate and address diverse needs from the outset represent the ideal form of inclusivity.

Moving on to diversity, consider the various ideas and perspectives shared during the meeting. Students contribute different thoughts and approaches to the project without anyone considering it unusual. The diversity in their ideas is embraced, and no one makes comments or thinks anything of the differences – it's simply appreciated as a natural part of the collaborative learning environment.

Balancing access and engagement

The foundations of a truly inclusive education rest upon two pillars: access and engagement. Access guarantees that every student, regardless of background or identity, can enter the classroom doors. This encompasses policies and structures that ensure free attendance for all, dismantling barriers based on age, gender, ethnicity, socioeconomic status, ability, health, or language. However, simply attending school isn't enough. For inclusion to flourish, engagement becomes paramount. Engagement focuses on the quality of the learning experience. It necessitates relevant, meaningful, and empowering lessons that foster personal growth and academic success. This dimension translates to pedagogical practices and curriculum design that effectively cater to diverse needs and learning styles.

The two concepts are linked. Without access, even the most engaging curriculum remains out of reach. Conversely, if students enter the classroom but disengage from the learning process, physical presence translates to only minimal benefit. Achieving both necessitates a nurturing school culture that upholds high standards for every student, fostering a belief in their individual potential.

Key policies

Now that we have set the groundwork for SEND, let's introduce you to some key provisions and policies for pupils with SEND in the UK. At the heart of our approach is the belief that all children should be safe, happy, accepted, and recognised for their strengths, and interventions should be planned using a strength-based approach.

SEND code of practice 0-25

The SEND Code of Practice provides statutory guidance for organisations that work with and support children and young people with SEND. It covers the age range from birth to 25 and sets out the processes and procedures that schools, local authorities, and other agencies should follow to meet the needs of students with SEND. According to the Code of Practice, 'a child or young person has SEN if they have a learning difficulty or disability' that calls for 'provision that is additional to or different from that made generally for other children or young people of the same age by mainstream schools.'

Education, Health, and Care (EHC) plans

The EHCP is a key component of the SEND system in the UK. It replaces the Statement of Special Educational Needs and is a legally binding document that outlines the specific support and provision that a child or young person with SEND requires. EHCPs are designed to support individuals up to the age of 25.

Local offer

Local authorities are required to publish a Local Offer, which is a comprehensive guide to the support and services available for children and young people with SEND in a particular area. This includes information about education, health, and social care services.

Inclusive education

The UK promotes the principle of inclusive education, emphasising that children with SEND should, wherever possible, be educated in mainstream schools. Schools are expected to make reasonable adjustments to accommodate the needs of all students.

SEN support

Schools are required to provide special educational provisions for children with SEND through a system known as SEN Support. This involves identifying the needs of the child, planning appropriate support, and reviewing progress regularly.

Annual reviews

For students with an EHCP, there is a legal requirement for an annual review to assess the child or young person's progress and the effectiveness of the support provided and to make any necessary changes to the plan.

Disability discrimination legislation

The Equality Act 2010 in the UK includes provisions related to disability discrimination, ensuring that children and young people with disabilities, including those with SEND, are protected from discrimination in education.

The definition is set out in section 6 of the Equality Act 2010. It is someone defined as having a disability if they have a physical or mental impairment, and that impairment has a substantial and long-term adverse effect on their ability to do normal day-to-day activities.

Parental involvement

The involvement of parents in the decision-making process and their collaboration with schools and local authorities is emphasised to ensure that the needs of the child are properly understood and addressed (Inclusive Provision for Students with Special Educational Needs and/or Disabilities A Resourced Provision Toolkit, n.d.).

It's important to stay informed about the latest updates and revisions to the SEND Code of Practice and related policies by referring to official government publications and guidance from the Department for Education in the UK.

In our area, we also have access to SEN Matters, a key publication in promoting awareness and signposting schools to available resources, including an SEN support line for educators, conferences, training, and SEN support guidance. It also recommends publishing the Parent Guide to SEND on your school or college website (sen.hias.hants.gov.uk, n.d.).

Undiagnosed SEND needs and pupils without an EHCP

Children with special educational needs (SEND) who do not possess an Education, Health, and Care Plan (EHCP) are entitled to receive support while attending school. Here's a breakdown of the assistance available:

School responsibilities

Identification and assessment

Schools are responsible for identifying children with SEND and evaluating their requirements, often involving collaboration with parents and professionals.

SEN Support: Following the assessment, schools should offer 'SEN Support,' which encompasses various interventions and adjustments to facilitate the child's learning and participation, including:

- Tailoring lessons and materials to suit the child's needs
- Providing individual or small group support from a teacher or teaching assistant

- Making modifications to assessments and exams for fairness
- Supplying specialised equipment or software to aid learning
- Maintaining regular communication with parents regarding the child's progress and support

Planning and review

Schools should devise a 'Support Plan' detailing specific interventions and goals for the child, which should be regularly reviewed and shared with parents. If the SEN Support proves ineffective, the school should consider revising the plan or initiating an EHC needs assessment.

Additional resources

Parents retain the right to request an EHC needs assessment at any point, which can be arranged through the Local Authority (LA). Independent advice and support organisations such as IPSEA and SENDIAS can offer assistance in navigating the process and understanding the child's rights.

Important points to consider

Even in the absence of an EHCP, schools are legally obligated to make reasonable adjustments for children with SEND. The level and nature of support will vary depending on the individual needs of the child.

Supporting SEND in your classroom

The SEND Code of Practice groups needs into four broad areas to support schools to plan the provision that they offer:

- Cognition and learning
- Communication and interaction
- Social, emotional, and mental health
- Sensory and physical needs

Thinking about these basic needs is a good starting point, but to make a real impact, we need to delve deeper and really understand each child. Educators should grasp the unique aspects of each student's needs and how these connect to the classroom atmosphere and the subjects they're teaching. A child with a physical disability might also have a learning disability, but that doesn't mean the physical needs cause the learning challenges. The whole idea of Special Educational Needs and Disabilities (SEND) is shifting our focus from just looking at a condition or diagnosis to understanding each student's unique learning needs. The big question isn't, 'What works for kids with dyslexia?' It's more like, 'What does this specific student need to shine?'

Differentiation in the classroom

Use effective scaffolding to aid the learning of students, fostering independent learning skills.

- Provide individualised resources to facilitate learning
- Encourage students to engage in collaborative learning with their peers, promoting mutual learning experiences
- Incorporate visual aids to support learning
- Collaborate with staff to share expertise and best practices within the classroom environment
- Learning Support Assistants (LSAs) can offer support to students

Collaborating with parents and carers is really important:

- It establishes a unified approach bridging home and school
- Parents and carers receive assistance in comprehending their child's needs and strengths while also being encouraged to share their expertise
- Discussions about parents' and carers' expectations can happen, and the school ensures that its input is realistic
- Parents/carers are informed about the role of external professionals and what to expect from them. The school supports the relationship between parents and external professionals.

Involving children and young people in their EHCPs and reviews

The Department for Education recognises the vital role of including children and young people's aspirations and desired outcomes within their Education, Health, and Care (EHC) plans. It is included in paragraphs 9.21–9.24 of the Special Educational Needs and Disability Code of Practice: 0 to 25 years, which provides statutory guidance for professionals on how to include children, young people, and their parents in their individual process of assessment and production of an EHC plan. This guidance confirms that the needs of the child and young person should sit at the heart of the assessment and planning process. This empowers them as individuals and promotes holistic development, particularly for those with disabilities.

Beyond their individual plans, children and young people themselves have emphasised key areas crucial for their participation, not only in crafting their EHCPs but also in broader decision-making. These principles serve as a valuable guide for all educators and professionals supporting children and young people.

Ensure their dreams and aspirations are acknowledged, even if they appear impractical to family or professionals. Recognising aspirations and striving towards them provides disabled children and young individuals with valid objectives and promotes skill development.

Keep the young person at the forefront, both in planning and discussions regarding support. EHCPs should be crafted and executed with the child or young person's needs and aspirations as the central focus. It's crucial that the plan includes information about the individual, is developed with their involvement, and is aimed at supporting them in achieving agreed-upon outcomes and goals.

Remain open-minded, truly listen, empathise, and inspire. Children and young individuals express the desire for adults to trust their decision-making abilities and to be available for guidance and support when necessary. Above all, they seek professionals who believe in their capabilities and their potential to fulfil their dreams.

Approach meetings with an open mind, ensuring awareness of the child or young person's accessibility needs beforehand and using clear language without technical jargon. Remember that the child, young person, and their family are experts in their support requirements.

Be innovative during meetings. Some children and young individuals may not feel comfortable in formal settings. Creating a relaxed atmosphere may involve involving trusted adults or friends for support, holding meetings in informal venues, providing various activities or materials, offering frequent breaks, and ensuring the availability of the young person's preferred communication method.

Refrain from sharing personal information without informing the child and parents about the recipient and the purpose. Privacy is essential, and concerns about personal information, including mental health, emotional well-being, personal care needs, and details about home life, have been voiced by young people. Incidents of bullying, particularly by adults, are particularly sensitive issues.

Remember that success is diverse. A child or young person may excel in one area while requiring additional support in another. Maintain an open mindset regarding the various types of assistance needed.

SEND safeguarding

As well as the statutory safeguarding training you will receive, it is important to consider specifics for children and young people with SEND.

Safeguarding considerations for children with SEND (Special Educational Needs and Disabilities) encompass a range of specific factors to ensure their safety and well-being. These considerations are crucial due to the increased vulnerabilities that children with SEND may face. Here are some key aspects to consider:

Understanding individual needs

Recognise that children with SEND have diverse needs, and their vulnerabilities may vary depending on their specific disabilities or conditions. It's essential to understand how their disability impacts their ability to communicate, comprehend, and protect themselves from harm.

Communication

Children with SEND may have communication barriers, making it challenging for them to express concerns or disclose instances of abuse or neglect. Therefore, it's important to establish alternative communication methods, such as using visual aids, simplified language, or assistive communication devices, to facilitate effective communication.

Recognising signs of abuse or neglect

Be vigilant in identifying potential signs of abuse or neglect, considering both physical and behavioural indicators. Since children with SEND may exhibit different behavioural responses or physical manifestations compared to typically developing children, it's essential to be familiar with these differences and consider them when assessing safeguarding concerns.

Tailored safeguarding procedures

Develop and implement safeguarding procedures that are specifically tailored to accommodate the needs of children with SEND. This may include adapting reporting mechanisms, conducting assessments in a sensitive and accessible manner, and providing additional support or accommodations during safeguarding investigations.

Training and awareness

All staff members, including teachers, support staff, and caregivers, should receive comprehensive training on safeguarding children with SEND. This training should cover recognising signs of abuse, understanding specific vulnerabilities, implementing appropriate safeguarding protocols, and promoting inclusive practices that prioritise the safety and well-being of children with SEND.

Collaboration and multi-agency working

Establish effective collaboration and communication channels with relevant agencies and professionals involved in supporting children with SEND, including social services, healthcare providers, educational professionals, and advocacy organisations. This collaborative approach facilitates early intervention, holistic support, and coordinated responses to safeguarding concerns.

Empowering children and young people

Empower children and young people with SEND by providing them with age-appropriate information about their rights, personal boundaries, and safety strategies. Encourage self-advocacy skills and foster an environment where children feel comfortable expressing their concerns and seeking help when needed.

Accessibility and accommodations

Ensure that safeguarding policies, procedures, and support services are accessible and inclusive for children with SEND. This includes providing accommodations such as accessible formats, interpreters, or additional support personnel to ensure that children with diverse needs can fully participate in safeguarding processes.

Preparing for adulthood

Preparing for adulthood support usually focuses on four pathways, helping young people to achieve the best outcome in:

- Higher education or employment
- Independent living and housing options
- Participating in the local community and society and having positive relationships
- Good health

This is relevant to all individuals working with children and young people with SEN or disabilities, especially those aged 14 and above. The framework outlines how professionals in education, health, and social care should assist young people in preparing for adulthood, achieving optimal outcomes in employment, independent living, health, and community involvement. The principles apply universally to young people with SEN or disabilities, except where specified for those with Education, Health, and Care (EHC) plans only. Establishing high aspirations is vital for success, with discussions on long-term goals ideally commencing well before Year 9, focusing on individual strengths, capabilities, and desired outcomes.

Guiding children and young people with SEN towards increased independence and employability can be life-changing. Preparing for adulthood entails preparing for higher education or employment, exploring various employment avenues such as self-employment and assistance from supported employment agencies. It also involves promoting independent living with choices, control, and support over their accommodation and living arrangements, as well as fostering participation in society and maintaining healthy lifestyles into adulthood.

SEND and mental health

- 54% of people with a learning disability have a mental health problem
- Children with learning disabilities are four and a half times more likely to have a mental health problem than children without a learning disability

(Mental Health Foundation, 2023)

It can be particularly hard to identify mental health difficulties in a child with SEND needs, but the key is in knowing the child or young person and looking for changes in behaviour. Children with special educational needs may encounter various social, emotional, and mental health challenges, posing obstacles to their learning. However, identifying mental health issues can be challenging due to symptom overlaps with conditions like autism or Attention Deficit Hyperactive Disorder (ADHD). Promoting mental health and well-being is important for all children, particularly if the child or young person has special educational needs. Children need to develop the skills to understand and express their emotions and to develop strategies for coping with the ups and downs of life.

Possible signs to look out for:

- Showing withdrawal
- Experiencing hyperactivity and difficulty focusing

- Restless and fidgety behaviour
- Expressing feelings of sadness
- Demonstrating unusual anxiety
- Experiencing disrupted sleep patterns or increased sleep
- Engaging in self-harm
- Expressing feelings of anger or fear
- Posing unusual questions
- Experiencing changes in eating habits
- Experiencing frequent tummy aches or headaches

(TheSchoolRun, n.d.)

The following strategies and activities can be helpful in supporting children and young people with SEND and mental health needs:

- **Offer choices**

  Children with special educational needs often experience a lack of control over their own lives. Try to support them in making choices to maximise their independence.
- **Support emotional intelligence**

  Support children to develop the skills to understand and express their emotions from an early age, using pictures, signs, and other communication aids.
- **Set up a worry box**

  Start a worry box, especially if they have high anxiety levels. At the end of each day, talk about all the things they're worrying about and encourage them to put them in the box. Every now and then, open the box and talk about each worry, how they are feeling, and share some ways to handle the worry.
- **Express emotions**

  Challenging behaviours are usually signs that they are unhappy about something. Try to work out the message behind them. Encourage children to express and release their emotions in ways that suit them – whether that's through art, music, movement, etc. Self-talk can often help a child with special educational needs process their feelings effectively, so try not to discourage it.
- **Acknowledge and label feelings**

  Identify feelings as they arise. For example, if a child cries, tell them you understand they are sad and back this up with any communication aids you are using.
- **Write it down**

  Sometimes, it's easier for children to write down how they're feeling, rather than expressing it verbally. The process of writing can help calm their anger and frustration. If they find it difficult to tell you what's upsetting them, try asking them to draw or paint a picture.
- **Channel energy**

  Many children with special educational needs have their own unique way of coping. Find out what works for them. If a child or young person expresses their feelings in physically aggressive ways, try to channel this energy appropriately, for example, through sport or banging a drum.

- **Try different coping strategies**

  Teach strategies for coping with difficult situations, such as deep breathing and counting to 10 or down from 10. Cards are useful for allowing children with special educational needs to leave a situation they find uncomfortable; they can use the card to tell people they want to leave.

- **Encourage friendships**

  Having friends and close social relationships is important for all children. Loneliness is often a large factor in mental ill-health.

Myth: Children with SEND are less intelligent than their peers.

Truth: Intelligence is not determined by the presence of SEND. Children with SEND often have unique strengths and abilities in various areas, and with appropriate support and accommodations, they can achieve academic success and reach their full potential.

Myth: Children with SEND cannot be included in mainstream education.

Truth: Inclusive education is a fundamental right for all children, including those with SEND. With the right support and accommodations, children with SEND can thrive in mainstream educational settings alongside their peers, contributing to a more diverse and inclusive learning environment.

Myth: Children with SEND will always require special treatment and accommodations.

Truth: While children with SEND may require additional support and accommodations to access learning, they are capable of learning and growing like any other child. With the right support, they can develop the necessary skills to become independent and successful learners, contributing positively to society.

Resources

- Special Educational Needs and Disabilities (SEND) Code of Practice: This official guidance document provides information on identifying and supporting children with SEND in educational settings.
- National Autistic Society (NAS): The NAS offers a range of resources, including guides, training materials, and support networks specifically tailored to children with autism spectrum disorders (ASD).
- British Dyslexia Association (BDA): The BDA provides resources, training, and information for supporting children with dyslexia and other specific learning difficulties.
- Makaton: Makaton is a language program that uses signs and symbols to support communication and language development for children with communication difficulties, including those with SEND.
- Special Educational Needs and Disability Information, Advice, and Support Services (SENDIASS): SENDIASS offers information, advice, and support to parents, carers, and professionals working with children with SEND.
- The Communication Trust: This organisation provides resources and training to support children with speech, language, and communication needs (SLCN).

- Twinkl: Twinkl is an online platform that offers a wide range of educational resources, including materials specifically designed to support children with special educational needs and disabilities (SEND). Twinkl provides a variety of printable worksheets, lesson plans, interactive activities, visual aids, and more, covering various subjects and topics tailored to different age groups and learning needs. These resources can be accessed by educators, parents, and caregivers to support the learning and development of children with SEND in both classroom and home environments.
- Special Educational Needs and Inclusion Support Services (SENISS): SENISS offers a range of resources and support services for schools, teachers, and professionals working with children with SEND.
- National Association for Special Educational Needs (NASEN): NASEN provides resources, training, and support for professionals working with children with SEND, including information on inclusive teaching practices and strategies.
- Department for Education (DfE): The DfE website offers guidance and resources for supporting children with SEND in educational settings, including information on legal requirements and best practices.
- Local Authority SEND Support: Local authorities often provide resources and support services for children with SEND, including specialist teaching support, training for teachers, and access to specialist equipment and resources.

References

Department for Education. (2014). SEND code of practice: 0 to 25 years. *GOV.UK*. [online] Available at: www.gov.uk/government/publications/send-code-of-practice-0-to-25

Department for Education. (2023). SEND and alternative provision improvement plan. *GOV.UK*. [online] Available at: www.gov.uk/government/publications/send-and-alternative-provision-improvement-plan

GOV.UK. (2012). Children with special educational needs and disabilities (SEND). *GOV.UK*. [online] Available at: www.gov.uk/children-with-special-educational-needs

Inclusive Provision for Students with Special Educational Needs and/or Disabilities a Resourced Provision Toolkit Acknowledgements. (n.d.). Available at: www.southampton.ac.uk/~assets/doc/Resource%20Provision%20Toolkit%20-%20FINAL-1.pdf [Accessed 14 Feb. 2024].

Mental Health Foundation. (2023). *People with learning disabilities: Statistics*. [online] Available at: www.mentalhealth.org.uk/explore-mental-health/statistics/people-learning-disabilities-statistics#:~:text=Data%20has%20shown%20that%20people

TheSchoolRun. (n.d.). *Positive mental health tips for parents of SEN children*. [online] Available at: www.theschoolrun.com/positive-mental-health-tips-parents-sen-children#:~:text=Encourage%20children%20to%20express%20and [Accessed 15 Feb. 2024].

sen.hias.hants.gov.uk. (n.d.). *SEN Moodle: All courses*. [online] Available at: https://sen.hias.hants.gov.uk/course/index.php?categoryid=29 [Accessed 14 Feb. 2024].

9 Neurodiversity

Chapter introduction

How would you define 'neurodiversity'? Neurodiversity recognises that we all think and act in different ways due to variations in the human genome. Just as with any other individual characteristics, such as ethnicity, sexuality, or gender, we each have a 'neurotype' (Grant and Kara, 2021). While around 75% of the population is thought to be neurotypical, the other 25% is 'neurodivergent'. Neurodivergent (ND) individuals have less typical variations, including, but not exhaustively, Attention Deficit Hyperactivity Disorder (ADHD), Autism Spectrum Disorder (ASD), and dyspraxia, but importantly, each presentation and experience is unique, and many of these ND diagnoses present on a spectrum. Being inclusive of people who are neurodivergent can help create a more equitable society that values and celebrates differences. Neurodiversity is the idea that diversity in all forms is a source of strength, celebrating differences in the ways our brains work and embracing the idea that people with unique cognitive and neurological differences can bring talent, creativity, and diverse perspectives. This chapter looks at neurodivergent conditions such as Autism and ADHD and shares strategies that may support neurodivergent learners in accessing the curriculum and developing social skills. This chapter also includes an expert voice from Dr Sarah Alix, who works for the Sigma Trust as the Teacher Training Programme Director.

Why understanding neurodivergent conditions is important

Part of the challenge of supporting people who are neurodivergent is that many of these conditions have only recently been recognised across the globe. For example, in the United Kingdom, ADHD was first recognised as a valid condition as recently as 2000, when the National Institute of Clinical Excellence (NICE) released a report on the condition. However, ADHD wasn't officially recognised as an adult condition until 2008. In the history of the world, to consider that our understanding and recognition of such conditions is as recent as the last couple of decades is troublesome as it means some people may be more cynical about the existence of such conditions, having not encountered the official diagnosis before. Part of the difficulty can also present in the comorbidity, namely the coexistence of more than one neurodivergent condition. This is why we must

DOI: 10.4324/9781032697932-9

continue talking about these conditions to reduce prejudice and support inclusivity and understanding.

Neurodiversity in schools

So, how can we support young people with neurodivergent conditions in our classrooms? Let's begin by exploring some of the conditions we may encounter and the symptoms and behaviours that may present, namely in ADHD, ASD, Tourette syndrome, dyslexia, dyscalculia, and dyspraxia.

Attention deficit hyperactivity disorder (ADHD)

Attention-deficit hyperactivity disorder (ADHD) can be defined as a set of symptoms, including inattentiveness, impulsivity, and hyperactivity, that may manifest in emotional, psychological, or learning issues (Furman, 2005). ADHD is more frequently diagnosed in boys than girls. For pupils with ADHD, behaviour management strategies may be ineffective as the need for instant gratification, as opposed to delayed gratification of a house point or sticker at the end of the day, and impulsivity may mean that consequences are also less considered. When interested in a topic, or 'hyperfocused', learners with ADHD can be highly motivated and very creative, and thus, we must remember to appreciate the benefits and joys that neurodivergent conditions can bring and create to add beauty to our world. It is important to highlight that around 2 to 3 in 10 people with the condition have problems with concentrating and focusing, but *not* with hyperactivity or impulsiveness, and in this case, the 'H' for hyperactivity is removed from the title, being known as attention deficit disorder (ADD); ADD may be harder to diagnose without the more obvious element of hyperactivity (NHS, 2024). In the UK, a research survey of 10,438 children between the ages of 5 and 15 years found that 3.62% of boys and 0.85% of girls had ADHD (ADHD UK, 2024).

As we will see with some of the other conditions explored in what follows, some of the symptoms of ADHD can be comorbid and confused with symptoms of other conditions.

Autism spectrum disorder (ASD)

Autism Spectrum Disorder (ASD) is an umbrella term for a group of neurodevelopmental disorders, including autism, Asperger's syndrome (AS), and pervasive developmental disorder-not otherwise specified (PDD-NOS) (Sharma et al., 2018). Behaviours of a person with autism may be different from one person to the next, hence the word 'spectrum' being used in the title, but as highlighted in the new diagnostic criteria for ASD, the two core areas that present are difficulties with social communication, and the repetitive behaviours or hyper-interest in a topic or certain topics (Sharma et al., 2018). More than one in 100 people are on the autism spectrum, and there are around 700,000 autistic adults and children in the UK (National Autistic Society, 2024).

Tourette syndrome, or Gilles de la Tourette syndrome (GTS)

Gilles de la Tourette syndrome (GTS) is a childhood-onset neurodevelopmental disorder which presents through 'tics', which may be physical or verbal twitches (Robertson et al., 2017). In Tourette syndrome, tics usually present before age ten and often improve as the child grows, decreasing into adulthood. Tourette syndrome presents tics on a spectrum of severity, with those tics at the more severe end – such as coprolalia (swearing tics) and self-injurious behaviours – sometimes leading to a poorer quality of life (Robertson et al., 2017). Tourette syndrome affects up to 1% of the population.

Dyslexia

Dyslexia is a neurodevelopmental learning disability that can present as difficulty in reading and spelling and slow word recognition (Peterson and Pennington, 2012). A learner with dyslexia processes codes differently, and thus, this condition can affect spoken language, written language, and language comprehension. Approximately 1 in 10-20 people in the UK have dyslexia (Safespot, 2024).

Dyscalculia

Dyscalculia, also known as developmental dyscalculia (DD), involves specific difficulties in making sense of numbers, number symbolisation, and also issues with working memory (Von Aster and Shalev, 2007). Approximately 1 in 20 people have dyscalculia, and 50% of people with dyscalculia have also dyslexia (Safespot, 2024).

Dyspraxia

Dyspraxia is a condition, also known as Developmental Coordination Disorder (DCD), which involves motor-based difficulties in balance and movement. A large number of school-aged children present with motor-based performance problems that have significant negative effects on their ability to participate fully in the daily activities of home, school, and play (Polatajko and Cantin, 2005). It is thought dyspraxia affects up to 6% of the population, with up to 2% being severely affected (Foundation for People with Learning Difficulties, 2024).

So, how can we shift our thinking around neurodivergent learners?

In the following contribution, Dr Sarah Alix encourages us to reflect upon our mindset when thinking about what it means to be neurodivergent and how the key is through a positive approach to inclusion in our schools and wider society.

***

Neurodiversity in schools; changing thinking and perceptions, by Dr Sarah Alix

Everyone has subtle individual differences in how they process information and how they respond to it. How we process information is as unique as our fingerprints. In schools, the education model is designed to accommodate and teach to the broadest category of differences, that of the 'neurotypical' learner, which is approximately 85% of the population. There are many studies on neurodiversity which indicate that in the UK, approximately 15-20% of people are neurodivergent, and the rest of the population is classed as neurotypical. However, depending on the study conducted, it is thought that potentially up to 30-40% of the world could be classed as neurodivergent in some form and sit outside the neurotypical framework of learning and processing.

Our SEND and neurodivergent pupils fit into the 15-20% of the population within our class, and it can be challenging to accommodate their needs on a daily basis when balancing all of the jobs that we have to do as teachers.

The medical model

The medical model is currently the model that has been in place for decades within our schools. It is a model in which everyone who fits into the majority in the way that they learn is seen as being 'neurotypical'. The medical model implies that there is a 'right' way of functioning and processing, which is the model in which the education system is built, but changes are being made, and knowledge around neurodiversity and how we think about it within our schools is increasing. The medical model implies that anyone who processes information differently has something wrong with them. These pupils are seen to have a deficit or an impairment or be described as having a disorder. These 'impairments' are seen to fall short of what is a normal, neurotypical cognitive way of learning.

The medical model 'aspires towards normalization, symptom reduction, and elimination of conditions based on deficits to cause functional impairment in life activities' (Kapp et al., 2013). The aim of the medical model is to alleviate the symptoms of the disorder, to get rid of any symptoms or unwanted behaviours so that the person 'fits in' to the expectations and 'norms' of the neurotypical population. Rolfe (2019) argues that the medical model believes that any deviations from the neurotypical population and expectations are an impairment within the child that needs to be addressed.

Neurodiversity is key in challenging this model; it does not believe that there is a right or wrong way to function or for cognitive processing; they are just different for different learners and to different extents. The medical model is socially constructed by neurotypical learners, and the neurodiversity model aims to deconstruct the medical model and begin to view learning and individuality differently and as equal. Slorach (2016) argues that these differences in cognitive functioning are part of our natural human variation, just as other elements of human development and differences are. It is normal to have variation within our species, and how our brains and minds work is just one of these ways.

Instead of thinking 'disorders' or 'impairments', we need to make a shift in our own think-ing and understanding to know that different processing is normal, natural, and ok! It may take a learner longer to master something, they may need something to be repeated more times, or they may need you to show it to them in a different way.

Developing positive attitudes towards neurodiversity in society

We need to develop our language around differences in society to a more positive framing. There has been a shift in language from the use of 'autism awareness day/week/month' to 'autism acceptance'. This is a really important shift of language for neurodiversity. We don't just want everyone in society to be aware of a neuro-difference. We need (and have the right) for society to be accepting of neuro-difference and to ensure that everyone has the same rights and opportunities, regardless of whether they are neurotypical or neuro-divergent. We see acceptance in other areas of difference, such as gender and race, and we now need to ensure that neurodivergent individuals also receive acceptance as part of society. Everyone has the right to any difference to be embraced and to be treated with dignity and respect.

The current model in society expects neurodivergent people to change, for exam-ple, to change their behaviour to fit into a more neurotypical society and to be more sociable or to give eye contact and to fit in with a set of norms that have been imple-mented by neurotypical people. In effect, it is similar to asking other minority groups to dress differently to be accepted. It is highly prejudicial and discriminatory, and it is not acceptable.

We are beginning to know much more about neurodiversity, both through research and through individuals reading up more about differences and the neurodiversity model. Making a shift in school towards a model of neurodiversity will promote a model of the acceptance of difference within society – very much a move that is needed.

Dr Sarah Alix works for the Sigma Trust as the Teacher Training Programme Director. She has many publications on Neurodiversity and SEND. www.dr-sarah-alix.com

***

To summarise, neurodiversity is the diversity of human minds. It's important to be inclu-sive of people with neurodiversity because it can lead to:

- Improved productivity
- Neurodiverse people often have strengths like creativity, focus, and pattern recognition. This can lead to more innovation in the workplace.
- Increased empathy
- Neurodiverse people often have heightened empathy and understanding due to their own experiences. This can lead to a more compassionate workplace where employees better support each other.
- More accurate understanding
- Celebrating neurodiversity can help challenge harmful and inaccurate stereotypes that can damage the mental health and self-esteem of neurodivergent people.

Myths

Myth: We must promote terms such as 'autism awareness' to help show our support for neurodivergent conditions.

Truth: We are now encouraging the term 'acceptance' instead of 'awareness', which encompasses a more inclusive approach.

Myth: Being neurodivergent has a correlation with lower academic achievement.

Truth: Neurodivergent people may have different strengths and weaknesses than people whose brains develop more typically. These differences can cause challenges in many areas, including reading and writing, communication, social interaction, coordination, motor skills, and learning disabilities, but this does not mean they are less academic; it just means they may struggle accessing the curriculum or assessments.

Myth: All neurodivergent people are similar.

Truth: In reality, neurodiversity is a broad term that encompasses various conditions, such as autism, ADHD, dyspraxia, dyslexia, dyscalculia, and Tourette's syndrome. Everyone sits at a different place on the cognitive spectrum, so the way we think, behave, and process information is unique to each individual.

References

ADHD UK. (2024). *About ADHD*. Available at: https://adhduk.co.uk/about-adhd/

Foundation for People with Learning Difficulties. (2024). *Dyspraxia*. Available at: www.learningdisabilities.org.uk/learning-disabilities/a-to-z/d/dyspraxia

Furman, L. (2005). What is Attention-Deficit Hyperactivity Disorder (ADHD)? *Journal of Child Neurology*, 20(12), pp. 994–1002. Available at: https://journals.sagepub.com/doi/abs/10.1177/0883073805020012 1301?casa_token=UWZr-bk-nOsAAAAA:fKVyhf05S7d4WU9fHpG51vMOJq92fOkjteHRvS6QfpCl-PfQGxcG1yoJeBq-e56zSMhUG2JejBns

Grant, A., & Kara, H. (2021). Considering the Autistic advantage in qualitative research: the strengths of Autistic researchers. *Contemporary Social Science*, 16(5), 589–603. https://doi.org/10.1080/21582041.2021.1998589

Kapp, S., Gillespie-Lyncg, K., Sherman, L. and Hutman, T. (2013). Deficit, difference, or both? Autism and neurodiversity. *Developmental Psychology*, 49(1), pp. 59–71.

National Autistic Society. (2024). *What is autism?* Available at: www.autism.org.uk/advice-and-guidance/what-is-autism

NHS. (2024). *Attention Deficit Hyperactivity Disorder (ADHD)*. Available at: www.nhs.uk/conditions/attention-deficit-hyperactivity-disorder-adhd/symptoms/

Peterson, R.L. and Pennington, B.F. (2012). Developmental dyslexia. *The Lancet*, 379(9830), pp. 1997–2007. Available at: www.thelancet.com/journals/lancet/article/PIIS0140-6736(12)60198-6/abstract

Polatajko, H.J. and Cantin, N. (2005). Developmental coordination disorder (dyspraxia): An overview of the state of the art. *Seminars in Pediatric Neurology*. Dec. 12(4), pp. 250–258. WB Saunders. Available at: www.sciencedirect.com/science/article/pii/S1071909105000859?casa_token=YYmdYsraKrYAAAAA:1DgQlfncWv8sBxjNkszLXbFBor3Hn4EmWiSD55v9ugBBZ7beTO3Bg_K1Xs4adhfOzcEZTpMJQA

Robertson, M.M., Eapen, V., Singer, H.S., Martino, D., Scharf, J.M., Paschou, P., Roessner, V., Woods, D.W., Hariz, M., Mathews, C.A. and Črnčec, R. (2017). Gilles de la Tourette syndrome. *Nature Reviews Disease Primers*, 3(1), pp. 1–20. Available at: www.nature.com/articles/nrdp201697

Rolfe, S. (2019). Models of SEND: The impact of political and economic influences on policy and provision. *British Journal of Special Education*, 46(4), pp. 423–444.

Safespot. (2024). *Dyslexia & dyscalculia*. Available at: https://safespot.org.uk/safespotopedia/dyslexia-dyscalculia/#:~:text=Approximately%201%20in%2010%2D20,in%2020%20people%20have%20dyscalculia

Sharma, S.R., Gonda, X. and Tarazi, F.I. (2018). Autism spectrum disorder: Classification, diagnosis and therapy. *Pharmacology & Therapeutics*, 190, pp. 91–104. Available at: www.sciencedirect.com/science/article/pii/S0163725818300871?casa_token=14UIKMkTCC4AAAAA:C62BwXe_3qxskDhQBDO3FxGySHuPhNdpxFmGjvTjmjB7LrUN-fRHqqMeOndw7YWnFfhLNGuGig

Slorach, R. (2016). *A very capitalist condition: A history and politics of disability*. London: Bookmarks Publications.

Von Aster, M.G. and Shalev, R.S. (2007). Number development and developmental dyscalculia. *Developmental Medicine & Child Neurology*, 49(11), pp. 868–873. Available at: https://onlinelibrary.wiley.com/doi/full/10.1111/j.1469-8749.2007.00868.x

10 Social media

Chapter introduction

Often, people think the best option when it comes to social media is to prevent young people and children from using online platforms to avoid harm. You only have to type a sentence like 'children and social media' in a search engine online to see articles come up about 'risks' and 'challenges' and 'dangers'. But perhaps the better option is to have purposeful conversations about positive social media usage, to better prepare students to navigate online spaces safely and with enjoyment. This chapter shares strategies for supporting social media interactions and connections and also considers how social media can support education, inspiration, and ambitions for the young people in our society, complete with a thoughtful contribution from Ted Samaras, Instructional Technology Coach.

Social media

'Social media' can be defined as a 'group of Internet-based applications that build on the ideological and technological foundations of the Web 2.0 and that allow the creation and exchange of user-generated content' (Kaplan and Haenlein, 2011: 60). Social media encapsulates ways that individuals can create, share and exchange ideas and information in a virtual space or online community. In recent years, social media platforms have 'penetrated deeply' into the mechanics of our everyday lives, affecting both our informal interactions and our professional routines (Fisher, 2015: 72).

Social media is the 'latest innovation in computer-mediated communication that poses serious challenges to existing institutions' (van Dijck and Poell, 2013), such as the institutions of mass media and the government. The rapid development and integration of such cultural tools have forced us to adapt to a new cultural reality. On a daily basis, news, information, and select entertainment are at our fingertips and no longer a privilege for the few. Fast-growing networks like TikTok, Instagram, Facebook, and Twitter, with millions of active users, are 'rapidly penetrating public communication, affecting the operational and institutional power balance of media systems' (van Dijck and Poell, 2013: 3).

We may question why there are so many children using these networks when there are age restrictions on the registrations for most of them. As D'Lima and Higgins (2021) highlight, professing to have an age restriction may purely be tokenistic, as when we look into the

DOI: 10.4324/9781032697932-10

statistics for social media use by children, the Office of Communications (OfCom, 2019) found that 21% of 8-to-11-year olds in the United Kingdom have social networking profiles, despite the majority of social media having age restrictions limiting use to those above 13 years (for example, Snapchat; TikTok; Instagram; National Society for the Prevention of Cruelty to Children (NSPCC, 2020; Ofcom, 2019). Similarly, 78% of young people under 13 years had a social networking profile, according to the Comres survey of 1,200 young people aged between 10 and 18 (Coughlan, 2016). Having age limits on these sites also causes moral issues for parents and schools, who may not wish to admit children are using these platforms whilst under-age, which means our curriculum is not robust or relevant enough as it omits the use of social media entirely for this reason (D'Lima and HIggins, 2021).

The role of social media in building identities

Waggoner (2013) noted that users could see their online selves as having equal status with their offline selves; the two selves, then, are not different but the same entity in different contexts. If not seeing the two as identical – participants wish to 'keep them as close together as possible, and not adopt new persona' (Bullingham and Vasconcelos, 2013: 9). By looking into the motivations behind social media use, the relationships between this phenomenon and individuals' well-being may begin to become somewhat more transparent.

Tajfel and Turner (1985) emphasise the importance of two key influences on identity: personal identity and self-concept versus the social context within which self-concept is situated. Later, Badiou (2014) talks about the 'subject' and the 'situation'. Identities are considered here as being fluid, on being entities that are reliant on the membership within social groups. This dependence offers a new conflict in the identity debate. Ultimately, identity gets down to the problem of the subject versus agency (Badiou, 2014), with the first issue addressing mind-body duality: am I uniquely and only my body? Or do I transcend/transform/transgress my body? Can there be a disembodied me? The process of growing up and ageing locates the body as a vessel in time, which presents further questions: will I survive my body? And if I do, will I (now) know about it then? The second issue around identity addresses free will versus determinism. If I am socially constructed and fluid (or even just a collection of hormonally driven associated behaviours), am I responsible for my acts?

A further debate around identity is that of performativity, introduced by Butler (1990). Butler expanded upon the notion of a socially constructed identity by introducing performativity and the extent to which an individual's identity is discursively constructed. Performativity relates to the discursive construction of identity (McKinlay, 2010). Butler's key concept is performativity: how gender identity is embodied and enacted rather than a more or less adequate reflection of some underlying bodily reality. Butler draws on Foucault in several respects, not least her stress on the physicality of individual and social life and her concern to understand identity as a social process. Identity is always provisional rather than complete, a profoundly ambiguous and unstable moment. Performativity is not reducible to performance, and the degree of choice involved in identity construction both makes it appear more 'natural' for the individual and also open to reinterpretation (McKinlay, 2010).

So, why are children using social media?

Take a moment to reflect. If you have accounts on social media platforms: Why? Why do you post a status or a photograph? Why do you follow somebody online or add a 'friend'? How many minutes (or hours!) a day do you spend scrolling, and why? The answer to this last one will likely be 'because you enjoy it'. It is the same for children and young people: the enjoyment of learning, or being connected, of feeling part of something.

Or perhaps it is the fear of not being part of something, namely 'the Fear of Missing Out' (FOMO). A study by D'Lima and Higgins (2021) found children enjoyed using social media and managed risks with assertiveness and initiative. However, conflict between competing motivations and underlying assumptions regarding stranger interaction could place children at risk. We need the creation of a more relevant and aware social media strategy in our primary schools; however, until then, the best we can do as educators consider how we can support some of these conversations around safe and enjoyable social media use in our classrooms.

Here are three key strategies for supporting positive social media use amongst children and young people:

Strategy 1: boundaries and good habits

The vulnerability for young people comes through the social connection that smartphones offer; the 24/7 pipeline of connectivity, the pressure of posting on social media platforms, and the analytics of 'likes' and engagement can be overwhelming for a child trying to establish their identity in the world.

- Talk to children about screen time and look at how to set limits on apps if they find it hard to limit their usage
- Model good habits as an adult; avoid using your phone when you eat and put phones away when having a conversation with somebody face to face
- Remind children what they see online is only a snapshot of something that has been created to gain engagement; it is likely not real or telling the whole story

Strategy 2: openness about inappropriate material and use

Parents, carers, and teachers need to have open conversations with their children about things they may encounter online and how to react or behave when we leave timeless digital footprints online. We must prepare children for a future intertwined with technology by helping them reflect upon how social media serves them and being able to appreciate when to delete apps or how to navigate these social spaces in a healthy way.

- Encourage children to reflect on why they sign up for social media sites. What does the platform give them?
- Remind children they can delete accounts and apps when they feel they no longer enjoy them.
- Ensure children are aware that someone else being inappropriate towards them is not their fault; they should not feel guilt or shame about speaking up and telling someone about what has happened.

- Talk about how to set adult settings on different platforms to reduce the amount of inappropriate content they may see, and let them know you are there to listen if they see something that upsets them.

Strategy 3: celebrating positives

Just as many of us as adults enjoy using social media for a range of purposes, so many young people find these same joys.

- Help children understand how they can learn through social media
- Look at ways for children to make health connections with material they relate to and are interested in
- Consider how social media is a great way to share things about our lives but with healthy limits and boundaries

The bottom line must be that whilst social media can open up our lives, it also presents a place where things we post may never fully disappear. Remind your learners that things they post can be found in the future; what about when they go for a job interview, for example, and their prospective employer might find a status or image they posted? Is it appropriate? Is it kind? Could it harm their opportunities? If we have these conversations with children and young people, rather than pretending they are not using social media, we can hopefully prepare them to navigate these spaces safely and with lifelong enjoyment and fulfilment.

To end this chapter, this contribution from Ted Samaras encourages us to consider the positives of children using social media.

Why shouldn't we be scared of children using social media?
By Ted Samaras, instructional technology coach

When we consider how our children use social media, we need to look at ourselves for the answers. We need to be honest about its pitfalls and limitations but not paralyzed by the fear of them. Just like with any emerging technology (i.e., automobile, airplane, Internet, etc.), there are risks that can be identified, addressed, and managed. It is human nature to focus on negative and sensational stories, particularly regarding social media. However, there are many positives to our children using social media while being fully aware that further research needs to be conducted and communities need continuous improvement in guidance and modeling of appropriate behaviors. We should be thoughtful about how children use social media and intentional in our expectations.

An example of the positive impact of social media is increased communication and collaboration. The opportunities for connections that our children can make with others are tremendous. It allows them to meet other children who are similar to them when they feel alone, meet children who are different from them to broaden their perspectives and have access to experiences that they might not have had otherwise. Social media can push past digital divides and economic boundaries and bring us closer together. In fact, this contribution that you are currently reading is rooted in connections that I have made with the authors via social media across continents and would not have happened without these platforms.

In order for children to have an increased chance of having a positive experience with social media, we must take the opportunity to model proper use of social media and set expectations and norms. When our children get driver's licenses, we tell them that it is not them that we worry about but the other drivers on the road. We try to equip them the best we can for when they get on the road. We provide driver's education classes, practice in empty parking lots, permitted driving on the road with a guardian, etc. On the road of social media, we must do the same thing. We enact laws and pass regulations, but we still need to equip our children with how to deal with things that can happen and help them build resilience and problem-solving skills rather than live with fear and avoidance. By introducing social media to them in a structured and supervised environment, we can take the opportunity to nurture their learning, model best practices, and introduce them to all of the positives that social media has to offer.

As we evolve as a society, we will continue to create new products and technologies and will be responsible for designing, adopting, and modifying how they are used and their impact. We should not proceed in fear of this evolution, but rather, we should move forward with thoughtful consideration and a growth mindset to help our children have a positive and productive relationship with all they will experience, including social media.

***

Myth: Social media is dangerous for children.

Truth: So, whilst there are definitely dangers that children may encounter online, we must also accept that there are positives and joys to be found through learning, connection, and empowerment through knowledge sharing. The important thing is for us to help facilitate open conversations around what is - and isn't - appropriate and equip children and young people with skills and understanding of what to do when they are upset by something online, and to recognise ways they can protect themselves and keep themselves safe when going online.

Myth: Using social media gives children issues with body image and ruins their confidence.

Truth: If children do not understand filters and photoshopping before navigating social media platforms, there is a risk that these unreal standards can affect their self-image; however, if we help children to see that most things online have been manipulated - including news, not just images - this can help provide a balance. Some social media opportunities, such as through creating their own video content, can help increase users' confidence and ambition.

Myth: We should ban smartphones and ensure children are not using social media sites until they are the correct age stated on the platform.

Truth: Whilst this may have been the ideal before smartphones became deeply integrated into our society - and pockets! - the realist approach now is to mitigate risk and harm through the purposeful conversations we have with young people about their internet use. There are joys and positives to be found through the global connection social media offers; it is our service as adults to help children and young people understand how to navigate this network or, in some cases, how to avoid it.

References

Badiou, A. (2014 but composed of selected earlier writings). *Infinite thought: Truth and the return of 179 philosophy*. (O. Feltham and J. Clemens, Eds.). London and New York: Bloomsbury Academic.

Bullingham, L. and Vasconcelos, A.C. (2013). 'The presentation of self in the online world': Goffman and the study of online identities. *Journal of Information Science*, 39(1), pp. 101–112.

Butler, J. (1990; Anniversary edition 1999). *Gender trouble: Feminism and the subversion of identity*. New York: Routledge.

Coughlan, S. (2016). Safer internet day: Young ignore 'social media age limit'. *British Broadcasting Corporation (BBC) News*. Available at: www.bbc.co.uk/news/education-35524429 [Accessed 28 Jun. 2020].

D'Lima, P. and Higgins, A. (2021). Social media engagement and Fear of Missing Out (FOMO) in primary school children. *Educational Psychology in Practice*, 37(3), pp. 320–338. Available at: www.tandfonline.com/doi/full/10.1080/02667363.2021.1947200?casa_token=YeiL5Bvk598AAAAA%3AFO95u-R9iGPjiDgHa4OPjBy69UDWW6clDz96YRXqSx4lRfvWhgtkXn12codLQgQYFGG5yIdbYOdO

Fisher, E. (2015). Class struggles in the digital frontier: Audience labour theory and social media users. *Information, Communication and Society*, 18(9), p. 1108.

Kaplan, A.M. and Haenlein, M. (2011). Two hearts in three-quarter time: How to waltz the social media/viral marketing dance. *Business Horizons*, 54(3), pp. 253–263.

McKinlay, A. (2010). Performativity and the politics of identity: Putting Butler to work. *Critical Perspectives on Accounting*, 21(3), pp. 232–242.

National Society for the Prevention of Cruelty to Children (NSPCC). (2020). *Netaware: Your guide to social networks, apps and games*. Available at: www.net-aware.org.uk/ [Accessed 28 Jun. 2020].

OfCom (2019). Children and parents: Media use and attitudes report 2019. Available at https://www.ofcom.org.uk/siteassets/resources/documents/research-and-data/media-literacy-research/children/childrens-media-literacy-2019/children-media-use-attitudes-2019-report.pdf?v=324598

Tajfel, H. and Turner, J.C. (1985). An integrative theory of intergroup conflict. *The Social Psychology of Intergroup Relations*, 33, p. 47.

van Dijck, J. and Poell, T. (2013). Understanding social media logic . *Media and Communication*. 12 Aug. 1(1), pp. 2–14.

Waggoner, Z. (2013). *My avatar, my self: Identity in video role-playing games* (p. 200). McFarland: eBook. Available at: https://play.google.com/store/books/details/My_Avatar_My_Self_Identity_in_Video_Role_Playing_G?id=uf9QosYeuX4C

11 Poverty and child poverty

Quote: 'Mum and me, we are having to choose between using electric on hot water, the washing machine or cooking food, we can't afford to do more than one'.

More than 1 in 5 people in the UK (22%) were in poverty in 2021-2022 – 14.4 million people. This included:

- 8.1 million (or around 2 in 10) working-age adults
- 4.2 million (or nearly 3 in 10) children
- 2.1 million (or around 1 in 6) pensioners

(Joseph Rowntree Foundation, January 2024)

The UK has greater regional disparities compared to many other developed nations (Levelling Up the United Kingdom, 2022). These variations encompass a range of socioeconomic indicators, including productivity, wage levels, educational attainment, and health outcomes. Big cities and towns by the coast often have more crime. And areas with lots of poverty, like old mining towns or suburbs and seaside towns, struggle the most. These gaps aren't just between different parts of the country – they can be right within the same town or city. Despite the potential for change, certain discrepancies have persisted over a significant period of time. Furthermore, several prominent cities in the UK, including Birmingham, Manchester, Leeds, Glasgow, and Cardiff, are behind their international counterparts in terms of both productivity and income levels.

Key facts from the Trussel Trust 2022/2023 report:

Food banks in the Trussell Trust network have seen the highest levels of need ever, even superseding the peak reached during the pandemic.

This is representative of the increasing numbers of people experiencing financial hardship due to the cost-of-living crisis. In December 2022, the Joseph Rowntree Foundation (JRF) reported that for all low-income households in the bottom 40% of incomes, 62% were going without essentials. This means that they had reported going hungry, cutting down the size of meals, skipping meals in the last 30 days, or going without basics like showers or adequate clothing since June 2022.

The Trussel Trust 'Hunger in the UK' report (June 2023) examines the scale and drivers of food insecurity and food bank use in the UK.

DOI: 10.4324/9781032697932-11

14% of all UK adults (or their households) have experienced food insecurity in the last 12 months. This means that at some point over this period, they have run out of food and been unable to afford more, and/or reduced meal size, eaten less, gone hungry, or lost weight due to lack of money.

More than half of households facing food insecurity, and three-quarters of individuals referred to food banks within the Trussell Trust network indicate that they or a member of their household are disabled.

Families with children face a heightened risk of food insecurity, with nearly half (47%) of all food-insecure households including children under the age of 16 (Bull et al., 2023).

Structural inequalities play a significant role in shaping hardship and food insecurity. People from ethnic minority backgrounds, women, individuals who identify as LGBTQ+, those who have sought asylum or applied for it in the past, and individuals who were in care during childhood are disproportionately represented among those experiencing food insecurity and seeking food assistance.

Patterns of adversity are seen amongst people across the UK who have experienced food insecurity in the previous 12 months.

Turn2Us report in 2021 found:

- 10% of people who had experienced food insecurity had faced a parental or family relationship breakdown in the previous 12 months – compared to just 3% of people who had not experienced food insecurity
- People who had experienced food insecurity were also more likely to have faced another household or relationship breakdown (11% compared to 2%)
- Increased likelihood of becoming long-term sick or disabled (9% compared to 2%)
- Have experienced domestic violence or abuse (9% compared to 0.4%)
- 2% of the general population have experienced three or more adverse events in the last year; this rose to one in five (21%) people referred to food banks
- Four times more likely to have experienced a relationship breakdown
- More likely to have experienced the death of a partner or other bereavement than people in the general population (18% compared to 13%)

In work poverty

A report published by Mental Health at Work states:

According to the UK Poverty 2023 report by the Joseph Rowntree Foundation (JRF) published in January 2023, over 1 in 10 of all workers (11%) reported living in a household in poverty in 2020/21. Almost two thirds (61%) of working-age adults in poverty lived in a household where at least one adult was working.

In-work poverty occurs when a working person's income, after housing costs, is less than 60% of the national average, and they don't earn enough to meet the cost of living (calculated using data from the ONS households below average income statistics) (CIPD, n.d).

Despite wage increases, the combination of a cost-of-living crisis and soaring housing costs has resulted in a further decline in living standards for many. While work can positively influence mental health by fostering feelings of autonomy, confidence, and fulfilment, a significant proportion of low-paid jobs fail to meet these criteria, lacking security and opportunities for advancement. The proliferation of 'zero-hours' contracts has become a prominent feature of the UK economy, exacerbating job insecurity.

Research demonstrates that low wages, job instability, and unpredictable income contribute to a sense of powerlessness among workers, impacting their mental well-being and interpersonal relationships. Additionally, caregiving responsibilities and health issues often prevent individuals from increasing their working hours, further limiting their financial stability. Recognising intersectionality is crucial, as certain groups, such as those with mental health issues, disabilities, or women, are disproportionately affected by these challenges.

According to Gov.uk, 71% of children growing up in poverty live in a household where at least one person is in work (CPAG, 2023).

Child poverty

Children have consistently had the highest poverty rates. Reports paint a stark picture of the reality faced by many children. Child Poverty action group reports (September 2023):

> 4.2 million children in the UK are growing up in poverty. That's 9 children in an average classroom of 30. The causal relationship between child poverty and educational outcomes is well established, with children from lower-income households less likely to achieve than their more affluent peers. This results in unequal life chances and futures, with children growing up in poverty earning less as adults.

The report from the Centre for Young Lives think tank (March 2024) suggests that children growing up in poverty are likely to be at increased risk of not attending school. Data found that over half (57%) of those identified as persistently absent from school were eligible for FSM. It also found that children eligible for FSM were three times more likely to become persistently absent at some point over their school career compared with their peers who did not receive FSM. The Guardian reports a girl was not attending school because she had to share her only pair of shoes with her mother – meaning she could not go to school if her mother needed to wear shoes that day (Adams and editor, 2024). Rising fuel costs, caring needs, hunger, ill health, and mental health (parent and child) all create barriers to attending school.

The findings reveal a concerning escalation in child poverty within schools, which is significantly impeding children's ability to learn. Staff frequently observe students who are fatigued, hungry, anxious, unable to focus, and lacking the necessary materials to engage fully with the curriculum. Addressing poverty-related needs within the school community often diverts staff from their primary responsibilities, extending beyond their designated roles and expertise. This strain not only impacts the effectiveness of schools but exacts a heavy toll on the well-being of children.

People working in schools witness the impact of poverty on children and families daily, and the scale and severity of the problem means schools and staff are reeling. The Education Anti-Poverty Coalition, convened by the Child Poverty Action Group, conducted a first-of-its-kind survey of professionals working in every role in schools in England in September 2023. A growing proportion of school staff report diminished time and capacity to fulfil other aspects of their roles due to the repercussions of child poverty. Specifically, 79% of school staff report having less time and capacity for other duties because of the effects of child poverty. Similarly, there is a noticeable increase in the number of staff (74%) witnessing children from impoverished backgrounds falling further behind in their education compared to previous years.

- 89% believe that child poverty in their school has increased in the last two academic years
- 88% of school staff reported that increasing numbers of families in their school who previously appeared to be managing financially were now struggling to cope
- 82% believe that the reason poverty is having a greater effect on children's education is because the depth of poverty has worsened over the last two academic years
- 78% say they are noticing more families struggling with uniform and P.E. kit requirements
- 72% say more children come to school in ill-fitting or worn-out clothes
- 68% report that more children do not have enough money to buy enough food
- 46% say children are struggling to concentrate on learning due to hunger and fatigue

(CPAG, 2023)

Additionally, schools face an array of additional challenges, including financial constraints resulting in significant staff reductions, escalating operational costs, deteriorating infrastructure, inadequate funding for students with special educational needs and disabilities, and substantial cuts to essential services. The pervasive issue of child poverty undermines the entire education system, impacting everyone involved.

The impact

Beyond the immediate challenges of financial hardship, child poverty has a profound impact on various aspects of life, including stigma, health outcomes, and educational opportunities.

Child poverty often carries a significant stigma, both within communities and in broader societal perceptions. Stereotypes and misconceptions about poverty can lead to the stigmatisation of children and families experiencing financial hardship. This stigma can manifest in various forms, including social exclusion, discrimination, and feelings of shame or embarrassment. Children living in poverty may internalise these negative perceptions, leading to low self-esteem, diminished confidence, and a sense of hopelessness about their future prospects. Research (Inglis et al., 2022) has shown that children living in poverty often face social exclusion and discrimination from their peers, teachers, and other community members. Children from low-income families are more likely to experience peer rejection and victimisation, leading to feelings of isolation and alienation. The stigma associated with poverty can evoke feelings of shame and embarrassment among children and families, impacting their mental health and well-being. Children living in poverty may internalise negative perceptions and stereotypes about their socioeconomic status, leading to low self-esteem, diminished confidence, and a sense of hopelessness about their future prospects.

Stigma can create significant barriers to accessing support and resources for families experiencing poverty. Fear of judgement or societal condemnation may deter families from seeking assistance, exacerbating their financial hardships and limiting their access to essential services. A report by the Joseph Rowntree Foundation in 2022 highlights the impact of stigma on help-seeking behaviour among low-income families in the UK.

Secondly, the impact of child poverty on health outcomes is profound and enduring. Growing up in poverty exposes children to a range of health risks, including inadequate nutrition, substandard housing conditions, limited access to healthcare services, and heightened exposure to environmental toxins. These factors contribute to higher rates of physical and mental health problems among children living in poverty, including malnutrition, chronic illnesses, developmental delays, and mental health disorders such as anxiety and depression.

Children growing up in poverty often experience food insecurity and inadequate access to nutritious meals. Research conducted by the National Institute for Health and Care Research (NIHR) found that food insecurity among children in the UK is associated with poor dietary intake, leading to nutritional deficiencies and compromised health outcomes (Brazzelli and Cruickshank, 2018).

Poverty is closely linked to substandard housing conditions, including overcrowding, dampness, and poor sanitation. A report by Shelter highlighted the impact of inadequate housing on children's health, with findings showing higher rates of respiratory illnesses, infections, and mental health problems among children living in poor-quality housing (Harker, 2006).

Children from low-income families often face barriers to accessing healthcare services, including financial constraints, transportation issues, and long waiting times. Poverty is also associated with increased exposure to environmental toxins and pollutants, including air pollution, lead, and pesticides. In addition to ambient air pollution from traffic, heating, and industry, children's health is also threatened by other airborne pollutants, like second-hand smoke, damp, and mould (European Environment Agency, 2023).

The National Child Mortality Database (NCMD) reported living in temporary accommodation was a factor in the unexpected deaths of 55 children between 1 April 2019 and 31 March 2023, according to official reviewers. It found that 42 of those who died were less than a year old.

Temporary accommodation can include bed and breakfasts, hostels, and temporary housing, and is often supplied by councils. A shortage of social housing and soaring private rents have led some town halls to resort to places that are damp, cold, and overcrowded (Booth, 2024).

Poverty is a significant risk factor for the development of mental health disorders among children and adolescents. Research conducted by the Mental Health Foundation found that children living in poverty are more likely to experience anxiety, depression, and behavioural problems compared to their more affluent peers (Mental Health Foundation, 2023). Research also found that the stress and instability associated with poverty can have long-term effects on children's health, increasing their vulnerability to chronic diseases and reducing their life expectancy compared to their more affluent peers. The report highlighted the link between childhood poverty and poor health outcomes in adulthood, emphasising the need for early intervention and support (Mental Health at Work, 2024).

Poverty also significantly impacts parental mental health. People with mental health issues are also more likely to be lower paid than those without mental health issues, and money worries can exacerbate these (Gable and Florisson, 2023). The research also found 'people are 3.7 times more likely to say they experience poor mental health when they also lack confidence in being able to afford an unexpected expense'.

Child poverty in the UK has a profound impact on educational outcomes and opportunities, with children from low-income households facing significant barriers to academic success. Studies have documented the detrimental effects of poverty on educational attainment, highlighting the urgent need for targeted interventions and support. Children growing up in poverty often lack access to essential educational resources, including textbooks, school supplies, and technology. Research conducted by the Education Policy Institute (EPI) found that children from disadvantaged backgrounds are less likely to have access to educational resources at home, hindering their ability to engage in learning activities outside of school. The evidence also shows that the home learning environment (HLE), including how often children read with their parents, learn the alphabet and numbers, sing songs, play games, and go on educational visits, is crucial for the development of skills that determine school attainment. These include reading, verbal and spelling abilities, and positive behaviour, well-being, and enjoyment of school. Children living in poverty were found to be significantly less likely to experience a rich home learning environment (Education Policy Institute, 2018).

Poverty is closely linked to unstable home environments, including family instability, parental unemployment, and housing insecurity. There is also evidence that people who experience ACEs are more likely to experience poverty as adults. When children experience poverty and trauma at the same time, the impacts can be even more profound and damaging and can extend well beyond childhood. There is a clear link between childhood disadvantage, low educational attainment, and future poverty. This is largely due to challenges with access and engagement around education (Poverty and trauma, 2020).

Barriers to seeking help and support

Turn2us Life events and financial insecurity found the following barriers:

Only 45% of people surveyed said they would know where to seek financial support in the future. This indicates that a significant portion of individuals may not know where to turn when in need, potentially leading to delays in seeking assistance as they first have to search for available support services.

Shame, stigma, and a reluctance to seek help are significant factors contributing to delayed or avoided searches for support (jrf.org.uk, 2022). The survey suggests that only half of UK residents would feel comfortable seeking financial support from the government, 42% from their local council, and only 27% from a charity. Additionally, half of the respondents would wait until their situation became very serious before seeking financial assistance (Life events and financial insecurity, n.d.).

The findings raise concerns about the impact of stress, anxiety, and depression on delays in seeking help, highlighting the need for mental health support alongside financial assistance.

Thirty-five percent of survey respondents agreed that they would be too stressed to seek help in the event of a life event, indicating that immediate mental health impacts could hinder seeking necessary support. This risk is particularly alarming for individuals already vulnerable to poor mental health, potentially leading to a cycle of deteriorating mental well-being and financial resilience.

In addition to lack of awareness, shame, and stigma, negative perceptions of the welfare system present significant barriers to seeking help. Many respondents reported feeling unfairly treated when seeking welfare support, often citing negative experiences with the Department for Work and Pensions (DWP). These negative perceptions and experiences can deter individuals from seeking assistance in times of need.

What can we do?

In school and in the classroom

Teachers can play a crucial role in supporting children living in poverty during lessons by implementing several strategies:

- Create a supportive environment. Foster a welcoming and inclusive classroom atmosphere where all students feel valued and supported. Recognise and respect the diverse backgrounds and experiences of each student. Challenge stigma and discrimination, even jokes and 'banter'.
- Build positive relationships with students based on trust, respect, and empathy. Take the time to get to know each student individually and show genuine care and concern for their well-being. Offer emotional support and encouragement to students facing challenges related to poverty.
- Create opportunities for open dialogue and provide a safe space for students to express their feelings and concerns.
- Implement trauma-informed practices to support students who may have experienced adversity or trauma related to poverty. Provide a safe and nurturing environment that recognises the impact of adverse experiences on learning and behaviour.
- Offer mentorship programs or peer support groups where students can connect with older peers or mentors who have overcome similar challenges related to poverty. These programs can provide guidance, encouragement, and positive role models for students.
- Collaborate with school counsellors, social workers, and other support staff to identify and address the specific needs of students living in poverty. Develop individualised support plans and coordinate interventions to ensure that students receive comprehensive support both inside and outside the classroom.
- Incorporate culturally relevant content and experiences into lessons to make learning meaningful and relatable for students from different backgrounds. Validate students' identities and perspectives by including diverse voices in the curriculum.
- Be mindful of students' basic needs, such as hunger, hygiene, and clothing. Teachers can discreetly provide access to hygiene products and clothing assistance for students in need.

- Provide flexible learning materials that accommodate various learning styles and abilities. Offer a variety of resources, including digital and printed materials, to ensure accessibility for all students. When setting homework, remember that not everyone has access to a computer or even a quiet place to work at home.
- Provide opportunities for experiential learning and real-world application of knowledge, such as internships, job shadowing, or community service projects. These experiences can help students develop valuable skills, build confidence, and explore potential career pathways despite economic challenges.
- Offer financial literacy education and life skills training to equip students with the knowledge and skills they need to navigate financial challenges and make informed decisions about their future. Topics may include budgeting, saving, banking, and understanding credit.
- Promote social justice and equity in the classroom by discussing issues of poverty, inequality, and discrimination. Encourage students to critically examine systemic barriers and advocate for positive change in their community.
- Encourage students to express their thoughts and emotions about money through art journaling. Provide art supplies such as coloured pencils, markers, and collage materials, and prompt students to create visual representations of their financial worries, hopes, and aspirations. Art journaling can serve as a therapeutic outlet for processing emotions and reducing stress.
- Provide writing prompts related to money and financial well-being, such as 'Write a letter to your future self describing your financial goals' or 'Create a short story about a character overcoming financial challenges'. Encourage students to explore their thoughts and feelings about money through storytelling and self-reflection.
- Invite students to create their own podcast episodes focused on money management and financial literacy. Students can research topics such as budgeting, saving, and investing, then record audio segments sharing tips, advice, and personal anecdotes related to money management. This activity not only fosters creativity but also promotes financial education and empowerment.
- Financial Literacy Board Game: Design a board game that teaches players about money management skills and financial concepts. Students can work in groups to brainstorm game rules, create game pieces, and design the game board. Encourage creativity and innovation as students incorporate themes of budgeting, earning, and spending into their game design.
- Healthy budget cooking lessons and learning how to use leftovers are valuable skills that can help individuals and families save money, reduce food waste, and eat nutritious meals. Include nutrition advice, meal planning, and batch cooking.
- Connect students and their families with community resources and support services that can address their specific needs, such as food assistance programs and academic support programs.
- Advocate for policies and initiatives that address the root causes of poverty and inequality. Collaborate with colleagues and community stakeholders to advocate for equitable resources and opportunities for all students.

Myth: Child poverty in the UK only affects families who are unemployed.

Truth: In the UK, child poverty remains a significant issue, with approximately 4.3 million children living in poverty, according to recent statistics from the End Child Poverty coalition. This represents nearly one-third of all children in the country.

Myth: Child poverty in the UK only affects urban areas.

Truth: Child poverty exists in both urban and rural areas across the country. While urban areas may have higher concentrations of poverty due to factors like population density and higher living costs, rural communities also experience significant levels of child poverty, often exacerbated by issues such as isolation, limited access to services, and seasonal employment fluctuations.

Myth: Child poverty is the result of parental irresponsibility or poor financial management.

Truth: Research shows that factors beyond parental control, such as structural inequalities, systemic barriers, and economic downturns, play significant roles in driving child poverty rates. Blaming parents overlooks the complex socioeconomic factors that contribute to the problem.

Signposting for support

36% of people referred to food banks in the Trussell Trust network received no advice from other services before their latest referral to the food bank.

Citizens Advice Bureau (CAB): Citizens Advice offers free, confidential advice on a wide range of issues, including benefits, debt, housing, and employment rights. You can find your nearest CAB office or access their online resources through their website www.citizensadvice.org.uk/

Trussell Trust Foodbanks: The Trussell Trust operates a network of food banks across the UK, providing emergency food parcels to individuals and families in crisis. You can find your nearest food bank and access their services through the Trussell Trust website www.trusselltrust.org/

Turn2us: Turn2us is a charity that helps people in financial hardship to access welfare benefits, charitable grants, and support services. They provide an online benefits calculator, grant search tool, and helpline for individuals seeking assistance www.turn2us.org.uk/

Shelter: Shelter provides support and advice to people facing homelessness or housing issues. They offer online resources, helplines, and face-to-face support services to help individuals find suitable accommodation and navigate housing-related challenges www.shelter.org.uk/

Child Poverty Action Group (CPAG): CPAG campaigns for policies and practices that reduce child poverty and improve the lives of low-income families. They offer advice, information, and resources to individuals and organisations working to address child poverty in the UK https://cpag.org.uk/

Local Welfare Assistance Schemes: Many local authorities operate welfare assistance schemes that provide emergency financial support to residents facing crisis situations. You can contact your local council to inquire about the availability of these schemes in your area.

Jobcentre Plus: Jobcentre Plus offices offer support and guidance to individuals seeking employment, including access to benefits and financial assistance for those who are unemployed or on a low-income www.gov.uk/contact-jobcentre-plus

Community Support Groups: Many local community organisations and charities provide support to individuals and families in need, including food aid, financial assistance, and practical help. You can search online or inquire at your local council office for information about community support groups in your area.

References

Adams, R. and editor, R.A.E. (2024). Government to fund school 'attendance mentors' in worst-hit areas of England. *The Guardian.* [online] 5 Jan. Available at: www.theguardian.com/education/2024/jan/05/government-fund-school-attendance-mentors-worst-hit-areas-england [Accessed 25 Mar. 2024].

Booth, R. and correspondent, R.B.S. affairs (2024). Temporary housing 'a factor in 55 child deaths in England since 2019'. *The Guardian.* [online] 4 Mar. Available at: www.theguardian.com/society/2024/mar/04/temporary-accommodation-a-factor-in-child-deaths-in-england-review-finds?CMP=Share_iOSApp_Other [Accessed 25 Mar. 2024].

Brazzelli, M. and Cruickshank, M. (2018). Child food insecurity in the UK: Evidence on its extent, nature and effects and what can be done to address it: A rapid review 2. *Name of External Assessment Group (EAG) and Project Lead Aberdeen Health Technology Assessment Group.* [online] Available at: https://njl-admin.nihr.ac.uk/document/download/2025189 [Accessed 25 Mar. 2024].

Bull, R., Miles, C., Newbury, E., Nichols, A. and Weekes, T. (2023). *Hunger in the UK.* [online] The Trussell Trust. Available at: https://www.trusselltrust.org/wp-content/uploads/sites/2/2023/08/2023-The-Trussell-Trust-Hunger-in-the-UK-report-web-updated-10Aug23.pdf.

Child Poverty Action Group. (2023). *'There is only so much we can do' - School staff in England | CPAG.* [online] Available at: https://cpag.org.uk/news/there-only-so-much-we-can-do-school-staff-england#:~:text=4.2%20million%20children%20in%20the

CIPD. (n.d.). *CIPD | Tackling in-work poverty.* [online] Available at: www.cipd.org/uk/knowledge/guides/in-work-poverty/#gref [Accessed 25 Mar. 2024].

CPAG. (2023). *Official Child Poverty statistics: 350,000 more children in poverty and numbers will rise| CPAG.* [online] cpag.org.uk. Available at: https://cpag.org.uk/news/official-child-poverty-statistics-350000-more-children-and-numbers-will-rise.

Education Policy Institute. (2018). *The education policy institute.* [online] Available at: https://epi.org.uk/

European Environment Agency. (2023). *Air pollution and children's health - European environment agency.* [online] www.eea.europa.eu. Available at: www.eea.europa.eu/publications/air-pollution-and-childrens-health

Gable, O. and Florisson, R. (2023). *Limiting choices: Why people risk insecure work.* [online] Available at: www.lancaster.ac.uk/media/lancaster-university/content-assets/documents/lums/work-foundation/reports/limiting-choices.pdf

Harker, L. (2006). Chance of a lifetime: The impact of bad housing on children's lives. *Shelter.* [online] Available at: https://assets.ctfassets.net/6sxvmndnpn0s/4LTXp3mya7ligRmNG8x9KK/6922b5a4c6ea756ea94da71ebdc001a5/Chance_of_a_Lifetime.pdf

Inglis, G., Jenkins, P., McHardy, F., Sosu, E. and Wilson, C. (2022). Poverty stigma, mental health, and well-being: A rapid review and synthesis of quantitative and qualitative research. *Journal of Community & Applied Social Psychology,* 33(4). https://doi.org/10.1002/casp.2677

Joseph Rowntree Foundation. (2024). UK poverty 2024: The essential guide to understanding poverty in the UK | Joseph Rowntree foundation. [online] Available at: www.jrf.org.uk/uk-

Levelling up the United Kingdom. (2022). Available at: https://assets.publishing.service.gov.uk/media/61fd3ca28fa8f5388e9781c6/Levelling_up_the_UK_white_paper.pdf

Life events and financial insecurity. (n.d.). Available at: www.turn2us.org.uk/T2UWebsite/media/Documents/PDFs/Life-Events-Executive-Summary-Final.pdf

Mental Health at Work. (2024). *The mental health impact on people suffering in-work poverty*. [online] Available at: www.mentalhealthatwork.org.uk/resource/the-mental-health-impact-on-people-suffering-poverty-in-work/?read=more [Accessed 25 Mar. 2024].

Mental Health Foundation. (2023). *Poverty: Statistics*. [online] Available at: www.mentalhealth.org.uk/explore-mental-health/statistics/poverty-statistics#:~:text=Analysis%20of%20data%20from%20the

National Child Mortality Database. (n.d.). *NCMD | The national child mortality database*. [online] Available at: www.ncmd.info/

Poverty and trauma. (2020). Available at: www.therobertsontrust.org.uk/media/uivjx4p0/poverty_and_trauma_briefing.pdf

poverty-2024-the-essential-guide-to-understanding-poverty-in-themuk#:~:text=More%20than%201%20in%205

School staff in England on the impact of poverty on children and school life. (2023). Available at: https://cpag.org.uk/sites/default/files/2023-10/%27There%20is%20only%20so%20much%20we%20can%20do%27%20School%20staff%20in%20England%20on%20the%20impact%20of%20poverty%20on%20children%20and%20school%20life.pdf

www.jrf.org.uk. (2022). How we can flush out poverty stigma from our systems and services | Joseph Rowntree foundation. [online] Available at: www.jrf.org.uk/how-we-can-flush-out-poverty-stigma-from-our-systems-and-services

12 Climate crisis

Quote: 'I am so worried about the climate crisis; it feels like we're running out of time to save the planet. What kind of world will we be living in if things keep going the way they are?'

The world is getting hotter, and humans are the cause, without question. It has been predicted that in ten years' time, the damage that human activities have inflicted on the planet's climate will be irreversible.

Young Minds' 'Deconstructing the system: young people's voices on mental health, society and inequality' report (2024) states that 87% of young people worry about climate change. Eco-anxiety is growing among young people. Researchers at the University of Bath found that climate change and inadequate governmental responses are linked with climate anxiety and distress in children and young people globally. The level of distress young people feel over climate change is a threat to their health and well-being. It also makes them trust the Government even less due to a perceived lack of action on environmental issues.

There has been a 68% average decline in the population sizes of mammals, birds, amphibians, reptiles, and fish between 1970 and 2016.

Extreme weather events have detrimental effects on biodiversity and wildlife. For instance, in Australia at the end of 2019 and the beginning of 2020, fires exacerbated by climate conditions ravaged 97 square kilometres of forest and surrounding habitats.

Climate change significantly impacts oceans and bodies of water, such as warming temperatures, acidification, coral bleaching, and other detrimental effects.

The ocean has absorbed a substantial amount of increased heat; approximately 90% of the heat generated by rising emissions has been absorbed by the ocean.

Global sea levels have risen by approximately 8 inches, or 20 centimetres, over the past century.

Coral reefs face particularly acute vulnerability to climate change. The Great Barrier Reef in Australia has suffered substantial coral loss since the 1990s, with estimates suggesting a decline of half its corals.

Annually, over 12 million hectares of land are lost to desertification, land degradation, and drought.

Human activities have irrevocably altered at least three-quarters of land-based environments and more than 66% of marine environments.

DOI: 10.4324/9781032697932-12

Ice glaciers are receding in Greenland, the Alps, the Himalayas, the Andes, the Rockies, Africa, and Alaska.

Between 1993 and 2019, Greenland witnessed an average loss of 279 billion tons of ice annually, while Antarctica experienced a loss of 148 billion tons of ice each year. To put this into perspective, this ice loss is roughly equivalent in weight to the entirety of Mount Everest.

68% of extreme weather events investigated over the past two decades were either intensified or made more probable by human-induced climate change.

There has been a reported 53.7% increase in heat-related mortality among individuals over 65 years old over the past two decades, a trend likely to persist as temperatures continue to rise.

In 2020, extreme weather, alongside conflicts and economic shocks, pushed at least 155 million people into acute food insecurity.

Climate and mental health

YouGov and Woodland Trust published their survey in February 2023:

- 16-24s more likely to be 'very worried' about climate change vs. age 50+, with nearly one in three (31%) 'very worried' compared to 23% of 50-64-year-olds and 18% of those aged 65 and over
- 20% of people aged 16-24 would be willing to have fewer children than they would like to address climate change
- Almost one in three people aged 16-24 (33%) are scared when hearing about climate change
- 75% of people would be willing to plant a tree
- 86% of people feel that being outdoors and among nature has a positive impact on their mental health
- Only 9% of people aged 16-24 feel like they have influence in making decisions about climate change

Climate security

Climate security refers to the effects of the climate crisis on peace and stability, particularly in vulnerable and conflict-ridden environments (UNDP Climate Promise). The impacts of climate change can worsen food, water, and livelihood insecurity, resulting in competition over natural resources, social disruptions, and displacement. The UN Refugee Agency (UNHRC UK, n.d.) reports that in 2022, a staggering 84% of refugees and asylum seekers originated from countries highly vulnerable to climate-related risks, particularly vulnerable groups, including women, girls, and other marginalised communities, who bear disproportionate risks and burdens from climate change due to prevailing societal roles, responsibilities, and cultural norms.

These factors can escalate tensions, foster conflict, and destabilise a country or region. In regions already afflicted by conflict, climate change can exacerbate or prolong existing conflicts, presenting obstacles to achieving and maintaining peace. By investing in climate action, there is an opportunity to enhance collaboration, restore confidence, and mend societal bonds in fragile and conflict-affected areas.

United Nations climate change action

The Paris Agreement, the Kyoto Protocol, and the Convention are key international agreements aimed at addressing climate change. E They represent concerted global efforts to combat climate change and safeguard the environment for current and future generations.

The Paris Agreement is a landmark international treaty that aims to combat climate change by limiting global warming to well below 2 degrees Celsius above pre-industrial levels, with efforts to limit the temperature increase to 1.5 degrees Celsius. It was adopted in 2015 at the United Nations Framework Convention on Climate Change (UNFCCC, 2017) Conference of the Parties (COP21) in Paris, France. The agreement outlines commitments from participating countries to reduce greenhouse gas emissions, enhance resilience to climate impacts, and provide financial and technological support to developing nations.

The Kyoto Protocol is an international treaty aimed at mitigating climate change by setting binding targets for reducing greenhouse gas emissions. It was adopted in 1997 as an extension of the United Nations Framework Convention on Climate Change (UNFCCC). The protocol requires participating developed countries to reduce their emissions of six greenhouse gases to levels below those of 1990. It also established mechanisms such as emissions trading and clean development projects to help countries meet their targets. Although the protocol has faced challenges and limitations, it represented a significant step forward in international efforts to address climate change.

The Convention refers to the United Nations Framework Convention on Climate Change (UNFCCC), a landmark international treaty established in 1992 with the objective of addressing global warming and its impacts on the environment. The Convention sets forth principles and guidelines for international cooperation on climate change mitigation, adaptation, and sustainable development. It serves as the foundation for subsequent agreements and protocols aimed at reducing greenhouse gas emissions and fostering climate resilience worldwide.

Things we can all do about climate change

Plant trees, plants, and flowers. Trees are crucial in combating climate change by absorbing and storing carbon dioxide. Many flowers attract pollinators like bees, butterflies, and birds. By providing habitat and food sources for these pollinators, you're supporting biodiversity, which is essential for ecosystem health. Healthy ecosystems play a role in sequestering carbon and regulating the climate.

Make mindful choices about your food consumption by opting for locally sourced and in-season products. This reduces the carbon footprint associated with transportation. And try growing some of your own fruits and vegetables.

Consider reducing or eliminating meat consumption, as the livestock sector contributes significantly to greenhouse gas emissions.

Take simple steps to minimise single-use plastics in your daily life. Use reusable water bottles, coffee cups, and shopping bags. Choose products packaged in glass or alternative materials and consider eco-friendly alternatives for household items like washing-up sponges.

Use public transport whenever possible. Many companies are transitioning to electric vehicles to reduce pollution.

Practice energy-saving habits like turning off lights and unplugging appliances when not in use. Invest in energy-efficient housing, appliances, and smart technologies to further reduce energy consumption and lower utility bills. You can also consider switching to energy providers that offer renewable energy options to reduce reliance on fossil fuels.

Talking about the climate crisis

Talking to children and teenagers about the climate crisis, particularly if they are very anxious and worried, should aim to provide support, information, and empowerment. Here are some key topics and strategies to consider:

Acknowledge their feelings: Begin by acknowledging and validating their concerns about the climate crisis. Let them know that it's normal to feel anxious or worried about such a significant issue.

Provide accurate information: Offer factual information about the climate crisis, including its causes, impacts, and potential solutions. Help them understand the science behind climate change and dispel any misconceptions or misinformation they may have encountered.

Discuss coping strategies: Explore healthy coping strategies for managing anxiety and stress related to the climate crisis. Encourage activities such as mindfulness, meditation, spending time in nature, and engaging in positive actions like volunteering or advocacy.

Focus on empowerment: Empower them to take action and make a difference in addressing the climate crisis. Encourage them to get involved in environmental initiatives, advocacy campaigns, or community projects aimed at promoting sustainability and resilience.

Highlight positive examples: Share stories of individuals, communities, and organisations that are making a positive impact in the fight against climate change. Highlight examples of innovative solutions, grassroots movements, and collective action that inspire hope and optimism.

Promote resilience: Discuss the importance of resilience and adaptation in the face of climate change. Help them to develop skills and strategies for coping with uncertainty, building community connections, and fostering personal resilience.

Encourage self-care: Emphasise the importance of self-care and well-being during times of heightened anxiety. Encourage them to prioritise activities that promote mental and emotional health, such as getting enough sleep, eating well, exercising regularly, and seeking support from trusted friends, family members, or mental health professionals.

Maintain open communication: Keep the lines of communication open and encourage them to express their thoughts, feelings, and questions about the climate crisis. Listen actively, without judgement, and provide a supportive space for them to share their concerns and ideas.

Activities for the classroom

Integrating climate teaching and activities into the classroom provides numerous benefits that extend beyond academic achievement to encompass personal growth, social responsibility, and environmental stewardship, preparing students to thrive in a rapidly changing world.

Here are some ideas you can try:

- Use online simulations or interactive models to demonstrate the greenhouse effect, carbon cycle, and impacts of climate change.
- Analyse real-life case studies of communities affected by climate change, such as coastal erosion, wildfires, or droughts.
- Discuss current events related to climate change, allowing students to explore news articles and scientific reports to understand ongoing developments.
- Organise debates on controversial topics related to climate change, such as the role of government policies, renewable energy solutions, or climate change denial.
- Project-based tasks where students research climate change topics and propose solutions or actions. Projects could include creating awareness campaigns, designing sustainable urban plans, or developing renewable energy models.
- Set up investigations where students collect and analyse data on local weather patterns, carbon footprints, or biodiversity changes.
- Integrate art projects into the curriculum, allowing students to express their understanding of climate change through drawings, paintings, or multimedia presentations.
- Encourage creative writing assignments where students imagine future scenarios impacted by climate change or write persuasive speeches advocating for environmental action.
- Explore interdisciplinary connections by incorporating climate change topics into subjects like science, geography, mathematics, language arts, and social studies.
- Take students on field trips to local ecosystems, parks, or environmental centres to observe firsthand the effects of climate change on biodiversity and ecosystems.
- Arrange outdoor activities like nature walks, tree planting, or water quality testing to foster environmental stewardship and appreciation.
- Invite guest speakers, such as scientists, activists, or policymakers, to share their expertise and experiences related to climate change.
- Arrange virtual or in-person interviews with local professionals working in fields relevant to climate science, renewable energy, or environmental conservation.
- Empower students to act by initiating school-wide sustainability projects, such as recycling programs, energy audits, or community garden initiatives.
- Encourage student-led initiatives to advocate for policy changes, participate in climate strikes, or engage in community activism focused on climate justice.
- Community planting days can be a community-building activity that raises awareness about environmental issues, including climate change. Community gardens and green spaces foster a sense of stewardship and can lead to broader efforts to address environmental challenges.

Setting up a nature group

Creating a student-led nature group in schools empowers students to take ownership of environmental initiatives and drive positive change within their school community.

Start by conducting a survey or holding a meeting to gauge student interest in forming a nature group. Encourage students to express their ideas, concerns, and motivations for getting involved.

Facilitate the selection of a student leadership team to spearhead the establishment and operation of the nature group. This team could include roles such as president, vice president, secretary, treasurer, and project coordinators.

Collaboratively set goals and objectives for the nature group based on student interests and priorities. Encourage the leadership team to brainstorm ideas and develop a vision for the group's activities and impact.

Empower the student leadership team to recruit members for the nature and eco group from across different grade levels and backgrounds. Utilise creative strategies such as posters, social media announcements, and classroom presentations to attract participants.

Establish an organisational structure for the nature group, including regular meetings, decision-making processes, and communication channels. Encourage transparency, inclusivity, and democratic participation in group activities.

Task the group with planning and organising nature-based projects and eco-friendly initiatives within the school community. Encourage creativity, collaboration, and innovation in project selection and implementation.

Provide opportunities for student leaders to develop leadership, communication, teamwork, and problem-solving skills through their involvement in the nature group. Offer training, workshops, and mentorship to support their personal and professional growth.

Facilitate partnerships and collaboration with local environmental organisations, businesses, government agencies, and community groups. Encourage student leaders to network, seek support, and leverage resources to amplify the impact of their initiatives.

Encourage them to regularly evaluate the effectiveness of group activities and reflect on lessons learned.

Celebrate the achievements and contributions of student leaders and members of the nature group. Acknowledge their efforts through awards, certificates, public recognition, and social media highlights to inspire others and reinforce the value of student-led initiatives.

Establishing a student-led nature and eco group in schools offers a multitude of benefits for participating students, including:

Students can develop and practise leadership skills by taking on roles such as president, vice president, project coordinator, or treasurer within the group. They learn how to organise events, delegate tasks, make decisions, and collaborate effectively with peers and stakeholders.

Participation in nature group activities fosters a deeper understanding of environmental issues, sustainability principles, and the importance of conservation efforts. Students gain firsthand experience in addressing real-world challenges and making a positive impact on the environment.

Students feel empowered to take action and make a difference in their school community and beyond. They develop a sense of agency and responsibility for creating positive change, which boosts their self-confidence and motivation to tackle environmental issues.

The nature group provides a platform for students to engage with their peers, teachers, parents/carers, and local community members in meaningful ways. Through collaborative projects and partnerships, students build connections, foster social cohesion, and strengthen community ties.

Participation in nature group activities enhances students' communication, teamwork, problem-solving, and critical thinking skills. They learn how to plan and execute projects, adapt to challenges, and evaluate outcomes, which are valuable skills for academic and future career success.

Engaging in outdoor activities and spending time in nature has been shown to reduce stress and anxiety and improve overall well-being. Students benefit from spending time outdoors, connecting with nature, and participating in hands-on environmental projects, which can promote mental health and resilience and help to reduce anxiety about climate change.

Being part of a nature group gives students a sense of purpose and fulfilment as they work towards common goals related to environmental conservation and sustainability. They feel a sense of pride in contributing to positive changes in their school and community.

By actively participating in environmental initiatives, students develop a sense of responsibility and stewardship towards the environment. They learn to appreciate and respect nature and cultivate a lifelong commitment to protecting the planet for future generations.

Myth: Young people are not significantly affected by the climate crisis.
Truth: The climate crisis profoundly impacts young people, both now and in the future. They face the long-term consequences of climate change, including extreme weather events, rising sea levels, food and water shortages, and displacement from their homes. Additionally, young people are inheriting a planet with a degraded environment, which will impact their quality of life and economic prospects.
Myth: Young people are not capable of contributing meaningfully to addressing the climate crisis.
Truth: Young people play a crucial role in climate action and are driving significant change worldwide. They are leading protests, advocating for policy reforms, implementing sustainability initiatives, and raising awareness about environmental issues. Many youth-led organisations and movements are at the forefront of efforts to combat climate change and promote environmental justice.
Myth: Climate change is an abstract concept for young people, and they are not concerned about it.
Truth: Young people are deeply concerned about the climate crisis. They recognise the urgent need for action to mitigate its effects and are demanding that governments, businesses, and communities take decisive steps to address climate change. Young activists are mobilising their peers and amplifying their voices to push for tangible solutions and hold decision-makers accountable.

Useful websites

Clean Air Task Force: www.catf.us/

Union of Concerned Scientists: www.ucsusa.org/

Carbon180: https://carbon180.org/

Greenpeace: www.greenpeace.org/

Earth Justice: https://earthjustice.org/

Rainforest Alliance: www.rainforest-alliance.org/

Climate Foundation: www.climatefoundation.org/

Climate Emergency Fund: www.climateemergencyfund.org/

Friends of the Earth: https://friendsoftheearth.uk/

Environmental Defense Fund: www.edf.org/

Woodland Trust: www.woodlandtrust.org.uk/

Find Out More: A Guide to NASA's Global Climate Change Website https://science.nasa.gov/climate-change/what-is-climate-change/

This website provides a high-level overview of some of the known causes, effects and indications of global climate change:

Evidence. Brief descriptions of some of the key scientific observations that our planet is undergoing abrupt climate change. https://science.nasa.gov/climate-change/evidence/

Causes. A concise discussion of the primary climate change causes on our planet. https://science.nasa.gov/climate-change/causes/

Effects. A look at some of the likely future effects of climate change, including U.S. regional effects. https://science.nasa.gov/climate-change/effects/

Vital Signs. Graphs and animated time series showing real-time climate change data, including atmospheric carbon dioxide, global temperature, sea ice extent, and ice sheet volume. https://climate.nasa.gov/vital-signs/carbon-dioxide/?intent=121

Earth Minute. This fun video series explains various Earth science topics, including some climate change topics. https://science.nasa.gov/earth/multimedia/earth-minute/

References

Charity Digital. (n.d.). *Climate change facts you need to know in 2024*. [online] Available at: https://charitydigital.org.uk/topics/climate-change-facts-you-need-to-know-in-2024-10655 [Accessed 27 Mar. 2024].

Trust, W. (2023). Young people's climate anxiety soaring. *Woodland Trust*. [online] Available at: www.woodlandtrust.org.uk/press-centre/2023/03/young-people-climate-anxiety-green-space-access/#:~:text=16%2D24s%20more%20likely%20to

UNDP Climate Promise. (n.d.a). *The climate dictionary: An everyday guide to climate change*. [online] Available at: https://climatepromise.undp.org/news-and-stories/climate-dictionary-everyday-guide-climate-change#:~:text=Climate%20change%20refers%20to%20the

UNDP Climate Promise. (n.d.b). *What is climate security and why is it important?* [online] Available at: https://climatepromise.undp.org/news-and-stories/what-climate-security-and-why-it-important

UNHCR UK. (n.d.). *Climate change and disaster displacement*. [online] Available at: www.unhcr.org/uk/what-we-do/build-better-futures/environment-disasters-and-climate-change/climate-change-and#:~:text=Climate%20change%20is%20increasingly%20linked [Accessed 27 Mar. 2024].

United Nations. (2017). UNFCCC. *Unfccc.int*. [online] Available at: https://unfccc.int/

Young Minds. (2024). *Deconstructing the system | Mental health report*. [online] Available at: www.youngminds.org.uk/about-us/reports-and-impact/deconstructing-the-system/global-issues-and-their-impact-on-young-people/#:~:text=Climate%20crisis%20and%20conflict&text=Researchers%20at%20the%20University%20of

13 Refugees

Chapter introduction

Have you supported refugees and asylum seekers in your school community? In this chapter, we explore the terms 'refugees', 'asylum seekers', and 'immigrants' and consider some of the barriers to learning that may be encountered by children with English as an Additional Language, and thus some of the support strategies that can be employed in our classrooms and schools to reduce these barriers.

The School of Sanctuary is a beacon for good provision when welcoming refugees to the school community, but what does it mean to have refugee children in our classrooms, and how can we support them in sharing their voices and integrating them into our school life? The second half of this chapter offers the expert voice of Jeannette Baxter, who leads a special event called 'A Day of Welcome' that aims to build a culture of welcome and understanding for people seeking sanctuary.

Empathy and compassion

Let us begin this chapter with some reflective questions:

What is empathy?
What is compassion?
How do they differ?

Empathy can be understood as an awareness and ability to understand somebody else's feelings and perspective, whilst **compassion** comes from a place of action and pity in wanting to help someone because of their suffering or circumstances.

How can we develop empathy and compassion in our learners; in fact, we must question how this is even possible. Essentially, at the heart of a safe classroom space must be inclusivity for all, and to provide this, empathy and compassion are key.

DOI: 10.4324/9781032697932-13

Refugees, asylum seekers, migrants, and immigrants

To better be able to support refugees and asylum seekers in our schools, it is important to ensure we understand the different terms:

'**Refugees**' are people forced to flee their country because of war, persecution, or violence; a refugee has a well-founded fear of persecution on the basis of their race, sexuality, religion, nationality, political opinion, or membership in a particular social group.

'**Asylum seekers**' are people seeking protection from war, persecution, or violence but who have not yet had their refugee status evaluated by the authorities.

'**Migrants**' are people who choose to move to another country for other reasons (to be with family, for better job prospects, etc.).

'**Immigrants**' are people who move to live in a country other than that of their birth, where they do not possess nationality.

The UK media is increasingly publishing reports of refugee migration, many of which are negative in tone. During teacher training, it is likely that the focus of the modules may have been on how to teach, as opposed to who you are teaching, especially when it comes to teaching children who have moved to our country from a totally different country or culture, and sometimes under circumstances of war, and thus harbouring trauma and loss from all they are leaving behind. Additionally, these children may not speak much English, or even any English at all, adding a more complex dynamic to how we can support them once they arrive in our classrooms. As teachers, we may not be able to fully explain to our pupils the tangled reasons why so many people have to live like this, nor what the solutions might be, but what we can do is help them appreciate that there are real people behind the statistics – and as educators, we all know that empathy can be a powerful force for change.

EAL and SEND

It is important we also appreciate that English as an Additional Language (EAL) is not a Special Education Need or Disability (SEND) in and of itself. Although some children with EAL may also have SEND, these are two very separate entities.

As The Bell Foundation (2024) highlights, learning EAL is not the same as having SEND; however, there may be a need for language support as the child will need to access the curriculum in English. For children with EAL, however, diagnosis of need can sometimes be more difficult due to communication and assessment.

The Bell Foundation (2024) estimates that almost 230,000 children are both EAL and SEND in schools in England alone, though understandably, this figure may not be accurate due to the complex nature of diagnosis in these cases.

Strategies to support refugee learners

When it comes to supporting refugees and asylum seekers in our classrooms, the situation will likely vary depending on the children's backgrounds and experiences. There may be children who have recently witnessed war and may struggle to leave their parents or even go into a classroom through fear. There may be children who have not been in school for a long period of time, whilst others may have been educated recently. To help understand the best way to support them, the key will be through communication with the parents and carers; however, again, the language barrier can make these discussions difficult. Where possible, see if another member of staff or even a parent could help bridge the language gap if they speak that language and act as a translator. Otherwise, a free online translating tool can be useful - speak or type into the translator, and then let it translate your words for the parent to listen to. Consider using visuals and pictures where necessary, such as on any letters or emails home.

Also, remember the student may be feeling a loss for what they have left behind; give them space to talk about their home country or culture if they wish to; find their birth country on a map, plot their route from there to your school, allow for conversation - as age appropriate - about their relocation and situation by looking at items in the news.

Resources to support refugee learners

Depending on where you are based in the world, your country may have its own set of resources from your government, authorities, or councils around how to support refugees in your community. There are also many charities that offer resources and information that could be useful for you to explore, particularly around English as an Additional Language aspect; some of these are listed:

The Bell Foundation
https://www.bell-foundation.org.uk/
Through generating and applying evidence, The Bell Foundation aims to improve policy, practices, and systems to enable children, adults, and communities in the UK who speak English as an Additional Language (EAL) to overcome disadvantages through language education.
Naldic
https://naldic.org.uk/
NALDIC provides a welcoming, vibrant, professional forum for learning more about English as an Additional Language (EAL) and bilingual learners in schools.
The British Council
https://www.naldic.org.uk/eal-advocacy/eal-news-summary/020113.html

As the 2011 UK census shows, almost one in eight or 13% of UK residents were born outside the UK; what better time for the British Council to expand its activities in the UK? In its most recent foray into UK EAL and ESOL, the British Council has recently published 'Innovations in English Language Teaching to Migrants and Refugees'. The publication includes 14 papers covering a range of EAL and ESOL topics. According to Melissa Cudmore, Senior Adviser for English and Examinations at the British Council, the international organisation has 'recently started to extend our work to the UK, connecting with the ESOL (English for speakers of other languages) communities by launching our first ESOL-specific website' and to organise events for EFL, ESOL and EAL practitioners.

In the second half of this chapter, Jeannette Baxter tells us more about the 'Day of Welcome' and shares further information on what it looks like to support refuge-seeking pupils and their families.

A day of welcome: building a culture of welcome in schools for people seeking sanctuary, by Jeannette Baxter

A Day of Welcome is a collaboration between UK Schools of Sanctuary and Anglia Ruskin University, led by Jake Rose-Brown and Jeannette Baxter. It is an annual day of solidarity and learning that aims to build a culture of welcome and understanding for people seeking sanctuary. A Day of Welcome supports children and young people in understanding the importance of building welcoming communities and helps schools to educate and support refugee and sanctuary-seeking pupils and their families better. A Day of Welcome is open to primary and secondary schools across the UK, and it takes place on the Friday before Refugee Week to maximise engagement in local and national activities.

The Day of Welcome's key aims are:

- Support schools to foster a culture of welcome, belonging, and solidarity for those seeking sanctuary.
- Help teachers to uncover and share stories of refugee migration, local and global, past and present.
- Assist schools to educate and support refugee pupils and their families better.

A day of welcome: the human stories behind the statistics

According to the United Nations High Commissioner for Refugees (UNHCR), the number of forcibly displaced people worldwide is estimated at 110.8 million. This figure encompasses 'refugees, asylum seekers, internally displaced people, and other people in need of international protection', people who have been 'forcibly displaced from their homes due to persecution, conflict, violence, human rights violations and events seriously disturbing to public order'. 40% of all people seeking sanctuary are children.

Whilst these statistics communicate the scale of global displacement today, what gets lost in them, and particularly in the media reporting of them, are the human stories. A Day of Welcome started life in Norfolk in 2018 when reports about the so-called 'Refugee Crisis' were dominating national media, and anti-immigrant discourse and behaviour were on the rise locally. As educators, we felt strongly that it was our responsibility to help children and young people make sense of the overwhelming number of media stories and images of refugees and asylum seekers coming to the UK. As part of this, we wanted to tackle media myths about refugees and asylum seekers prevalent in some newspapers and media outlets and develop evidence-based learning and teaching materials that counter these myths and show the positive contributions that refugees and asylum seekers make to our society and culture.

To develop the Day of Welcome, we formed a partnership with a Norwich charity that supports refugees and people seeking asylum to integrate into the local community, and with a group of their clients aged between 18 and 55, we established key aims for the project. We have since established a formal project advisory board made up of local people with lived experience, including recently settled refugees with children in local schools. Our experts, by experience, ensure refugee agency and voice in the shaping and delivery of the Day of Welcome.

In its first year, A Day of Welcome engaged 57 schools across Norfolk, involving 23,374 pupils (aged between 4-18 years) and teachers. We have gradually grown the Day of Welcome year on year across the United Kingdom, and in 2023, more than 530 schools, representing tens of thousands of pupils, took part in building communities of welcome and solidarity.

What does a Day of Welcome look like?

In every school, the Day of Welcome will look different. We offer more than 60 research-informed activities, teaching resources, training opportunities, and live events that schools can pick and choose from. Some schools may take a whole day off curriculum where every lesson explores the topics of refugee migration; some schools may engage in their own refugee heritage project. Others may simply choose to do one of our range of lessons and activities. With this in mind, we have incorporated live author webcasts into our Day of Welcome offer, bringing thousands of pupils into direct conversation with the likes of Miriam Halahmy, Dina Nayeri, Victoria Jamieson, Omar Muhamed, Michael Rosen, and Edmund de Waal.

However schools choose to participate in the Day of Welcome, our aim is to make it easy and engaging for them. We provide all participating schools with a toolkit that supports them when planning their Day of Welcome, and if they are unable to join us on the day, schools are invited to use our resources throughout Refugee Week or at any other time to support their curriculum learning. Our teacher evaluations evidence the quality, adaptability, and relevance of our resources:

> The materials, lesson and webinars are very well thought and help the children understand more about refugees, asylum seekers and their experiences.
>
> We use A Day of Welcome each year to review the 'Welcome' Greetings that we use in school: at the beginning of our celebration assembly each Friday children are greeted with 'Welcome' in 24 languages which reflect the languages spoken by members of the school community (including staff) and those linked to our local area.
>
> There were several poignant moments during this year's Day of Welcome. We currently have 2 Ukrainian refugees with us & the activities and events helped the children to really relate.
>
> The discussions around school on the day showed a greater understanding of refugees and migration. These conversations have continued throughout the term and pupils link the concepts to their other learning.
>
> (Teachers' Evaluation data, Day of Welcome 2023)

Creativity into community

A key element of the Day of Welcome resources is a creative response, whereby pupils are asked to respond creatively or artistically to the refugee migration histories they have been learning about and discussing. Examples include letter-writing to historical migrant groups, creating 'Welcome' cards for recently settled families, and visual poems of solidarity in collaboration with local refugee groups and families.

Feedback from teachers shows us that creative activities are particularly powerful ways of encouraging pupils to think about different reasons why people are forced to seek sanctuary and to imagine what that must be like, to flee your homeland and to leave your family, friends, and job behind, and to resettle in a new country, in a new culture, potentially learning a new language and a new way of life.

> Our Year 12 pupils delivered sessions for Year 7 pupils using the creative resources which you supplied. The pupils then created an art display which stands near our reception area where it is seen by all.
>
> (Teachers' Evaluation data, Day of Welcome 2023)

Building wider communities of welcome

We all have a role to play in fostering a culture of kindness, and as the centre of our communities, the potential impact of schools is huge. The Day of Welcome empowers teachers to unlock this potential by providing resources that are tailored to the contexts of various local areas and counties, from Norwich to Cardiff and beyond, and which help school communities to understand how people seeking safety have played a part in making their own cities, towns, and local communities the places they are today. Our work with schools to date shows us that involving refugee families in the Day of Welcome activities and events strengthens links between refugee and host communities and enhances understanding of sanctuary-seeking, both past and present.

> I enjoyed a lot working on the Day of Welcome project because it engaged local schools, teachers and refugee groups. I appreciated how they [Basque Child refugees] needed to be welcomed warmly to ease their troubles as my children felt such a necessity of welcoming at the school when arriving in the UK.
>
> (An expert by experience on the Haven's East project, which uncovered little-known stories of Basque child refugee migration to 1930s East Anglia)

Beyond learning in the classroom, schools can also use the Day of Welcome to focus on fundraising activities for local organisations that support refugees and people seeking sanctuary. This is a simple way to send a clear message of support to refugee and sanctuary-seeking children in the school as well as their families and friends. For example, schools in Norwich alone have raised tens of thousands of pounds to support recently settled families to furnish their new homes with essential items and to provide bikes, equipment, and cycle proficiency training for local refugees and people seeking asylum.

Refugee education: a rapidly evolving landscape

Schools have never before been more at the forefront of receiving and supporting those forcibly displaced: the recent, sudden arrival of people from Ukraine,

Afghanistan and changes to the dispersal of families seeking asylum across the UK mean schools are increasingly the first supportive institution refugee children and families come into contact with.

(UK Schools of Sanctuary)

The increasing displacement of people from countries all over the world means that we have to be highly responsive to the educational and emotional needs and contexts of children seeking sanctuary. In collaboration with our partners, such as UK Schools of Sanctuary, Refugee Week, and Amnesty International, we produce guidance for teachers that supports them to talk about sanctuary seeking in the classroom and to plan and adapt these conversations and activities if the school has refugee or asylum-seeking pupils. Since 2021, we have developed our refugee education offer to include the facilitation of free teacher training – 'Teaching About Refugees' – to support schools to teach with, for, and about refugees. We trialled this initially in Norfolk with 40 teachers, and its success has led to the partnership between UK Schools of Sanctuary and UNHCR to deliver the training across the Schools of Sanctuary Network. We also offer teachers live sessions and workshops focussing on the International Rescue Committee's Healing Classrooms programme, which supports schools and educators to develop inclusive and nurturing learning spaces where refugee and asylum-seeking pupils feel safe and supported to learn academic, social, and emotional skills to develop their full potential.

From a day of welcome to a school of sanctuary

Children often feel passionately about standing with those who are most marginalised and disadvantaged and Schools of Sanctuary support students to develop the knowledge, skills and confident to take action and make change.

(UK Schools of Sanctuary)

We are proud to develop the Day of Welcome in partnership with UK Schools of Sanctuary, a national network of over 400 primary and secondary schools, nurseries, and sixth forms, all committed to creating a culture of welcome and inclusion for refugees and people seeking asylum.

Many schools use the Day of Welcome as a starting point to launch their journey to becoming a School of Sanctuary. In Norfolk, the Day of Welcome has become a mandatory event for schools aspiring to the School of Sanctuary Award and has enabled 15 Norfolk schools to achieve Schools of Sanctuary status, with a further 25 currently working towards the award.

Working together with our local communities and our national and international partners, the Day of Welcome aspires to support every school to be a safe, welcoming, and inclusive place for everyone. Will you join us?

For further information about the Day of Welcome, please contact Jeannette Baxter: Jeannette.Baxter@aru.ac.uk.

***

Myths

Myth: Asylum seekers, refugees, and immigrants are interchangeable terms.

Truth: No, they can mean very different things; see the definitions provided near the start of this chapter if you need to revisit these.

Myth: Having English as an Additional Language is a Special Educational Need.

Truth: No, although some children who have EAL may also have SEND, and the process of diagnosis may be more difficult due to communication barriers.

Myth: Refugees will likely be lower academically.

Truth: Being a refugee is not a determiner of being less able; however, if they have moved to a place where the school curriculum is being delivered in a language that they do not speak or at least are not proficient in, then it is unlikely they will excel on assessments that are also in this language. Given time, being bilingual or multilingual can, in fact, enhance academic attainment.

Reference

The Bell Foundation. (2024). *Learners with special educational needs or disabilities*. Available at: https://www.bell-foundation.org.uk/eal-programme/guidance/schools-and-leaders/learners-with-special-educational-needs-or-disabilities/

14 Gender diversity and sexual orientation

Quote: 'I want to come out as trans but I am really scared of being bullied or people not understanding'.

Gender diversity

Understanding gender identity is complex and diverse, best considered as a spectrum rather than a strict binary between male and female. Developing a positive sense of gender identity is an important part of growing up for all children and young people. It is essential that educational settings develop both their own and pupil and student understanding of the spectrum of gender identity and provide support to trans, gender questioning, and non-binary pupils, students, and staff.

'Transgender' and 'trans' serve as encompassing terms for individuals whose gender differs from or doesn't align entirely with the sex assigned to them at birth. There are diverse expressions of being transgender and engaging in discussions with the individual, and if applicable, their family, to understand their desires and requirements is a fundamental approach.

Support for trans children and young people should be embedded across policies and curricula. This will help schools meet the Public Sector Duty of the Equality Act and eliminate unlawful discrimination, harassment, and victimisation, advance equality of opportunity, and foster good relations. Creating safe, trans-inclusive learning environments is crucial to reduce and prevent harm to trans and non-binary children and young people, but it will also be of benefit to all as gender stereotyping, sexism, homophobia, biphobia, and transphobia are challenged.

When children and young people's understanding of their own gender differs from the expectations of those around them, this can be very challenging, and young people and their families can experience high levels of distress. Some children and adolescents may explore their gender identity for various reasons and in diverse ways, with some beginning this exploration at a young age.

- Supporting a gender-questioning child or adolescent does not necessarily mean a definitive transgender identity or any specific transition path.
- Prioritise listening to and respecting the child or young person's preferences while involving and supporting parents or caregivers (without compromising the young person's confidentiality).

DOI: 10.4324/9781032697932-14

- View transgender, non-binary, or gender-questioning individuals as enriching the school community and challenging gender norms and not a problem.
- Gender plays a significant role in identity development, and fostering a positive gender identity is a natural part of growing up.
- Implement gender-segregated activities only when justified.
- Embrace the understanding of gender as a spectrum broader than traditional male and female categories.
- Inclusive practices for transgender and non-binary individuals require challenging traditional notions of sex and gender.
- All members of the school or organisation community, including parents and caregivers, may require support in developing this understanding.
- No trans or non-binary young person should be made to feel that they are the ones who are causing problems.

This section aims to help develop an understanding of language and terminology related to sex and gender, but this is likely to change over time. Trans and non-binary children and young people should be asked how they identify in age-appropriate ways, and assumptions about gender identity based on dress and looks should be avoided.

Gender identity and key terms

When discussing transgender identities, it's crucial to distinguish between the sex assigned at birth (natal sex) and gender identity. Natal sex refers to biological characteristics like chromosomes, genitalia, and hormones, while gender identity pertains to one's internal sense of self and its expression. For transgender individuals, their natal sex differs from their gender identity. Each person's experience of this difference varies, with some identifying as fluid, non-binary, agender, or partially male/female. While terms like 'transgender' and 'trans' are generally accepted, individuals should have the opportunity to express their own identity rather than having labels imposed on them.

Trans: An umbrella term used to describe people who identify as, for example:

- Transgender
- Queer
- Gender-fluid
- Non-binary
- Both male and female (this may be at the same time or over time)
- Neither male or female
- A third gender or who have a gender identity which we do not yet have words to describe

Cisgender person

A person whose sex assigned at birth matches their gender identity. In other words, it is a term for non-trans people.

Transition

The steps a trans person may take to live in the gender they identify as. Transitioning will be different for each individual. The social transition could involve name and pronoun changes and dress differently. The medical transition could include hormone blockers, hormones, and surgeries. There is not a single route for transition: individuals' experiences are all different, and no one's transition is the same.

Trans boy or man

A person assigned female at birth who identifies as a boy or man.

Trans girl or woman

A person assigned male at birth who identifies as a girl or woman.

Non-binary

An umbrella term for a person who does not identify as (solely) male or (solely) female. Non-binary people may identify as both male and female, neither male nor female, or as another gender identity. This group is under the trans umbrella but may not consider themselves trans.

Intersex

A term used to describe a person who may have the biological attributes of both sexes or whose biological attributes do not fit with societal assumptions about what constitutes male or female bodies. Intersex people can identify as male, female, or non-binary. Intersex people may undergo elements of transition.

Sexual orientation

Gender identity refers to an individual's internal perception of themselves, including how they express it, and is distinct from sexual orientation, which pertains to romantic or sexual attraction. Both gender identity and sexual orientation are diverse and may evolve over time. Transgender individuals, like anyone else, may have various sexual orientations. While gender identity and sexual orientation are separate topics, this chapter primarily focuses on the former. However, there exists a correlation between transphobia, biphobia, and homophobia. Transgender individuals and those who deviate from gender stereotypes may encounter not only transphobic and sexist abuse but also homophobic and biphobic discrimination.

Gender expression

Gender is often viewed as a societal concept where children are taught to conform to behaviours associated with their assigned sex. This construct encompasses how gender is manifested through roles, attire, and activities. However, gender expression doesn't always correlate with gender identity or sexual orientation. For instance, a boy wearing a dress doesn't necessarily indicate transgender identity or gender questioning. Nonetheless, individuals who defy gender norms associated with their assigned sex may face transphobic reactions.

Experiences of trans children and young people

National data

The Trevor Project Data on Transgender Youth (2019) reports:

- Overall, 1.8% of youth identified as transgender.
- Transgender youth reported significantly increased rates of depression, suicidality, and victimisation compared to their cisgender peers. Notably, in the past year, one in three transgender youth reported attempting suicide, almost one-third reported being a victim of sexual violence, and more than half reported a two-week period of depression.

National Youth Chances Integrated Report 2016 reports:

- Not all gender-questioning children will grow up to be trans, but 40% of young people first thought they were trans aged 11 or under, compared to 25% of lesbian, gay, or bisexuals aged 11 or under.
- Just over 90% of LGBTQ young people report learning nothing about trans in their sex and relationships education.
- Nearly half of LGBTQ young people say their time at school was affected by discrimination or fear of discrimination.

The Stonewall School Report (2017) on the experiences of lesbian, gay, bi, and trans young people in Britain's schools revealed the following key findings:

- Nearly half of LGBT pupils (45%) - including 64%of trans pupils - are bullied for being LGBT in Britain's schools. This is down from 55% of lesbian, gay, and bi pupils who experienced bullying because of their sexual orientation in 2012 and 65% in 2007.
- Seven in ten LGBT pupils report that their school says that homophobic and biphobic bullying is wrong, up from half in 2012 and a quarter in 2007. However, just two in five LGBT pupils report that their schools say that transphobic bullying is wrong.
- More than four in five trans young people have self-harmed, as have three in five lesbian, gay, and bi young people who aren't trans.
- More than two in five trans young people have attempted to take their own life, and one in five lesbian, gay, and bi students who aren't trans have done the same.

Transgender young people face higher rates of discrimination, mental health issues, and violence compared to their cisgender peers. For example:

- Transgender youth are more likely to experience discrimination in various settings, including education, healthcare, and employment.

- Studies show that transgender youth have higher rates of depression, anxiety, and suicidal ideation compared to their cisgender counterparts. They may also face challenges accessing appropriate mental health support.
- Transgender youth are at a heightened risk of experiencing violence, including physical assault, harassment, and bullying. This violence can occur in schools, public spaces, and even within their own families.
- Transgender youth are disproportionately represented among homeless youth populations. Many face rejection or violence in their homes after coming out, leading to homelessness and housing instability.
- Transgender youth often encounter barriers to accessing gender-affirming healthcare, including hormone therapy and gender-affirming surgeries. This can impact their physical and mental well-being.

It's essential to recognise that challenges faced by transgender and gender-questioning and diverse children and young people are often rooted in societal attitudes rather than inherent aspects of their identities. Transphobia, characterised by irrational fear, hatred, and discrimination against transgender individuals and those who diverge from traditional gender norms, contributes to these challenges. Transphobia manifests in various forms, including pressure to conform to assigned genders, sexist bullying, and sexualised abuse, reflecting entrenched stereotypes about masculinity and femininity. Thus, addressing societal attitudes and combating transphobia is crucial for creating inclusive environments where all individuals can thrive regardless of their gender identity.

Sexual orientation

Sexual orientation refers to a person's romantic, emotional, or sexual attraction to others. It is distinct from gender identity. Sexual orientation includes categories such as heterosexual (attraction to people of the opposite gender), homosexual (attraction to people of the same gender), bisexual (attraction to people of more than one gender), pansexual (attraction regardless of gender), asexual (lack of sexual attraction), and others.

Stonewall, a UK-based charity advocating for LGBTQ+ rights, provides valuable insights into how sexual orientation, other than straight, affects young people. Here are some key statistics:

- 42% of LGBT+ school pupils have been bullied in the past year, double the number of non-LGBT+ pupils (21%).
- 48% of pupils have had little to no positive messaging about being LGBT+ at school in the last year.
- Half of LGBT pupils hear homophobic slurs 'frequently' or 'often' at school.
- Just one in five LGBT pupils have been taught about safe sex in relation to same-sex relationships.
- Two in five LGBT pupils (40%) are never taught anything about LGBT issues at school.
- Almost nine in ten secondary school teachers (86%) and almost half of primary school teachers (45%) say that pupils in their schools have experienced homophobic bullying.

- Discrimination and stigma faced by LGBTQ+ youth often lead to mental health issues. Stonewall reports that 52% of LGBTQ+ young people have self-harmed, and 44% have considered suicide.

The 'Positive Futures' report by Just Like Us (2021) explores the experiences of LGBTQ+ young people in UK schools and the impact of LGBTQ+ inclusive education.

The report emphasises the significance of LGBTQ+ inclusive education in creating safer and more supportive environments for LGBTQ+ young people in schools. Schools that provide LGBTQ+ inclusive education contribute to improved mental health and well-being among LGBTQ+ students, fostering a sense of belonging and acceptance. Despite progress in LGBTQ+ inclusion, the report highlights the continued need for greater inclusivity in schools, including comprehensive LGBTQ+ inclusive curriculum, policies, and support services. Positive representation of LGBTQ+ identities in school curricula, textbooks, and extracurricular activities plays a crucial role in challenging stereotypes and promoting acceptance among students. However, there remain persistent challenges and barriers faced by LGBTQ+ young people in schools, including bullying, harassment, lack of support, and inadequate teacher training on LGBTQ+ issues (Positive Futures How supporting LGBT+ young people enables them to thrive in adulthood, n.d.).

Equality Act, 2010

Under the Equality Act 2010, public sector organisations, including schools, must adhere to the Public Sector Equality Duty. This requires them to:

- Eliminate discrimination, harassment, victimisation, and other prohibited conduct.
- Promote equality of opportunity between individuals with and without relevant protected characteristics.
- Foster positive relations between individuals with and without relevant protected characteristics.
- The Act safeguards against discrimination based on specific 'protected characteristics', including age, disability, gender reassignment, marriage and civil partnership, pregnancy and maternity, race, religion or belief, sex, and sexual orientation.

Consequently, schools must ensure they do not discriminate against pupils and students based on the protected characteristic of gender reassignment, as well as other characteristics covered by the LGBTQ+ spectrum.

The Equality Act extends protection to individuals who are perceived as transgender or discriminated against due to their association with a transgender person. Gender reassignment, as defined in the Act, encompasses individuals who are considering, undergoing, or have undergone a process to change their sex characteristics. This definition means that pupils are protected under the Act if they are taking steps to live as a different gender, regardless of whether they are undergoing medical procedures.

Supporting an LGBTQ+ child or young person

Given the spectrum of LGBT, trans identities, and experiences, it is important that any support offered to a child or young person starts with identifying their individual needs. An initial conversation needs to show them that their experience is validated and supported. There may be additional challenges for young people from certain faith or cultural backgrounds or because of a special educational need or disability. It is important for us as educators to see all aspects of a young person's identity and experience and think about how to best support and respond. Some young people and their families may benefit from individual support from a service which you can signpost and refer to.

Developing a whole setting approach to supporting LGBTQ+ pupils

A comprehensive approach within educational settings is essential to ensure that everyone feels equally accepted and respected within the community. By adopting this approach, negative reactions toward LGBTQ+ learners and staff can be avoided or reduced. Implementing effective strategies across the entire setting also encourages an environment where young people feel comfortable coming out or undergoing transition. Educational settings should communicate their efforts in this regard to the broader school or setting community. Such a holistic approach benefits all community members by fostering greater understanding, not just for LGBTQ+ individuals.

A whole settings approach includes:

- Recognising and addressing LGBTQ+ issues and homophobia, biphobia, and transphobia within the policy framework and as integral to the approach toward equality and inclusion.
- Acknowledging the presence of LGBTQ+ individuals within the educational setting, including family members, staff, governors, pupils, and students, and embracing this diversity.
- Ensuring that the curriculum, particularly PSHE and activities related to spiritual, moral, social, and cultural development, challenges gender stereotypes, promotes gender equality, fosters a positive understanding of gender identity, and combats sexism and transphobia.
- Thoroughly assessing all aspects of the curriculum, resources, and teaching methods to promote inclusive practices that challenge stereotypes.
- Proactively addressing, documenting, and addressing incidents of abuse, harassment, and bullying and using this data to inform organisational improvements.
- Incorporating LGBTQ+ issues into equality training for staff and governors and promoting community-wide understanding of topics through training and other opportunities.
- Engaging in activities like LGBT History Month and Transgender Day of Visibility to highlight the presence and accomplishments of trans individuals.
- Providing information to all parents and caregivers about efforts to foster trans-inclusive environments within the educational setting and offering resources for them to learn more about trans identities if desired.

Curriculum and teaching and learning (including relationships and sex education)

PSHE curriculum should include opportunities to explore and raise awareness of issues of assigned sex, gender identity, sexual orientation, and transphobia and to make visible and celebrate lesbian, gay, bisexual, and trans people. Work to challenge sexism and champion gender equality will benefit all pupils. Therefore, inclusive practice is more than a one-off lesson; it is embedded in good equality practice. Ensure that any resources used to challenge gender stereotypes actively celebrate different families and members of the community and reflect LGBTQ+ people as positive role models.

Consider the teaching and learning approaches that you use, which may have the impact of making LGBTQ+ children and young people feel confused, excluded, or uncomfortable. For example, grouping learners by gender may have this impact, but there may still be times when single-gender work is needed. This may include aspects of relationship and sex education or to support the learning needs of particular groups (e.g., boys and literacy). Providing a clear need is identified, the Equality Act allows for such provision.

Particular care will need to be taken to ensure that relationships and sex education are inclusive of all genders.

Some examples:

- In referring to genitals, make it clear that 'most' rather than 'all boys have a penis and testicles' and 'most girls have a vulva and vagina'
- Start any teaching around puberty and bodies by highlighting that all people's bodies and genitals are different and that there will be a diverse range of responses to puberty (this will also be supportive to intersex pupils and students)
- Present sexual health information with an awareness that for trans young people, their body may not represent their gender identity
- Pre-planning and one-on-one support may be necessary to ensure the young person gets the information they need in a way that feels validating to their gender identity

Children and young people with special educational needs and disabilities

Young people with SEND may need additional support in understanding or accepting their own sexuality or identity, learning about those who are different from them, and understanding that difference is to be respected and celebrated. Staff, parents, carers, and wider professionals may need support in understanding that a SEND learner is just as likely to be LGBTQ+ as any other person. Indeed, lived experience and some developing incidence-based research are showing that there is a higher prevalence of those who question their gender identity in those on the autism spectrum. Ensure that their words or actions are not automatically attributed to their SEND; for example, preferences for clothing types or hair length are seen as a sensory need, or behaviours are described as a new special interest, fascination, curiosity, or phase. Whilst these may be true, it is important to listen without judgement so that expressions of questioning gender identity are not dismissed. Emotions related to sexual orientation and gender identity are complex for anyone to understand and express, and this could be exacerbated in those with communication and interaction difficulties. Some pupils with SEND may not see the need to communicate and may not understand that others don't already see them in the same way as they see themselves or know themselves to be due to them thinking everyone knows the same things they know and shares their one perspective. This could obviously lead to increased frustration and anxiety and impact negatively on well-being and mental health. They may benefit from social rules or scripts around what is socially acceptable and what is not, e.g., what it is OK or not OK to say or do in different contexts. It may be that some of these rules or expectations are different for different genders socially, and some things that had to be taught to the young person originally, e.g., the unwritten rules of using public toilets may need to be taught again to help the learner to socialise in their affirmed (rather than assigned) gender.

Remember:

- Follow the lead of the young person and, if appropriate, their family and protect confidentiality
- Consider all aspects of a young person's identity in the tailoring of support
- Transition is different for different people
- Pupils may need support in developing 'scripts' to respond to questions about their transition
- Make use of local and national support services

Scenarios and possible responses

Brighton and Hove council produced the following scenarios to offer support to staff (Trans Inclusion Schools Toolkit, 2017)

Scenario 1

Parent to school: 'All this talk about gender identity is confusing for children. They are too young to understand'.

A small minority of children have a very clear understanding that their assigned sex does not align with their gender identity from a young age. Working in educational settings to challenge gender stereotyping and explore a range of gender identities makes schools safer and more inclusive for all genders, not just those who are trans. For children who are comfortable in the gender assigned at birth, there is no confusion.

Scenario 2

Parent to school: 'My daughter doesn't want a boy changing next to her – what if he looks at her body?'

Underpinning this scenario is the idea that a trans girl is not a 'real girl', and this would be something that a whole-setting approach would challenge through training and awareness raising. A Human Rights response would be to state that the child is a girl and, as such, has the right under the Equality Act to change with the girls and to be treated fairly as such. In response to this parental concern, it would not be appropriate to remove the trans pupil from the changing rooms but to work together with the parent raising a concern and their child to find a different solution. It is the responsibility of members of staff to support both trans learners and cisgender learners to feel comfortable around one another and to ensure the safety and well-being of all in the changing rooms.

Scenario 3

Parent to school: 'It's not fair that he enters the 100 metres race for girls when he is a boy' or 'Won't she get injured playing rugby with boys?'

Underpinning this scenario is the idea that all boys or all girls share the same physical attributes and fails to acknowledge that there is a range of differences in physical strength and ability within single-gender groups. Trans boys are boys, not girls, and therefore, entitled to play rugby with boys and in consultation with relevant sporting bodies. Teachers already differentiate according to ability. Trans learners are entitled to access sporting opportunities equally to cisgender learners.

Scenario 4

Parent of a trans and gender-questioning pupil to the school. 'I refuse to allow my son to change his name or wear skirts'.

It is understandable that some parents and carers will struggle with their child questioning their gender identity, and it may be a long process to become more accepting of this change. This challenge should be acknowledged as difficult, and parents and carers can be referred for further support. The vast majority of parents and carers do their best to work alongside their child and can be reminded that a change of name, pronoun, or dress does not necessarily mean their child will follow any particular path into the future. However, the duty of care for schools is with the child, and educational settings need to accept that, in some cases, the school may be the only place the child feels safe to be themselves. Educational settings can offer a safe space with a trusted adult for the child to discuss their feelings and thoughts about their gender identity in the same way support would be offered to any vulnerable child. The child can also be reassured that you will continue to work with them, their parents and other relevant professionals to ensure they are supported. If a child is at risk of significant harm, then safeguarding procedures must be followed.

Scenario 5

A member of staff has been informed of a child's pronoun and name change but continues to use their original name and pronoun despite being reminded by the child in question.

Mistakes can be made with names and pronouns, and if a mistake is made, the member of staff should apologise and then move on. If it becomes clear that a staff member is deliberately using the incorrect name or pronoun for a learner, settings should follow their own systems for managing staff codes of conduct to address the issue.

Scenario 6

Trans girl to school: 'I have decided I am a boy after all, I think I might be gay'.

Everyone has a right to exploration, and for some children and young people, exploring gender identity is a part of understanding themselves and will pass over time. For others, this is the start of a longer journey of transitioning. It is vital that when a child or young person is exploring themselves, they feel safe, are supported, and are listened to by the people around them. If a child or young person does 'change their mind' about their gender identity, it is important they do not feel they are 'letting anyone down' or that they have caused an inconvenience in relation to practical changes in school. They should be supported in changing names and pronouns again if they want to, change uniform, gendered groups, and any other areas to ensure they remain comfortable in their gender identity and expression. Due to the age limits currently in place on hormone treatment (testosterone and oestrogen), under 16s do not have access to irreversible treatments.

Myth: Being gay is a choice or a result of upbringing or environment.
Truth: Sexual orientation, including being gay, is not a choice. It is a natural and inherent aspect of a person's identity that typically emerges without conscious decision-making. Research suggests that sexual orientation is influenced by a combination of genetic, hormonal, developmental, and environmental factors, but it is not something that can be changed or chosen.
Myth: Trans young people are just going through a phase and will grow out of it.
Truth: Gender identity is an inherent aspect of a person's identity, and for trans young people, their gender identity is valid and deserving of recognition and support. Gender identity is not a phase, and denying their identity can have harmful effects on their well-being.
Myth: Transitioning is always a quick and straightforward process for trans young people.
Truth: Transitioning is a complex and individualised journey that varies greatly for each young trans person, and it may involve multiple steps over an extended period of time, including social, medical, and legal aspects.

Resources

Gendered Intelligence: A UK-based organisation providing resources and training for schools to support trans and gender variant pupils. Website: genderedintelligence.co.uk

Mermaids: A UK charity offering resources, training, and support for schools and families of transgender children and young people. Website: mermaidsuk.org.uk

Stonewall: An organisation advocating for LGBTQ+ rights, providing guidance and resources for schools to create inclusive environments for all students, including trans pupils. Website: stonewall.org.uk

'Just Like Us' is a resource designed to support LGBTQ+ young people in educational settings, providing information, guidance, and advocacy to create inclusive environments. Website: https://www.justlikeus.org/

Transgender and Gender Nonconforming Supportive Schools Toolkit: A comprehensive resource developed by the Human Rights Campaign Foundation, offering guidance and best practices for schools to support transgender and gender nonconforming students. Website: hrc.org/resources/transgender-and-gender-nonconforming-supportive-schools-toolkit

TransEDU: A research project providing resources and guidance for educational institutions to support transgender students in higher education. Website: trans.ac.uk

The Proud Trust: A UK charity offering resources and training for schools to create LGBTQ+ inclusive environments, including support for transgender pupils. Website: theproudtrust.org

GLSEN (Gay, Lesbian & Straight Education Network): An organisation focused on creating safe and inclusive schools for LGBTQ+ students, offering resources and training for educators to support transgender and gender nonconforming youth. Website: glsen.org

Trans Student Educational Resources (TSER): An organisation run by trans students providing resources, advocacy, and support for trans youth in educational settings. Website: transstudent.org

Safe Schools Coalition: An international organisation working to create safe and inclusive schools for LGBTQ+ students, offering resources and support for educators to address issues related to gender identity and expression. Website: safeschoolscoalition.org

Inclusive Education for LGBTI+ Youth: A Whole School Approach: A resource developed by UNESCO providing guidance for schools on creating inclusive environments for LGBTQ+ students, including those who are transgender. Website: unesco.org/education/lgbti-youth-inclusive-education

References

Just Like Us. (2021). Just like us releases growing up LGBT+ report on bullying, schools and mental health. *Just Like Us*. [online] Available at: https://www.justlikeus.org/blog/2021/11/25/research-report-growing-up-lgbt-bullying/

Positive Futures How supporting LGBT+ young people enables them to thrive in adulthood. (n.d.). Available at: https://www.justlikeus.org/wp-content/uploads/2023/05/Positive-Futures-report-by-Just-Like-Us

Stonewall. (2017). School report (2017). *Stonewall*. [online] Available at: https://www.stonewall.org.uk/resources/school-report-2017

Trans Inclusion Schools Toolkit. (2017). Available at: https://www.bathnes.gov.uk/sites/default/files/siteimages/allsortsyouthproject_-_trans_inclusion_schools_toolkit_aug_2017.pdf [Accessed 16 Feb. 2024].

The Trevor Project. (2019). Data on transgender youth. *The Trevor Project*. [online] Available at: https://www.thetrevorproject.org/research-briefs/data-on-transgender-youth/

YOUTH CHANCES: 2016. (n.d.). Available at: https://metrocharity.org.uk/sites/default/files/2017-04/National%20Youth%20Chances%20Intergrated%20Report%202016.pdf

15 Sex and relationships

Quote: 'Will it hurt?'

The Relationships and Sex Education (RSE) Framework of 2021 is a comprehensive guideline outlining the essential components of RSE in schools (Department for Education, 2019). It emphasises the importance of providing age-appropriate and inclusive education on relationships, sexual health, and consent. The framework covers topics such as healthy relationships, puberty, contraception, sexually transmitted infections (STIs), and online safety. It aims to empower young people with accurate information, skills, and attitudes to make informed decisions about their relationships and sexual health. Additionally, the framework highlights the significance of promoting respect, equality, and diversity in RSE curriculum delivery.

The 2024 nationwide poll conducted by Censuswide and commissioned by the Sex Education Forum reveals a mixed picture of young people's experiences with Relationships and Sex Education (RSE) in schools (sexeducationforum.org.uk, 2024). While 50% of respondents rate their RSE provision as good or very good, only 43% feel personally represented and included by it. A significant portion of young people (22%) rely on online sources for information on pornography, with 15% citing pornography itself as their main source. The findings underscore a call for the government to enhance teacher confidence in delivering RSE (57%) and provide schools with more flexibility to cover relevant topics based on the needs of their students (52%).

Myths about RSE

In 2017, RSE was made mandatory. The statutory guidance was informed by research evidence, shaped by extensive consultation with expert groups, and was supported by MPs and organisations across the youth, health, and education sectors. However, 'the conversation around RSE in 2023 has been dominated by myths and misinformation, often from a small but vocal group of people who oppose many aspects of RSE, especially LGBT+ inclusive RSE' (sexeducationforum.org.uk, 2023).

Despite misconceptions, Relationships and Sex Education (RSE) plays a crucial role in safeguarding children's well-being and empowering them with essential knowledge

DOI: 10.4324/9781032697932-15

and skills. Contrary to the belief that RSE deprives children of innocence, a well-structured curriculum equips them with the understanding of appropriate behaviour, consent, and the confidence to seek help when needed, ultimately serving as a protective tool against abuse. Concerns about RSE providing excessive information prematurely are unfounded, as evidence suggests it actually delays the onset of sexual activity and promotes safer practices (sexeducationforum.org.uk, 2023). Additionally, fears that RSE introduces children to LGBT+ concepts ignore the necessity of inclusive education that reflects the diversity of society and fosters respect for all individuals. While some worry about external influences on RSE content and the possibility of teachers imposing personal beliefs, strict standards and proper training ensure unbiased delivery. It's crucial to involve parents in RSE education, but not all children receive adequate information at home, emphasising the importance of collaboration between schools and families. Despite challenges, investments in teacher training and professional development are necessary to ensure consistent and high-quality RSE delivery. Moreover, while doubts exist about the suitability of RSHE guidance, continuous feedback from stakeholders should guide updates to ensure its effectiveness in addressing the evolving needs of children and adolescents.

The importance of relationships and sex education (RSE)

Research by (Goldfarb and Lieberman, 2021) shows that the outcomes of RSE include recognising and respecting sexual diversity, learning about dating and preventing intimate partner violence, building healthy relationships, preventing child sexual abuse, improving social and emotional skills, and understanding media better. There's strong evidence supporting the idea of starting sex education in Primary school, making it gradual and lasting longer, including LGBTQ+ topics across the curriculum, and approaching healthy sexuality with a focus on fairness and equality.

By equipping children and young people with essential knowledge about their rights and distinguishing healthy from unhealthy and harmful behaviour, RSE reduces their vulnerability to abuse. According to the UN's international guidelines, children aged 5 to 8 should be able to identify bullying and violence as wrong, while those aged 12 to 15 ought to understand that sexual abuse, assault, intimate partner violence, and bullying violate human rights and are never the victim's fault.

In 2020, the government made learning about coercive control at school compulsory. However, research by Ulster University (UU) (n.d.), Queen's University Belfast (QUB), and the Northern Health Trust in 2023 reveals that fewer than one in six 16-year-olds are familiar with the concept of coercive control and its meaning. Coercive control, a form of domestic abuse characterised by threats, humiliation, and intimidation, became a criminal offense under domestic abuse laws in England, Wales in 2015, and Northern Ireland in 2022. However, only 16% of the more than 2,000 16-year-olds surveyed had heard of coercive control and understood its implications. Interestingly, more boys than girls reported knowledge of coercive control. While many participants recognised examples of abusive relationships, the study highlights limited evidence of how relationship and sex education (RSE) in schools address issues like coercive control.

Navigating personal discomfort about having conversations about relationships and sex

It can be difficult to have these conversations, and you may be worried about being embarrassed or saying the wrong thing.

- Start by reflecting on your own biases, discomfort, and attitudes towards discussing relationships and sex. Recognising and acknowledging personal discomfort is the first step towards overcoming it.
- Schools can offer training and workshops focused on building teachers' confidence and competence in discussing sensitive topics like sex and relationships. This can include sessions on communication skills, understanding diverse perspectives, and managing discomfort. If your school doesn't offer this, it could be something to take to SLT for consideration.
- Establishing a classroom atmosphere where students feel safe, respected, and supported is essential. You can foster open communication by emphasising non-judgmental attitudes and respect for diverse opinions.
- Tailor discussions and materials to the developmental level of students. Using age-appropriate language and resources helps alleviate discomfort and ensure students can engage meaningfully with the topic.
- Practice active listening skills to understand students' perspectives and concerns. Showing empathy and validating students' experiences creates a supportive environment where they feel comfortable discussing sensitive topics.
- Collaborate with colleagues. You can collaborate with colleagues, school counsellors, or external experts to share strategies and resources for discussing RSE effectively. Collaborative planning and support can alleviate individual discomfort and enhance overall teaching effectiveness.
- Set boundaries and self-care. Recognise the importance of setting boundaries and practicing self-care when discussing sensitive topics.
- Engage in ongoing reflection and evaluation of teaching practices related to discussing relationships and sex with students. Embrace opportunities for growth, learning from experiences, and adapting strategies to meet the needs of students over time better.

Effective communication

When discussing Relationships and Sex Education (RSE) with students, several effective communication strategies can support:

- Foster an atmosphere of trust and respect where students feel comfortable expressing themselves without fear of judgement.
- Establish ground rules that promote confidentiality and confidentiality, ensuring students feel safe sharing their thoughts and concerns.
- Address sensitive topics with sensitivity and empathy, acknowledging the diversity of experiences and perspectives among students.

- Practice active listening by giving students your full attention and providing nonverbal cues that indicate understanding.
- Validate students' feelings and experiences, acknowledging their emotions without judgement or dismissal.
- Encourage open dialogue by paraphrasing and reflecting on what students have shared, demonstrating empathy and understanding.
- Create opportunities for students to ask questions in a supportive and non-judgmental environment.
- Encourage curiosity and critical thinking by validating all questions and providing factual and age-appropriate answers.
- Foster a culture of mutual learning where both students and educators can engage in open and respectful discussions about RSE topics.
- Use language that is inclusive of all genders, sexual orientations, and identities, avoiding stereotypes or assumptions.
- Incorporate diverse perspectives and experiences into discussions to reflect the lived realities of students from various backgrounds.
- Respect students' preferred pronouns and identities, creating a welcoming environment for all and promoting acceptance and inclusion.

Addressing sensitive topics

Addressing sensitive topics in RSE is crucial for promoting a safe and inclusive learning environment and equipping students with essential knowledge and skills to navigate complex issues. These topics include consent and boundaries, pornography and its impact, and sexting and sending nudes.

Consent and boundaries

The #everyonesinvited movement brought to light the prevalence of various forms of sexual harassment and abuse that are often normalised within the peer cultures and interpersonal relationships of young people, as noted by Ofsted in 2021. While not all young people are directly involved in or affected by non-consensual sexual behaviours, it is evident that we need to talk about this. Addressing this issue involves more than simply warning young people about the risks and harms associated with sex and relationships; it requires empowering them to cultivate positive and healthy relationships. It's important to recognise that consent is not solely a matter of individual choice or limited to specific interpersonal relationships; it is a broader social and cultural phenomenon.

In 2019, the University of Edinburgh, commissioned by NHS Greater Glasgow and Clyde in partnership with NHS Lanarkshire and NHS Lothian, conducted qualitative research with young people aged 16–19 to explore their understanding of sexual consent and how a shift towards affirmative or enthusiastic consent could be facilitated. The research aimed to investigate barriers and motivators for young people regarding communicating and recognising enthusiastic mutual consent in sexual situations. The study utilised co-production with young advisors, focus groups, and individual interviews with young people from diverse backgrounds. The findings highlighted that while some young people had positive experiences of sexual communication, discomfort and embarrassment hindered many from discussing consent openly. The research revealed varying experiences of communicating consent, with some emphasising the importance of mutuality and reciprocity. Barriers to communication included fear of rejection or labelling, particularly among inexperienced individuals or those unfamiliar with their partners. Young people expressed nuanced understandings of consent across gender and sexuality lines, with some advocating for clearer verbal communication. The study suggested promoting messages on sexual consent through diverse and accessible support and education tailored to different preferences and styles, with particular attention on social media platforms. The report also emphasised the need for broader efforts to normalise discourse around sexual consent and challenge gender stereotypes within society (Mcmellon et al., 2019).

Educating students about consent involves teaching them to understand and respect personal boundaries and to recognise the importance of obtaining explicit and enthusiastic consent in all sexual encounters. Discussions about consent should emphasise communication, respect, and autonomy, empowering students to establish healthy boundaries in relationships.

Pornography and its impact

Children's Commissioner for England Dame Rachel de Souza said: 'For too long we have brushed the issue of pornography under the carpet as awkward, uncomfortable, or too difficult to solve – but we cannot shy away from discussing the nature, scale and impacts of online pornography' (Children's Commissioner for England, 2023).

A report released by the Children's Commissioner for England in May 2023 sheds light on the concerning correlation between children's exposure to pornography and subsequent harmful sexual behaviour or abuse. Testimonies from young individuals featured in the report illustrate the link between viewing violent pornography and experiencing harmful sexual behaviours. The research, which involved an analysis of documents detailing accounts of sexual violence among children, underscores the alarming role of unrestricted access to pornography in influencing harmful behaviour and abuse. Findings reveal that specific acts commonly depicted in pornography, such as strangulation and slapping, were referenced in 50% of the examined cases. Moreover, interviews with both police and children revealed direct connections between the perpetration of abuse and exposure to pornography. Recommendations include implementing age verification on platforms hosting pornography, providing support for child victims of crime, and ensuring safeguarding-first approaches in Relationships, Sex, and Health Education (RSHE) teaching. This report contributes crucial evidence to the ongoing debate surrounding children's access to harmful online content and underscores the imperative of safeguarding children from sexual abuse.

Addressing pornography in sex education involves helping students critically evaluate media messages and understand the potential impact of pornography on attitudes, behaviours, and relationships. Discussions should explore issues such as unrealistic depictions of sex, consent, body image, and gender roles, empowering students to make informed choices and develop healthy attitudes towards sexuality.

Sexting and sending nudes

Sending nudes refers to the act of sending naked or partially naked images or videos to another person. While this is often referred to as 'sexting', young people may use this term to discuss sharing sexual messages rather than imagery.

Young people can send nudes using various devices like phones, tablets, or laptops, and they can share them through any app, website, or game, including during live streams. This can also involve sharing them across devices using offline services like Airdrop or Bluetooth.

Creating or sharing sexual images or videos of a child under 18 is illegal, even if the person sharing is also a child. This includes sending sexual messages to a child, taking explicit photos or videos of themselves or others, sharing explicit images or videos of a child, and possessing, downloading, or storing explicit imagery of a child, even with their permission. Additionally, sharing explicit imagery of a child, even between children of the same age, is illegal. Although it's illegal for anyone to exchange nude or semi-nude imagery of a child, the legislation aims to protect children from harm. If an incident involving a young person sharing a nude image is reported to the police, it's unlikely that the child will face prosecution.

Some of the risks associated with sending and sharing nudes for children and young people include:

- Losing control of the image. Once an image is shared, it can be difficult or impossible to control who sees it or where it ends up.
- Individuals may use nude images to blackmail or bully others, threatening to share them publicly unless certain demands are met.
- Online sexual harassment involves receiving unwanted sexual contact on digital platforms. When nude images or videos are shared online without consent, it constitutes online sexual harassment. Examples of online sexual harassment behaviours also include spreading rumours or lies of a sexual nature, sharing nude images or videos without consent, photoshopping or editing images or videos in a sexualised manner, sending sexualised messages via private messages or public comments, pressuring someone to share nude images or videos through persistent messaging, using offensive or discriminatory sexual language, bullying based on gender or sexual orientation, and sending sexualised emojis or memes to embarrass or annoy others.

The UK Safer Internet Centre, a child protection organisation made up of the Internet Watch Foundation (IWF), SWGfL, and Childnet, initial reports show schoolchildren in the UK are now using AI to generate indecent images of other children (SIC, 2023). There are reported concerns that students are producing imagery that constitutes child sexual abuse material. This behaviour may stem from curiosity, sexual exploration, or other motives, but there is a risk of images spreading uncontrollably online, and this imagery can have detrimental effects on children and may be used for abuse or blackmail.

Inclusive RSE

SEND inclusive RSE

SEND (Special Educational Needs and Disabilities) inclusive RSE is essential to ensure that all students, regardless of their abilities, have access to comprehensive and meaningful sexual health and relationship education. Students with SEND have the same right to accurate and age-appropriate information about relationships, sexuality, and consent as their peers. Without inclusive RSE, they may be more vulnerable to misinformation or exploitation.

Inclusive RSE empowers students with SEND to understand and assert their rights, recognise abusive behaviours, and seek help if needed. It's crucial for their safety and well-being. Students with SEND may require additional support to navigate relationships and sexual health. Inclusive RSE equips them with the knowledge and skills to make informed decisions and advocate for themselves. In many countries, including the UK, there are legal requirements to provide inclusive RSE that meets the needs of all students, including those with SEND. Failing to do so may constitute discrimination.

Strategies for inclusive RSE Education:

- Adapt RSE materials to suit the diverse needs and abilities of students with SEND. Use accessible formats, such as language, visual aids, or multimedia resources.
- Implement teaching strategies that accommodate various learning needs. Offer multiple means of engagement, representation, and expression to ensure all students can participate meaningfully.
- Pair students with SEND with peer mentors or support buddies who can provide assistance and guidance in understanding RSE topics and navigating social situations.
- Use role-playing activities and real-life scenarios to help students practice communication skills, decision-making, and boundary-setting in relationships.
- Work closely with special education teachers, learning support assistants, and other professionals to identify students' specific needs and develop tailored RSE interventions and support plans.
- Engage parents and carers of students with SEND in discussions about RSE education, providing them with resources and guidance to support their child's learning at home.
- Encourage students with SEND to express their preferences, ask questions, and seek clarification about RSE topics. Foster a supportive environment where they feel comfortable discussing sensitive issues.

LGBT+ inclusive RSE

Research by Stewart et al. (2021) reports that 24% of LGBT+ young people did not receive sexual education from school, parents, or other family members, compared to only 9% of heterosexual young people. Instead, a higher percentage of LGBT+ young people learned about sexual matters from the internet, compared to 53% of heterosexual young people.

Research conducted by charity Just Like Us and Teacher Tapp in 2023 indicates that teachers are still as uncomfortable discussing LGBT+ topics with their pupils as they were two years ago. Despite efforts, progress in this area has stagnated, with approximately 15% of teachers reporting feeling either 'not very comfortable' or 'completely uncomfortable' addressing LGBT+ topics.

LGBT+ inclusion in education benefits all students. Creating a safe space for dialogue encourages empathy and understanding among students, fostering a culture of respect. Open discussions about LGBT+ topics can help reduce bullying and discrimination against students based on their sexual orientation or gender identity. Creating an LGBT+ inclusive environment in education doesn't just benefit LGBT+ students; it has positive effects on all, fostering a more inclusive, empathetic, and supportive educational community. Exposure to diverse perspectives and an inclusive environment that promotes acceptance of LGBT+ students can contribute to a reduction in bullying and discrimination overall. Learning about and understanding different sexual orientations and gender identities enhances social and emotional learning. Non-LGBT+ students develop empathy, compassion, and interpersonal skills that are valuable in diverse social settings.

There are barriers that teachers may encounter when discussing LGBT+ topics in schools. Teachers may feel unprepared, or lack training on how to address LGBT+ topics in the classroom, or some teachers may fear backlash from parents or carers, other staff or community members who may hold anti-LGBT+ views, or have concerns about navigating cultural or religious sensitivities in their communities which could make discussing LGBT+ topics challenging. A lack of inclusive educational materials and curriculum may also limit teachers' ability to incorporate LGBT+ topics into their lessons effectively. However, an LGBT+ inclusive environment creates a more supportive, tolerant, and enriching educational setting for all students, contributing to their personal growth, academic success, and preparation for a diverse and interconnected world.

Myth: RSE promotes early sexual activity.

Truth: Comprehensive RSE programs that include information about contraception, STI prevention, and healthy relationships have been shown to delay the onset of sexual activity and reduce risky behaviours among young people.

Myth: RSE undermines religious or cultural values.

Truth: RSE can be tailored to respect diverse religious and cultural beliefs while still providing essential information about sexual health and relationships. Inclusive RSE programs aim to promote respect for individual values and choices.

Myth: RSE is only about anatomy and biology.

Truth: While understanding anatomy and biology is an important component of RSE, comprehensive programs also cover topics such as consent, healthy relationships, communication skills, sexual orientation, gender identity, contraception, STI prevention, and decision-making. These programs provide young people with the knowledge and skills they need to navigate various aspects of sexuality and make informed choices throughout their lives.

Resources and signposting

Sex Education Forum (SEF)

> Website: https://sexeducationforum.org.uk/
> SEF provides guidance, training, and resources for teachers and educators to deliver effective RSE in schools. They offer various tools, lesson plans, and policy advice to support RSE implementation.

PSHE Association

> Website: https://www.pshe-association.org.uk/
> The PSHE Association offers a wide range of resources and support for PSHE (Personal, Social, Health and Economic education), including RSE. They provide curriculum guidance, lesson plans, and professional development opportunities for teachers.

Department for Education (DfE)

> Website: https://www.gov.uk/government/organisations/department-for-education
> The DfE website offers official guidance and statutory requirements for RSE in schools. Teachers can find information on the statutory guidance for RSE, updates, and additional resources provided by the government.

Stonewall Education

> Website: https://www.stonewall.org.uk/education
> Stonewall provides resources and support specifically focused on LGBTQ+ inclusive education. They offer training, lesson plans, and guidance for teachers to create inclusive learning environments for all students.

Just like us

> Website: https://www.justlikeus.org/
> Just Like Us provides various resources and initiatives for educators, including School Diversity Week, educational resources, training sessions and workshops for teachers, school staff, and students, Student Ambassador program and research and advocacy:

Brook

> Website: https://www.brook.org.uk/
> Brook is a sexual health charity that offers resources and support for young people and professionals. They provide guidance and training for teachers on topics related to sexual health, relationships, and RSE.

RSE Hub

> Website: https://rsehub.org.uk/
> RSE Hub is an online platform offering RSE resources, training, and support for educators. Teachers can access lesson plans, teaching materials, and guidance on delivering comprehensive RSE in schools.

NSPCC

> Website: https://www.nspcc.org.uk
> The NSPCC offers guidance and resources specifically tailored to teachers delivering relationships and sex education (RSE) in schools. These resources include lesson plans, teaching materials, and advice on addressing sensitive topics with students.

References

Children's Commissioner for England. (n.d.). *New evidence on pornography's influence on harmful sexual behaviour among children.* [online] Available at: https://www.childrenscommissioner.gov.uk/media-centre/new-evidence-on-pornographys-influence-on-harmful-sexual-behaviour-among-children/

Department for Education. (2019). Relationships education, Relationships and Sex Education (RSE) and health education. *GOV.UK.* [online] Available at: https://www.gov.uk/government/publications/relationships-education-relationships-and-sex-education-rse-and-health-education

Goldfarb, E.S. and Lieberman, L.D. (2021). Three decades of research: The case for comprehensive sex education. *Journal of Adolescent Health.* [online] 68(1), pp. 13–27. https://doi.org/10.1016/j.jadohealth.2020.07.036

Mcmellon, C., Berry, H. and Roesch-Marsh, A. (2019). *Young people's attitudes to and experiences of consent: Facilitators and barriers to recognising and communicating enthusiastic sexual consent document: Report of consultation with young people for NHSGG&C, 'young people's attitudes to and experiences of consent: Facilitators and barriers to recognising and communicating enthusiastic sexual consent'.* [online] Available at: https://www.sandyford.scot/media/4218/finalreport_nhsconsent-dec-2019.pdf [Accessed 11 Apr. 2024].

NSPCC. (2023). Sexting and sending nudes. *NSPCC.* [online] Available at: https://www.nspcc.org.uk/keeping-children-safe/online-safety/sexting-sending-nudes/

sexeducationforum.org.uk. (2023). *Busting the myths about RSE.* [online] Available at: https://www.sexeducationforum.org.uk/news/news/busting-myths-about-rse

sexeducationforum.org.uk. (2024). *Young people's RSE poll 2024.* [online] Available at: https://www.sexeducationforum.org.uk/resources/evidence/young-peoples-rse-poll-2024 [Accessed 11 Apr. 2024].

SIC, U. (2023). Children must understand risk as UK schools say pupils abusing AI to make sexual imagery of other children. *UK Safer Internet Centre.* [online] Available at: https://saferinternet.org.uk/blog/children-must-understand-risk-as-uk-schools-say-pupils-abusing-ai-to-make-sexual-imagery-of-other-children [Accessed 13 Mar. 2024].

Stewart, H., Adewoye, M., Bayliss, D. and Khandker, R. (2021). *Experiences of relationships and sex education, and sexual risk taking young people's views from LSYPE2 research brief November 2021.* [online] Available at: https://fs.hubspotusercontent00.net/hubfs/20248256/Evidence%20and%20research/SRE_and_sexual_risk-taking_research_brief_Nov21.pdf

Ulster University. (n.d.). *Coercive control: Report says few teens know about form of abuse.* [online] Available at: https://pure.ulster.ac.uk/en/clippings/coercive-control-report-says-few-teens-know-about-form-of-abuse

Us, J.L. (2024). Teachers still as uncomfortable discussing LGBT+ topics as they were two years ago, new research finds. *Just Like Us.* [online] Available at: https://www.justlikeus.org/blog/2024/02/01/teachers-uncomfortable-lgbt-2024-research/ [Accessed 11 Apr. 2024].

16 Toxic masculinity

Quote: 'Being a man means not showing weakness but it's a battle between trying to live up to these expectations and wanting to be myself'.

Talking about misogyny, misandry, and masculinity is crucial for understanding and address-ing gender dynamics and promoting healthy relationships with our pupils and students. It is especially important when considering young people, as it lays the foundation for their understanding of gender dynamics and relationships. Research by the Government Equali-ties Office in 2019 recommended: 'There is a real need for more engagement with men and boys, and all members of society across the UK from a young age about gender norms and inequalities'.

The Fawcett Society Commission on Gender Stereotypes in Early Childhood reports that newborn children are initially unaware of gendered expectations and attitudes. However, research suggests that by the age of two, most children become aware of the social signifi-cance of gender. Furthermore, by the end of primary school, children typically form distinct perceptions of the expected behaviours of boys and girls (Culhane and Bazeley, 2019). During their formative years, especially teenage, young people are particularly impressionable and are heavily influenced by societal norms and cultural messages regarding gender. Without open discussions about misogyny, misandry, and toxic masculinity, young people may inter-nalise harmful stereotypes and beliefs about themselves and others based on their gender. By engaging in conversations about these topics, educators, parents, and mentors can help young people critically analyse and challenge gender stereotypes and expectations. This empowers them to form healthier attitudes and behaviours towards themselves and others, fostering empathy, respect, and equality in their relationships.

It's crucial to acknowledge that men, boys, women, and girls are diverse groups, each influenced by various aspects of their identity and social standing. Factors such as age, social class, race, ethnicity, sexuality, and disability intersect with gender to shape individual expe-riences. Additionally, these factors contribute to the formation of gender norms, which can differ among various groups of men and boys across different contexts.

Social norms and gender norms are influential concepts for understanding the behaviours of individuals and the broader gender relations and inequalities in society. UNICEF defines social norms as 'the perceived informal, mostly unwritten, rules that define acceptable and

DOI: 10.4324/9781032697932-16

appropriate actions within a given group or community, thus guiding human behaviour' (www.sbcguidance.org, n.d.). It is important to also bear in mind that gendered social norms typically dictate the expected conduct of individuals who identify as male or female, as perceived by themselves or others. These norms are commonly constructed in a binary manner and often overlook or exclude non-binary or gender-fluid identities. Furthermore, they often adhere to heteronormativity, resulting in marginalisation of lesbian, gay, bisexual, and transgender individuals.

In discussions surrounding misogyny, misandry, and toxic masculinity, it is essential to recognise the ways in which they intersect and influence each other. For example, toxic masculinity can contribute to the perpetuation of misogyny by reinforcing harmful gender roles and attitudes towards women. Similarly, addressing misogyny and misandry requires challenging stereotypes and expectations associated with gender, including those related to toxic masculinity.

Addressing misogyny, misandry, and hyper and toxic masculinity early on can help prevent the perpetuation of harmful gender norms and reduce the likelihood of young people engaging in behaviours that contribute to gender-based discrimination, violence, and inequality.

Misogyny

This term refers to the deep-seated hatred or contempt for women and/or girls. It encompasses a range of behaviours, including discrimination, objectification, physical and verbal violence, and the reinforcement of traditional gender roles that limit women's opportunities and autonomy. Misogyny can spread throughout society, affecting how people interact and how institutions operate. It can show up subtly in language, actions, and societal rules. This widespread misogyny keeps women from fully participating in social, economic, and political areas, contributing to inequality.

Studies have been conducted into the responses and neural processing of sexist comments in the brain (Jin et al., 2023). Results actually show that experiencing sexism often leads to negative emotions like anger, sadness, and feeling upset. Brain activity in areas like the prefrontal regions and subcortical-limbic regions suggests that three processes are involved: emotional reaction, emotion regulation, and social cognitive processing. Meta-analysis of research has also found that with regards to emotional reactivity, females have been found to be more reactive to emotional stimuli, specifically unpleasant, threatening, or traumatic stimuli.

Examples of misogyny:

- Gender-based discrimination
  Women facing discrimination in the workplace, such as being paid less than men for the same work or being passed over for promotions based on their gender, is a clear example of misogyny.
- Objectification
  The objectification of women in media and advertising, where women are often portrayed solely for their physical appearance or as sexual objects, perpetuates misogynistic attitudes.

- Sexual harassment
  Unwanted advances, comments, or behaviours of a sexual nature directed towards women in the workplace or public spaces are examples of misogyny and contribute to a hostile environment for women.
- Violence against women
  Domestic violence, sexual assault, and other forms of gender-based violence are extreme manifestations of misogyny, reflecting a belief in the inherent inferiority or subjugation of women.
- Gender stereotypes
  Stereotypical beliefs about women's roles and abilities, such as the assumption that women are less capable leaders or that their primary role is in caregiving, reinforce misogynistic views and limit women's opportunities.
- Online harassment
  Women experiencing harassment, threats, and abuse online, often targeted at their gender or sexuality, is another example of misogyny in the digital realm. Amnesty reported:

> online abuse of women is widespread in the UK with one in five women having suffered online abuse or harassment. Almost half of women said the abuse or harassment they received was sexist or misogynistic, with a worrying 27% saying it threatened sexual or physical assault (www.amnesty.org.uk, n.d.).

Misandry

Misandry, the counterpart to misogyny, refers to the hatred or contempt for men and/or boys. While less commonly discussed, misandry represents a harmful attitude that can contribute to gender-based discrimination and prejudice. Similar to misogyny, misandry can manifest in various forms, such as stereotypes portraying men as inherently violent or emotionally stunted. Despite being less prevalent in mainstream discourse, misandry still warrants attention as it contributes to the perpetuation of harmful gender stereotypes and hinders efforts to achieve gender equality.

Examples of misandry:

- Stereotyping
  Portraying men as inherently violent, aggressive, emotionally stunted, or incompetent solely based on their gender is a form of misandry. Such stereotypes undermine men's individuality and contribute to unfair generalisations about their behaviour.
- Discrimination
  Instances where men face discrimination based solely on their gender, such as being denied certain opportunities or services, can be considered misandrist.
- Prejudice in family court
  Some argue that family court systems in some jurisdictions are biased against men, presuming them to be unfit parents solely based on their gender during custody battles. While this is a contentious issue, some view it as an example of institutionalised misandry.

- Media portrayals
  Media representations that depict men as bumbling or inept caregivers or incapable of emotional depth can perpetuate misandrist stereotypes.
- Dismissal of male victims
  Dismissing or minimising the experiences of male victims of domestic violence, sexual assault, or other forms of abuse, based on the belief that men cannot be victims or that their experiences are less important, is another form of misandry.

Hyper and toxic masculinity

Societal expectations regarding 'manhood' are prevalent and deep-rooted. We tend to appreciate qualities like kindness, empathy, and nurturing in women more than in men. Concurrently, men are often positively associated with traits such as protectiveness, while negative connotations are attached to emotional expression, as noted by the Pew Research Center. An influential concept in understanding masculinity is the notion of the 'Man Box', by Paul Kivel (n.d.). This refers to a set of rigid and restrictive norms or beliefs that are conveyed directly or indirectly by families, peers, education, and the media. These norms place immense pressure on boys and men to conform to specific standards, which can also be harmful to women. The 'Man Box' dictates that men should:

- Prioritise self-sufficiency
- Project toughness
- Prioritise physical appearance
- Adhere strictly to traditional gender roles, particularly regarding household chores and caregiving responsibilities
- Exhibit heterosexuality and show aversion to homosexuality
- Demonstrate sexual prowess
- Be willing to resort to violence
- Assert control over household decisions and women's independence

Mosher and Sirkin first introduced the concept of hypermasculinity in 1984, with the prefix 'hyper' denoting excess or going beyond. Hypermasculinity is characterised by a desire to exert control, command respect, and acquire power (Doherty, 2017). It often manifests in behaviours associated with both sexual and non-sexual violence among males, leading to impulsive acts of aggression. Two prominent traits of hypermasculinity include feelings of isolation and a compulsion for attention and notoriety. Hypermasculinity is closely linked to violence perpetrated by men against other men and also contributes to internalised violence directed at oneself.

Toxic masculinity is a term used to describe harmful and often outdated traits or characteristics associated with men; it refers to the cultural norms and expectations surrounding masculinity that are harmful to both men and women, as well as society at large. These norms often prioritise traits such as dominance, aggression, emotional repression, and the suppression of vulnerability. Toxic masculinity can lead to harmful behaviours, including violence and substance abuse. Society's pressure on men to embody traditional masculine traits goes against vulnerability and emotional expression, which contributes to mental health issues such as anxiety, depression, increased risk of suicide, and an inability to seek help for mental health issues. Priory released statistics on male suicide (Priory, 2021):

- 74% of all suicides in the UK involve men
- The rate of suicide in men (15.4 per 100,000) is over three times higher than in women (4.9 per 100,000)
- Men aged 45–64 have the highest rate of suicide by age (20 per 100,000)
- Suicide is the second biggest cause of death in young males (1–19 years old)

Dr Natasha Bijlani, a Consultant Psychiatrist at Priory Hospital Roehampton, said:

> Traditionally, men have been less likely to seek support for mental health issues. This is probably for a number of reasons including stigma and the traditional 'strong male' stereotype still prevalent in our society – the idea that expressing emotion is a sign of weakness.

In general, girls and women demonstrate a greater openness in discussing mental health, expressing their feelings to others rather than internalising their emotions. Surveys on mental health consistently show that up to 40% of men have never engaged in conversations about their mental well-being, even though more than three-quarters experience common symptoms such as anxiety, stress, or depression.

Toxic masculinity perpetuates harmful gender stereotypes and rigid gender roles, reinforces power imbalances, and contributes to the marginalisation of those who do not conform to traditional gender norms.

Assuming that men must fulfil roles such as protector, provider, or leader and linking men with traits like anger, self-centredness, and violence is unfair, problematic, and detrimental. Negative consequences arise from toxic masculinity when men avoid vulnerability, embrace homophobic beliefs, suppress personal traumas, or exhibit prejudiced behaviour towards women, contributing to broader societal issues. These effects include:

- Domestic abuse
- Gender-based violence
- Gun violence
- Homophobia
- Misogyny
- Rape culture
- Sexual assault
- Violence and aggression

According to Britt East, author of *A Gay Man's Guide to Life*, 'rigid interpretations of masculinity lead to fragility'. In an attempt to conform to these expectations, men often resort to violence, either outwardly through physical aggression or inwardly through depression, addiction, or suicide.

Incel culture

The term 'incel' is an abbreviation of 'involuntary celibate'. The Key has produced some excellent resources to support staff with this (Thekeysupport.com, 2019).

The 'manosphere' is a term used to describe an online subculture or community consisting primarily of men who share and discuss views related to masculinity, gender dynamics, and men's rights. It encompasses a range of online spaces such as forums, blogs, social media groups, and websites where men gather to discuss various topics, including relationships, dating, self-improvement, and societal issues from a male perspective.

The manosphere is diverse and includes different subgroups with varying ideologies and focuses. These subgroups may include men's rights activists (MRAs), pickup artists (PUAs), men going their own way (MGTOW), and incels (involuntary celibates), among others. While some discussions within the manosphere may be focused on legitimate concerns related to men's experiences and challenges, others promote misogynistic or harmful beliefs about women and gender relations.

The incel 'worldview'

The belief is that attractiveness is predetermined by genetic factors, shaping physical appearance. Consequently, some men are seen as more appealing to women, leading to others being labelled as 'involuntary celibates'. This belief fuels a social hierarchy centred around attractiveness.

Women are genetically inferior to men and are portrayed as manipulative individuals driven by a desire to reproduce with genetically superior men. Additionally, incels attribute male suffering to women's increased independence and autonomy.

The concept of 'pilling' is drawn from the film *The Matrix*. Taking the red pill symbolises awakening to the true nature of the world, including the social hierarchy determined by genetic factors, while the blue pill represents remaining detached from reality. This idea is also prominent in far-right ideology.

Incels typically communicate through online platforms like Reddit, where discussions range from sharing ideas about women's manipulative nature to expressing violent fantasies about women. Similar to other forms of radicalisation, users may initially encounter relatively mild content before being exposed to increasingly extreme views.

Recognising incel slang

Slang plays a significant role in the online communication of incels. For example, a 'Chad' is a man perceived to be sexually successful, characterised by intelligence, good looks, and charm. Incels often struggle with conflicting feelings toward these men, simultaneously despising them while also longing to emulate them. They believe that women are irresistibly attracted to Chads and will inevitably betray their partners ('cuck') for them.

A 'Stacy' refers to a woman who engages in sexual activity with numerous men, typically Chads. Stacies are often stereotyped as unintelligent, attractive, and promiscuous, with the term used to degrade women.

The use of incel slang is becoming more prevalent in everyday language, largely due to social media and the widespread circulation of memes. Consequently, our students may encounter this language and rhetoric, potentially adopting it without critical thought. Alternatively, and more concerning, they may become influenced by the incel ideology.

Here are some words to listen out for:

AWALT: An abbreviation for 'all women are like that'. This term is employed to belittle women and portray them in a negative way.

Beta: A term used to describe a man who is not perceived as an 'alpha' (Chads). Betas are often viewed as weak and avoidant of confrontation.

Femoid or Foid: A derogatory term used to refer to women, suggesting they are sub-human and intended to dehumanise them.

Normie: A term used to characterise individuals who are considered relatively neurotypical, possessing average intelligence and appearance.

Roastie: Another disparaging term for a woman. Incels use this term to describe women who they believe have stretched labia due to having had sexual relations with multiple men. While some use it ironically, many incels genuinely believe that a woman's labia can change shape based on her number of sexual partners.

What do we see in the classroom?

In school, boys and young men are often expected to adhere to dominant masculinity norms, which prioritise traits like toughness, athletic ability, social status, and a casual approach to schoolwork. However, outside the influence of peer pressure, boys tend to exhibit greater introspection and self-awareness.

Portrayals of men and masculinity in TV shows, advertisements, magazines, movies, and music videos often depict narrow, unrealistic, and stereotypical images. Additionally, the widespread availability of pornography frequently portrays men as dominant and women as mere sexual objects.

Research by Ipsos for King's College London's Policy Institute and the Global Institute for Women's Leadership indicates that boys and men from Generation Z are more inclined than older generations to perceive feminism as having caused more harm than good. One in four males aged 16 to 29 in the UK believe that it is more challenging to be a man than a woman. Furthermore, a fifth of those who are familiar with him now views the social media influencer Andrew Tate in a favourable light. The Canadian author Jordan Peterson, who says he speaks up for 'demoralised young men' is also seen favourably by 32% of 16-to-29-year-old men (Booth and correspondent, 2024).

In a survey conducted by PerryUndem, a research and polling firm, approximately three-quarters of girls aged 14 to 19 reported feeling judged as sexual objects or unsafe due to their gender. A significant majority of respondents stated that society prioritises physical attractiveness as the most crucial trait for females, a sentiment also echoed by adult women in previous surveys. Additionally, girls were more inclined than boys to express feeling pressured to prioritise others' emotions over their own (Miller, 2018).

Approximately half of the respondents reported hearing boys make sexual comments or jokes about girls on a daily basis, with a quarter of girls aged 10 to 13 experiencing this. Additionally, one-third of teenage girls reported hearing such comments from male family members.

Strategies

'Masculinity' and 'toxic masculinity' are distinct concepts, and it's crucial not to confuse them. Educating young people about toxic masculinity isn't about undermining masculine traits altogether. Rather, it addresses harmful aspects of traditional masculinity that negatively impact everyone and works to change the harmful ideas and expectations of masculinity that are at the roots of so much violence and abuse in society (Burrell et al., 2019).

Encouraging boys and young men to discuss their lives openly is vital. The most effective examples of practice included using positive, affirmative messages showing what men and boys can do to create change (American Psychological Association, 2018).

Reassure them their masculinity isn't diminished if they enjoy activities typically associated with femininity. There is immense pressure on boys and young men to conform to traditional masculine ideals, leading to stereotypes and judgments. Masculinity and femininity aren't mutually exclusive, and we should promote acceptance and encouragement of diverse interests and expressions.

Language plays a crucial role. Suicide is a leading cause of death among men under 40, and phrases like 'man up' contribute to the stigma surrounding men expressing vulnerability and seeking help.

Embrace challenging conversations! Engaging in open and honest discussions about these sensitive topics is essential for fostering understanding and promoting change. Our beliefs are shaped by our environment, and by confronting and questioning them, we can work towards creating a more inclusive and empathetic society. It is important to show you are not judging and remember that their beliefs may come from their family, friends, and communities or people that they admire.

Activities in the classroom

Promoting open conversations about toxic masculinity in the classroom can help pupils develop a deeper understanding of gender roles and stereotypes. Here are some activities to encourage such discussions that can be adapted for different age groups.

Discussions: Begin by defining toxic masculinity and discussing its characteristics. Provide examples from media, literature, or personal experiences to illustrate how toxic masculinity manifests in society.

Drama or tutor time activity: Divide students into small groups and provide them with scenarios depicting situations where toxic masculinity may be present (e.g., bullying, peer pressure, gender-based violence). Ask each group to role-play the scenario and discuss alternative, non-toxic responses.

Media analysis: Show students various media clips, advertisements, or movie scenes that portray stereotypical masculinity. Guide a discussion on how these portrayals reinforce toxic masculinity and its impact on individuals and society.

Guest speakers or panels: Invite guest speakers such as psychologists, activists, or community leaders to share their perspectives on toxic masculinity.

Reflective writing: Assign pupils reflective writing prompts related to toxic masculinity. Encourage them to explore personal experiences, societal influences, and potential ways to challenge toxic masculinity in their own lives and communities.

Intersectionality exploration: Explore the intersectionality of toxic masculinity with other social identities such as race, class, sexuality, and ability. Discuss how these intersecting factors shape experiences of toxic masculinity and its effects on marginalised communities.

Empathy-building exercises: Use empathy-building exercises, such as perspective-taking activities or storytelling, to help students understand the impact of toxic masculinity on individuals' mental health, relationships, and well-being.

Create a safe space: Establish classroom norms that promote respect, active listening, and inclusivity. Emphasise the importance of creating a safe space where students feel comfortable sharing their thoughts, experiences, and concerns about toxic masculinity without fear of judgement or ridicule.

Challenging gender roles: Provide examples of women and men going against expected gender roles (e.g., female scientists, male caregivers).

It is important to involve all of your pupils in discussions on toxic masculinity for several reasons:

Promoting gender equality: By including female, non-binary, and trans perspectives, discussions on toxic masculinity become more balanced and inclusive, fostering a deeper understanding of the impact of harmful gender norms on individuals of all genders.

Empowering voices: Involving all pupils empowers them to share their experiences, challenges, and perspectives related to toxic masculinity. It validates their voices and provides a platform for them to contribute to conversations about gender dynamics.

Building empathy and understanding: Hearing from all pupils helps cultivate empathy and understanding among all pupils. It allows them to gain insight into the lived experiences of individuals affected by toxic masculinity and its broader societal implications.

Challenging stereotypes: Including different perspectives challenges stereotypes about gender roles and behaviours. It highlights the diversity of experiences and perspectives among individuals, breaking down rigid and harmful stereotypes perpetuated by toxic masculinity.

Fostering inclusive environments: Involving all pupils in discussions on toxic masculinity contributes to creating inclusive learning environments where diverse viewpoints are valued and respected. It promotes a culture of mutual respect and empathy among students.

Encouraging critical thinking: Hearing diverse perspectives encourages critical thinking and reflection among pupils. It prompts them to question societal norms, challenge biases, and develop a more nuanced understanding of complex issues related to gender and masculinity.

Empowering advocacy: Engaging all pupils in discussions on toxic masculinity empowers them to become advocates for gender equality and social change. It equips them with the knowledge and skills to challenge harmful norms and promote healthier, more inclusive attitudes towards gender.

Empowering boys to challenge boys

Empowering your male pupils to challenge what they read and hear, particularly regarding toxic masculinity and harmful gender norms, is extremely powerful.

Promoting peer accountability: When boys challenge each other's behaviours and attitudes related to toxic masculinity, it promotes peer accountability. This means holding each other responsible for perpetuating harmful stereotypes and encouraging positive behaviour change.

Creating safe spaces: Boys challenging boys can create safe spaces for open dialogue about masculinity, allowing them to express their thoughts, concerns, and struggles without fear of judgement or ridicule. This fosters a supportive environment for addressing issues related to gender norms.

Changing perceptions: Boys challenging boys can help change perceptions of what it means to be masculine. By encouraging a broader definition of masculinity that includes traits like empathy, vulnerability, and emotional intelligence, they challenge traditional stereotypes and promote more inclusive ideals of masculinity.

Reducing peer pressure: Boys challenging boys can help reduce peer pressure to conform to toxic masculine norms. By openly discussing and rejecting behaviours like aggression, dominance, and emotional suppression, they create space for boys to express themselves authentically without feeling the need to conform to harmful stereotypes.

Supporting mental health: Challenging toxic masculinity can support boys' mental health by encouraging them to be more open about their emotions and seek help when needed. By fostering a culture of acceptance and support, boys can feel more comfortable addressing mental health issues and seeking support from their peers.

Building empathy: Boys who challenge boys can build empathy by encouraging boys to consider the perspectives and experiences of others. By promoting understanding and empathy, boys can develop more respectful and compassionate relationships with their peers and contribute to a more inclusive and supportive social environment.

Myth: Misogyny only affects women.

Truth: Misogyny not only impacts women but also perpetuates harmful gender stereotypes and norms that can negatively affect men and non-binary individuals as well. It contributes to a culture of inequality and discrimination based on gender.

Myth: Toxic masculinity benefits men.

Truth: Toxic masculinity, characterised by rigid gender norms emphasising dominance, aggression, and emotional suppression, harms men by limiting their emotional expression, promoting violence, and perpetuating harmful stereotypes. It can also lead to mental health issues and hinder healthy relationships.

Myth: Misogyny and toxic masculinity are natural behaviours.

Truth: Misogyny and toxic masculinity are social constructs rooted in historical and cultural norms. They are learned behaviours that can be unlearned through education, awareness, and challenging traditional gender roles. Addressing these issues is crucial for creating a more equitable and inclusive society for all genders.

References

American Psychological Association (2018). *APA GUIDELINES for psychological practice with boys and men*. [online] American Psychological Association. Available at: https://www.apa.org/about/policy/boys-men-practice-guidelines.pdf.

Booth, R. and correspondent, R.B.S. affairs (2024). Gen Z boys and men more likely than baby boomers to believe feminism harmful, says poll. *The Guardian*. [online] 1 Feb. Available at: https://www.theguardian.com/news/2024/feb/01/gen-z-boys-and-men-more-likely-than-baby-boomers-to-believe-feminism-harmful-says-poll?utm_source=instagram [Accessed 11 Mar. 2024].

Burrell, S., Ruxton, S. and Westmarland, N. (2019). *Changing gender norms: Engaging with men and boys research report prepared by*. [online] Available at: https://assets.publishing.service.gov.uk/media/60008afad3bf7f33b0de61f1/Changing_Gender_Norms-_Engaging_with_Men_and_Boys.pdf

Culhane, L. and Bazeley, A. (2019). *Gender stereotypes in early childhood a literature review*. [online] Available at: https://www.fawcettsociety.org.uk/Handlers/Download.ashx?IDMF=e8096848-cbdb-4e16-8713-ee0dadb3dcc5.

Doherty, B. (2017). *Merrimack college Merrimack college Merrimack Scholar Works Merrimack Scholar Works honors senior capstone projects honors program hyper masculinity; Influences and prevention in children hyper masculinity; Influences and prevention in children*. [online] Available at: https://scholarworks.merrimack.edu/cgi/viewcontent.cgi?article=1025&context=honors_capstones#:~:text=Males%20experiencing%20hyper%20masculinity%20often [Accessed 11 Mar. 2024].

Jin, M., Bizzego, A., Teng, J. H., Gabrieli, G. and Esposito, G. (2023). Neural processing of sexist comments: Associations between perceptions of sexism and prefrontal activity. *Brain Sciences*, [online] 13(4), p. 529. https://doi.org/10.3390/brainsci13040529

Kivel, P. (n.d.). *Boys will be men raising our sons for courage, caring, and community*. [online] Available at: https://paulkivel.com/wp-content/uploads/2015/07/info_bwbm.pdf [Accessed 29 Jun. 2024].

Miller, C.C. (2018). Many ways to be a girl, but one way to be a boy: The new gender rules. *The New York Times*. [online] 14 Sep. Available at: https://www.nytimes.com/2018/09/14/upshot/gender-stereotypes-survey-girls-boys.html

Practice, A.S.A. | C. of A. (n.d.). *Report Signals Tougher Standards on Harmful Gender Stereotypes in Ads*. [online] www.asa.org.uk. Available at: https://www.asa.org.uk/news/report-signals-tougher-standards-on-harmful-gender-stereotypes-in-ads.html.

Priory. (2021). Why are suicides so high amongst men? *Priory Group*. [online] Available at: https://www.priorygroup.com/blog/why-are-suicides-so-high-amongst-men

Thekeysupport.com. (2019). *Safeguarding training centre | The key*. [online] Available at: https://safeguarding.thekeysupport.com/ [Accessed 17 Jul. 2019].

www.amnesty.org.uk. (n.d.). *Online abuse of women widespread*. [online] Available at: https://www.amnesty.org.uk/online-abuse-women-widespread#:~:text=Online%20abuse%20of%20women%20is

www.sbcguidance.org. (n.d.). *Social norms | UNICEF SBC GUIDANCE*. [online] Available at: https://www.sbcguidance.org/do/social-norms.

17 Abuse

Chapter introduction

In this chapter, a range of forms of abuse are discussed, along with signs and symptoms of how to recognise that someone may be being abused. The effects of abuse are discussed to help understand how abuse can have lifelong implications. Christina Gabbitas explains more about 'County Lines' and the associated criminal activities that children can be exploited into by gangs. Paul Portlock-Smith shares a personal reflection on county lines and the criminal exploitation of children and young people. L.D. Smith also offers a thoughtful contribution on 'safeguarding' that considers the term 'professional curiosity', as introduced by the Department for Education in 2022.

Definition of abuse and types of abuse

What is abuse, and how many categories or types of abuse can you name?

'Child abuse' includes physical abuse, sexual abuse, and psychological abuse (WHO, 1999). Child abuse is often seen as being inflicted on children under 18 years old, although it is important to note that upper age limits that define child abuse vary by country or legislative area, with the upper age limit as young as 12 years of age in some regions (Collins et al., 2023).

The National Society for the Prevention of Cruelty to Children, NSPCC (2024: 1) defines child abuse as when:

> a child is harmed by an adult or another child – it can be over a period of time but can also be a one-off action. It can be physical, sexual or emotional and it can happen in person or online. It can also be a lack of love, care and attention – this is neglect.

The NSPCC (2024) lists 13 different forms of abuse, which are shared in what follows with definitions. Please note some of these are covered in other chapters within this book, in which case their chapter number is given in brackets:

1. Bullying and cyberbullying (Chapter 7): This is where an individual is targeted by a 'bully' who may harm or threaten to harm them or cause them distress.

DOI: 10.4324/9781032697932-17

2.   Child sexual exploitation: This is where someone uses the power they have over a child – such as through authority, age, gender, strength, or money – to take advantage of them sexually.

3.   Child trafficking: This is where children are procured, and often relocated, to be engaged in forced labour or sexual exploitation.

4.   Criminal exploitation and gangs: This is where children are used as tools to hide or transport drugs, weapons, or money, or they may be facilitated to beg or steal to gain funds. 'County Lines' refers to the illegal transportation of drugs between different areas, often crossing police and local authority boundaries, typically carried out by children or vulnerable individuals who are coerced by criminal gangs, discussed later in this chapter.

5.   Domestic abuse: Domestic abuse, sometimes referred to as 'domestic violence', usually involves an adult threatening or harming someone else – or others – in the home.

6.   Emotional abuse: Sometimes referred to as psychological abuse, emotional abuse is where someone intentionally humiliates, isolates, or ignores a child.

7.   Female genital mutilation: Female genital mutilation (FGM), also called 'female cutting' or 'female circumcision', is when a female's genitals are deliberately altered or removed for non-medical reasons. The Female Genital Mutilation Act 2003 makes it illegal to perform FGM in the UK; help or arrange for anyone to carry out FGM abroad on girls who are British Nationals or UK residents; help a girl to carry out FGM on herself; or fail to protect a girl under 16 who is known to be at risk of FGM. FGM carries a penalty of up to 14 years in prison (Thames Valley Police, 2024: 1).

8.   Grooming (Chapter 18): This is where an individual prepares a child for a purpose, usually sexual gratification or – with adults – financial gain.

9.   Neglect: This is where a child's basic needs are not met by their caregivers for an extended period, such as through lack of food, lack of hygiene and care, and lack of interaction.

10.   Non-recent abuse: This is where an adult was abused as a child, also referred to as 'historical abuse'.

11.   Online abuse (Chapter 10): This is where technology, such as through phones, tablets, or computers, is used to facilitate bullying – known as 'cyberbullying'.

12.   Physical abuse: This is where an individual intentionally hurts or bodily injures someone through any means, such as hitting, smacking, or inappropriate physical restraints or punishments.

13.   Sexual abuse (Chapter 18): Every child or young person under the age of 18 is at risk of child sexual exploitation; the only common link is that abusers often look for someone who appears vulnerable through a falling-out with a friendship group (The Upstream Project, 2024).

Spotting signs and symptoms of abuse

As you will have learnt in any safeguarding training that you have attended, spotting signs of abuse can be difficult and complex. The signs of child abuse may not always be apparent, and in some cases, such as sexual abuse or physical abuse, the child may not even understand that the behaviours happening are abuse as they may have no other situations to compare theirs to. The signs and symptoms of abuse can greatly vary depending on the type of abuse;

however, there are some common signs that a child may have some issues going on outside of school, such as:

- Becoming withdrawn
- Difficulty to socialise with peers
- Changes in personality or their behaviour
- Being aggressive irrationally and out of character
- Knowledge of adult issues not appropriate for the child's age
- Wearing long sleeves or trousers that keep them covered up
- Poor bond with caregiver
- Running away from home or going missing

(NSPCC, 2024)

It must be stressed that recognising some of these behaviours does not definitely mean a child is being abused but may be a red flag that there is a situation affecting their well-being. Ensure you know who to speak to within your school or college if you have a concern about one of the students and make sure you follow your institution's policies and procedures, along with the guidelines of any safeguarding training your institution has provided to you.

Report abuse in the education helpline

If you are based in the UK, NSPCC has launched a dedicated helpline for children and young people who have experienced abuse at school and for worried adults and professionals that need support and guidance, including for non-recent abuse. Call the new NSPCC helpline, Report Abuse in Education, on 0800 136 663 or email help@nspcc.org.uk

Effects of abuse

The effects of child abuse will manifest differently in all children affected, depending on the circumstances and severity of the abuse, but may include:

- Poor mental health and well-being
- Difficulty in accessing or engaging with their education
- Poor social connections and relationships through adulthood
- Adults with historic abuse may struggle with healthy relationships, or being a good parent
- Drug or alcohol dependance
- Criminal behaviour
- Repeating the abusive behaviours they were subject to, towards other people

(NSPCC, 2024)

The next two contributions look at a more recent phenomenon in the landscape of child abuse, namely that of criminal gang exploitation of children and young people through the employment of 'County Lines'.

***

County lines and associated topics - the importance of early intervention
Christina Gabbitas - author, coronation champion, and honorary member of the NSPCC council

The term 'County Lines' refers to the illegal transportation of drugs between different areas, often crossing police and local authority boundaries, typically carried out by children or vulnerable individuals who are coerced by criminal gangs. These operations are facilitated through a mobile phone line known as the 'County Line' for drug orders, as highlighted by the National Crime Agency.

In 2019, I was approached by the Humberside Police and Crime Commissioners Office to engage with young people about knife crime, following the success of my story 'Share Some Secrets', which encourages children to speak out against abuse. Upon researching the topic, I discovered a strong correlation between the presence of knives and drug activity. This led me to create a graphic-style story commissioned by the police, entitled 'No More Knives or County Lines', depicting a group of friends aged 10 to 16 being groomed by a gang leader named Steve.

After conducting in-depth research on county lines and related issues, I engaged with a diverse range of individuals, including an ex-gang member, individuals with lived experiences, young people, police cadets, and various law enforcement personnel, to craft stories that resonate with my target audience of young people. I strongly believe in the power of storytelling as an effective tool to captivate the attention of children and youth.

After visiting numerous schools with law enforcement teams, I was approached by North Yorkshire Police to write a sequel, titled 'Trapped in County Lines', aimed at age 12+, which portrays a stabbing fatality and a character going missing. In primary schools, I focus on educating children about grooming tactics and the concept of County Lines. In secondary schools, I discuss the sequel story and ensure students comprehend terms like cuckooing and debt bondage, which some may not be familiar with.

Utilising a graphic story style, I transformed each narrative into an animated format to enhance engagement during our sessions with children and young people. It is very reassuring to know that my work has influenced the perspectives and helped to safeguard some children, as acknowledged by teachers and policing teams.

My stories serve as a means to educate students about the potential consequences of involvement in criminal activities and where to seek help if needed. By incorporating elements such as a fatality and a 13-year-old boy going missing, the narratives prompt important conversations and raise awareness among teachers, students, and parents. Providing students with copies of the graphic-style stories encourages further discussions within families and communities.

The reality of organised crime groups operating within communities, as highlighted by a parent whose 13-year-old child was exploited, empasises the urgency for collective action and increased support to combat such issues. It is crucial for us to collaborate and take proactive measures to safeguard our children from the threats posed by criminal activities like county lines.

Reflecting on an Ofsted report from 2018 that stressed the importance of early intervention education on county lines in all schools, it is disappointing to note the lack of significant progress in implementing such measures over the past six years. To truly educate children about the world they live in, it is crucial to equip them with a foundational understanding of critical topics like County Lines.

Christina says: If you would like to learn more about my working partnerships, visit www.trappedincountylines.co.uk and www.nomoreknifecrime.co.uk

***

In this second contribution, Paul Portlock-Smith shares a personal reflection on county lines and criminal exploitation of children and young people.

County lines, by Paul Portlock-Smith, middle management SEND education

When I started teaching, being Primary trained and spending my formative teaching years in the economically deprived South Wales valleys, I had only a vague knowledge of County lines and drug culture in general.

Although teaching at that time in very economically deprived areas, there were always whispers about drugs and families involved in drugs, predominantly cannabis; there was never any concrete evidence, just hearsay.

This changed greatly when I moved into Special Education, working with pupils with SEBD (Social, Emotional, and Behavioural Difficulties). These pupils are amongst the most vulnerable in society, many coming from the most fractured family backgrounds, and many pupils spending time within the care system. These environments can sadly be breeding grounds for unscrupulous drug gangs to exploit the vulnerabilities that exist because of the poor socioeconomic conditions that exist in some of our poorest areas. Where there is poverty, exclusion, and alienation, there are always opportunities to exploit and coerce.

My experience of working with pupils who face some of the harshest living conditions, struggling to eat in some cases, is one where opportunities through education (in their eyes) are limited. Many pupils see and have seen dealers with money and connections and see this as something to aspire to and an easy way to succeed than through academic endeavour.

These pupils, who already feel marginalised and alienated, have already been excluded from a number of schools until they arrive at my school, so they can be quite easily radicalised (I mean radicalised in the sense that they can be coerced easily with the thought of reward albeit money or drugs or just to feel wanted as in part of a gang).

These drug gangs operating in my area operate the same all over the UK. They either offer money, clothing (especially trainers), or indeed drugs as a way of payment for the delivery of drugs or money to other dealers or addicts, or in some cases, they will fabricate a drug deal and then arrange for the young person to be 'mugged' on the way to a fictitious deal so that the young person believes they owe them for losing their money or drugs.

Some of our pupils transfer to us from inner City areas for their own safety, and it is not uncommon for a pupil to come to me (as young as ten) who has been running drugs, money, and even knives and guns between drug gangs within an inner city area. These young pupils often bear the scars of such a lifestyle with evident stab wounds inflicted by drug gang leaders because they didn't meet expectations or just to instil fear.

It is also too evident that even from such a tender age, this culture has consumed such young people, and they cannot see a way out. County lines take childhoods and thrive on the vulnerabilities of young, easily exploited children and their families, too.

We have had cases where dealers have moved into family homes, often targeting single parents who themselves may have drug habits, and their children/my pupils have been paid by either drugs, cigarettes, or small material gifts not to say anything when they get to school, if they get to school.

As whole communities struggle with poverty and as society continues to implode almost, this cycle will continue, and the exploitation will continue to grow.

***

In this third and final contribution, L.D. Smith opens up an insightful conversation around professional curiosity when it comes to recognising signs and symptoms of abuse as part of safeguarding children and young people.

Safeguarding: professional curiosity and safeguarding, by L.D. Smith

Most teachers are aware of the Keeping Children Safe in Education (KCSIE) statutory guidance that is published annually by the DfE to support teachers in their safeguarding and welfare duties (DfE, 2023). Every year, teachers and schools review the changes as preparation for the new academic year.

In 2022, a new term was introduced, 'professional curiosity'.

> Section 19: 'This should not prevent staff from having a professional curiosity' (DfE, 2022: 8, 2023: 9, own emphasis).
> Section 21: 'Exercising professional curiosity [own emphasis] and knowing what to look for is vital for the early identification of abuse and neglect' (DfE, 2022: 9, DfE, 2023: 9).

Professional curiosity has entered the teaching lexicon with little to no explanation or guidance. Research explores professional curiosity in relation to adults and families and those professions involved in probation services and health, such as social workers, outside of the realm of the classroom and school (Dickens et al., 2023). However, there is little to indicate what this should or would look like in the classroom.

In safeguarding, professional curiosity has not been well defined; however, attempts have been made to provide some clarity, such as indicating that it is the use of questions to gain clarity on a family situation and the ability to reduce uncertainty around the harm that may happen to a child and as 'exploratory behaviour' (Burton and Revell, 2018: 1512; Cramphorn and Maynard, 2023; Muirden and Appleton, 2022).

McDonald and Rogowski (2023) provide insight by acknowledging the emotional and relationship dimensions. Relationships are at the very heart of teaching, and relationship-based practices permeate the profession. To enable children's voices to be heard, there needs to be trust, respect, and the ability to have open, non-judgemental listening. However, it must be acknowledged that this takes an emotional toll on teachers.

Professional curiosity is characterised by our skills in questioning, respectfully challenging, and noticing inconsistencies as indicators of concern without being pushy, going beyond face value (Thacker et al., 2019; Muirden and Appleton, 2022). This requires teachers to be confident in their knowledge of their responsibilities as well as communication skills and critically evaluating or reflecting on the information received.

Professional curiosity may take many forms, including strategic and proactive small talk, also known as 'quiet challenges'. This is exemplified through how a teacher asks, 'How did you do that?' when noticing an injury, asking, 'How are you doing today?' when a student is unusually quiet, or asking about behaviours of concern in a conversation (McDonald and Rogowski, 2023). At the other side of the spectrum are uncomfortable conversations that seek verification (Phillips et al., 2022).

As teachers, we also need to be aware that there are limitations to professional curiosity due to the emotional toll it takes. We need to ensure that our well-being is taken care of, as stress, our own prejudices and assumptions, over-optimism, lack of confidence or knowledge, and desensitisation or risk saturation can all work to diminish our capacity for professional curiosity.

***

Myth:	Asking someone to send a naked photo or video isn't abuse.
Truth:	Offenders know how to charm a child or young person to coerce them into sending them photos and videos, even if they may not want to initially. Taking advantage of a young or vulnerable person is abuse (The Upstream Project, 2024).
Myth:	Abuse is the child's fault.
Truth:	Sometimes, it might be the fear of judgement or a sense of guilt and shame that prevents a young person from speaking up about something that has happened to them. The truth is the only person to blame is the offender.
Myth:	Parents or carers should have recognised their child was being abused. Teachers should have spotted the signs of abuse.
Truth:	Abusers may build relationships with the family to feel trusted by them to be allowed alone with the child. They may also pursue the child to keep quiet and cover up the abuse. Offenders may also threaten the young person that if anyone finds out, bad things will happen. For all of these reasons, spotting abuse can be difficult and complex.

References

Burton, V. and Revell, L. (2018). Professional curiosity in child protection: Thinking the unthinkable in a neo-liberal world. *The British Journal of Social Work*, 48(6), pp. 1508–1523. https://www.jstor.org/stable/26613473

Collins, S., Orth, T., Brunton, R. and Dryer, R. (2023). Child abuse and wellbeing: Examining the roles of self-compassion and fear of self. *Child Abuse & Neglect*, 138, p. 106089. Available at: https://www.sciencedirect.com/science/article/pii/S0145213423000704

Cramphorn, K. and Maynard, E. (2023). The professional in 'professional curiosity'; exploring the experiences of school-based pastoral staff and their use of curiosity with and about parents: An interpretative phenomenological analysis. *Pastoral Care in Education,* 41(1), pp. 84–104. https://doi.org/10.1080/02643944.2021.1977989

DfE. (2022). Keeping children safe in education 2022: Statutory guidance for schools and colleges, Crown, London. *Keeping Children Safe in Education 2023.* Available at: publishing.service.gov.uk [Accessed 19 Apr. 2024].

DfE. (2023). Keeping children safe in education 2023: Statutory guidance for schools and colleges, Crown, London. *Keeping Children Safe in Education 2023.* Available at: publishing.service.gov.uk [Accessed 19 Apr. 2024].

Dickens, J., Cook, L., Cossar, J., Okpokiri, C., Taylor, J. and Garstang, J. (2023). Re-envisaging professional curiosity and challenge: Messages for child protection practice from reviews of serious cases in England. *Children and Youth Services Review,* 152, pp. 1–9.

McDonald, L. and Rogowski, S. (2023). Troubled and troublesome teenagers: Towards critical and relationship-based practice. *The British Journal of Social Work.* Oct. 53(7), pp. 3419–3435. https://doi.org/10.1093/bjsw/bcad161

Muirden, C.E. and Appleton, J.V. (2022). Health and social care practitioners' experience of exercising professional curiosity in child protection practice: An integrated review. *Health and Social Care in the Community,* 30(6), pp. 3385–3903.

NSPCC. (2024). *What is child abuse?* Available at: https://www.nspcc.org.uk/what-is-child-abuse/

Phillips, J., Ainslie, S., Fowler, A. and Westaby, C. (2022). Putting professional curiosity into practice, HM inspectorate of probation, academic insight 2022/07.*SHURA.* Available at: http://shura.shu.ac.uk/30544/ [Accessed 19 Apr. 2024].

Thacker, H., Anka, A. and Penhale, B. (2019). Could curiosity save lives? An exploration into the value of employing professional curiosity and partnership work in safeguarding adults under the Care Act 2014. *The Journal of Adult Protection,* 21(5), pp. 252–267. https://doi.org/10.1108/JAP-04-2019-0014

Thames Valley Police. (2024). *Female genital multilation.* Available at: https://www.thamesvalley.police.uk/advice/advice-and-information/fgm/female-genital-mutilation-fgm/#:~:text=The%20Female%20Genital%20Mutilation%20Act,carry%20out%20FGM%20on%20herself

The Upstream Project (2024). Preventing child sexual abuse. Available at: https://www.theupstreamproject.org.uk/prevent

WHO, G. (1999). *Report of the consultation on child abuse prevention, 29–31 March 1999.* Geneva: World Health Organization.

18 Grooming

Chapter introduction

The previous chapter looked at abuse more generally, whilst this chapter will focus on grooming, often with sexual intent. Grooming is when a person (the 'offender') builds a relationship with a child, young person, or a vulnerable adult (the 'victim') so that they can abuse them and manipulate them into doing things. The abuse is often sexual or financial in nature, but it can also include other illegal acts. This chapter explores the definition of 'grooming', considers how to support someone who may be being groomed, and raises awareness of how to recognise grooming tactics and subsequent behaviours in the groomed victims. It is especially important to have these conversations now, as data gathered through the Freedom of Information Act by the NSPCC shows that almost 34,000 online grooming crimes against children were recorded in the last six years (NSPCC, 2023), with an 82% rise in online grooming crimes against children in the last five years. This chapter also offers an informative insight into the sexual grooming of children, contributed by Dr Theresa Redmond, Associate Professor and subject specialist in child sexual abuse and exploitation.

Grooming

Originally termed 'seduction' in the 1970s by investigators, the now preferred term 'grooming' encompasses a process that involves a person, over time, gaining access to – and control of – their victim (Lanning, 2018), and sometimes with their wider family, gaining their trust and a position of power over the individual, in preparation for the onset of abuse (CEOP, 2022). Grooming is often non-violent in nature, which helps the offender avoid being discovered.

The three core categories of grooming involve:

- Verbal coercion
- Grooming with drugs/alcohol
- Threatening or violent grooming

(Wolf and Pruitt, 2019)

Grooming strategies that may be employed by the offenders may include – but are not limited to – enticements, such as gifts, isolation from friends and family through spreading

DOI: 10.4324/9781032697932-18

false truths about those members, sexualisation, fantasy, secrecy, coercion, and authority (Ringenberg et al., 2022). A study conducted with adult survivors of child sexual abuse found that for most trauma symptoms, Threatening or Violent Grooming was a significant predictor of trauma symptom severity, with a key exception of verbal coercion as a significant predictor of sexual problems in adulthood (Wolf and Pruitt, 2019). Clearly, the effects of grooming and abuse can have lifelong impacts and effects on relationships; thus more reason we must aim to identify and support victims of grooming and sexual abuse as early as possible.

Recent statistics of online sexual abuse

While grooming and child sexual abuse have been in existence for centuries before the explosion of online communications, tools such as social media have provided easier access to children (Ringenberg et al., 2022). The number of offences and children affected by online sexual abuse is likely to be a lot higher than what's currently known to the police as not all people affected will speak out about their experience, but the NSPCC (2023: 1) shares some startling statistics:

- 6,350 Sexual Communication with a Child offences were recorded last year (2022/23). This is an 82% increase since 2017/2018 when this offence came into force
- More than 5,500 offences were against primary school children, with under-12s being affected by a quarter of cases
- Where the gender was known, 83% of online grooming offences were against girls

Where the means of communication was known:

- 150 different apps, games, and websites were used to groom children online
- 26% of online grooming offences against children took place on Snapchat
- 47% of online grooming offences took place on Meta-owned products such as Facebook, Instagram, and WhatsApp

(NSPCC, 2023: 1)

Spotting possible signs of grooming

Signs that a child may be being groomed include:

- Sudden changes in the child's behaviour, such as spending more or less time online where they may be seeking contact or avoiding contact through feeling scared
- Spending more time away or going missing from home or school
- Being secretive about how they are spending their time, including when using online devices

(NSPCC, 2024b)

Ensure you are aware of your school's procedures should you or another staff member have a concern around grooming.

***

In the following contribution, Dr Theresa Redmond, Associate Professor and subject specialist in child sexual abuse and exploitation, The Policing Institute for the Eastern Region, Anglia Ruskin University, UK, focuses on the sexual grooming of children. Dr Redmond's professional background comprises 12 years experience in social care and then 13 years in education as a Social Sciences and Citizenship teacher and Head of Department. Dr Redmond has worked as a frontline practitioner with children and young people experiencing child sexual abuse and exploitation (CSAE) and held a pastoral role in a secondary school supporting young people facing a range of challenges to their mental health and well-being. When she moved into research, Dr Redmond specialised in CSAE, particularly working with victims and survivors, and spent two years working as a researcher for the Independent Inquiry into Child Sexual Abuse.

'All the things they never told me about . . . the sexual grooming of children and young people', by Theresa Redmond

The words 'sexual grooming' and 'children' should never go together, but unfortunately, they do, far too often. Let's just think about this phrase, 'sexual grooming', for a moment. On its own, the word 'grooming' has safe, almost pleasurable connotations. We groom pets, animals, and ourselves, and, in this context, it can be an act of care or self-care. As soon as we add the word 'sexual' as a prefix, which we must in order to be explicit about what this really is, the tone darkens, twisting that innocuous meaning to something sinister and dangerous. This is exemplified in the NSPCC definition of sexual grooming as 'when someone builds a relationship, trust and emotional connection with a child or young person so they can manipulate, exploit and abuse them' (NSPCC, 2024a). Another meaning of 'grooming' relates to preparedness or training of some kind: being groomed to take over the family business. However, in the context of sexual grooming, children are essentially being prepared for sexual abuse, which 'involves forcing or enticing a child or young person to take part in sexual activities, whether or not the child is aware of what is happening' (IICSA, 2018: 18). A more recent type of sexual abuse is sextortion, whereby children can be sexually groomed to share sexualised images ('nudes') of themselves – usually with someone the child believes themselves to be in a relationship with (at least initially). These images are then used to coerce and blackmail the child in order to extort money, more sexual images of the child, or to get sexualised images of other children, such as a friend or sibling (Wolak et al., 2018).

Sexual grooming is a means to an end, and the end is child sexual abuse and exploitation (CSAE). CSAE has always occurred 'offline' through contact offences, but, as a consequence of the internet, the number of online CSAE offences is now growing exponentially. WeProtect, a global organisation tackling CSAE, states that online CSAE is 'one of the most urgent and defining issues of our generation' (WeProtect, 2021: 8). In 2022, online sexual abuse accounted for at least 32% of CSAE reports to UK police (VKPP, 2024), and the CyberTipline for the National Centre for Missing and Exploited Children received 32 million global reports of suspected CSAE (NCMEC, 2024). In 2021, 29.3 million items of CSAE materials (images, videos, live streaming) were removed from the internet, representing a 35% increase since 2020 (Hern, 2022). The Internet Watch Foundation reported a 257% increase in CSAE involving the sextortion of children in the first six months of 2023, with an increasingly large number of boys being targeted (IWF, 2023). These numbers should terrify and mobilise all of us because each number represents a child who has suffered sexual abuse, and who, in most cases, will have been sexually groomed beforehand. These children may be anonymous to us, but they *are* present in our communities, schools, and families right now.

Sexual grooming of a child is usually done by a person (or people) with power (due to age, status, or ability to instil fear) over a child or young person. The perpetrators of online CSAE offences are usually adult males, but it is important to note that children and young people can also perpetrate these kinds of harm against other children; for example, an analysis of police data from 2022 revealed that 52% of CSAE reports to police-involved children offending against other children, and 14 years old was the most common age (VKPP, 2024). Along with being manipulative and determined to achieve their goal, perpetrators of sexual grooming are often patient and perceived as trustworthy by the child while normalising sexualised behaviour and abuse. Sexual grooming is usually a process that may involve befriending, gaining trust, encouraging disinhibition (via drug and alcohol misuse), giving gifts, attention, and flattery, desensitising to sex using pornography, and eventually manipulating and/or coercing children to be involved in abusive sexual activity. This is interpersonal sexual grooming, and it needs to be understood as an often intense process between perpetrators and victims. It is an example of the psychological concept of 'graduated commitment', whereby individuals get locked into obedient or compliant behaviours in stages so small and incremental that it is hard to disentangle oneself (Milgram, 1963). So in some cases of sexual grooming, a child or young person may take the 'gifts' offered (alcohol, phones, money) and may comply with small requests such as 'sexual favours' or to send a 'nude' of themselves, all of which make it harder to be disobedient and non-compliant at later stages. Interpersonal sexual grooming is a common process in the sexual abuse of children, and it serves two very key roles: to prepare or position a child so that they are likely to comply with sexual activity with minimum fuss or fight and to create subsequent long term opportunities for the perpetrator to continue to carry out that sexual abuse.

A very challenging aspect of sexual grooming is that very often, the child or young person does not recognise it for what it is and therefore does not recognise the danger they are in or see themselves as a victim. Children who are being sexually groomed can often enjoy the attention, at least at first, because they are made to feel special, even loved, and so they may *appear* to be actively engaged in it, but children *do not* consent to their own sexual abuse. A child or young person may go along with an abusive situation because they have been manipulated, coerced, and feel trapped. They do not know how to get out of it, especially when they feel ashamed, which is an inherent part of any sexual abuse and a feeling that perpetrators rely on to keep their victims silent. As a result, it is generally uncommon for children to disclose (NSPCC, 2024a), and if or when they do, it is so important to listen, believe, and not blame or punish them.

There is another dimension to the wider context of sexual grooming and CSAE, and that is cultural sexual grooming, a pervasive form of sexual grooming which arguably facilitates interpersonal sexual grooming. The process *and* consequence of cultural sexual grooming is the sexualisation of children and young people through the ubiquitous mainstreaming of sexualised content and pornography via social media, marketing and advertising, television, film, and music (Papadopoulus, 2010; Dines, 2013). Research found that young people often feel 'victimised by a culture of commercial sexualisation', and highlights the impact pornography can have on their perceptions of relationships and sex (Shephard and Lewis, 2017: 12). These sexualised messages, which tend to hyper-masculinise males and objectify and sexualise girls and women, essentially 'teach' children and young people how to dress, act, behave, and pose for that very often sexualised selfie. This is tantamount to sexual grooming on a cultural level because these messages and social norms are internalised by children and young people, increasing their vulnerability to sexual grooming and abuse and impairing an empowered response to some increasingly harmful, normalised attitudes and behaviours regarding sex, sexuality, gender and a young person's exploration and expression of these things (Papadopoulus, 2010). It is to be expected that children and young people take an active role in presenting a particular version of themselves (particularly online) – as a young, sexualised being – but it is a version that has been crafted by this wider dominant and normalised process of cultural sexual grooming.

Schools do not exist in a vacuum; they are a microcosm of this wider societal context and a primary site of secondary socialisation, whereby social norms like these are established and reinforced (Russell et al., 2016). Research conducted in secondary schools described sexualised behaviour as 'the new norm' for young people, and 'sexually charged behaviour drives young people's physical interactions' in school corridors and playgrounds 'and permeates through to their 24-hour-a-day life online' (Fixers Investigates, 2016: 2). Although there are no quick fixes, schools are in a unique position to help challenge students' pervasive exposure to a sexualised and sexualising socio-cultural context, which positions sexualised behaviours as normal and expected, and consequently increases a child's exposure and vulnerability to sexual grooming. This paper has aimed to offer a starting point for teachers and school staff to develop a more insightful understanding of sexual grooming as complex and nebulous and as a cultural and interpersonal process that can often make the victims *appear* complicit. Historically, this has led to victim-blaming responses instead of supportive ones, which has often worked more in the favour of the perpetrators than the victims. If school leaders support their staff to develop a more insightful awareness of the nature and complexities of sexual grooming and understanding that it is a powerful tool in an abuser's toolbox, designed to increase the pliability, compliance, and vulnerability of a child or young person – teachers will be better able to support students to develop healthier, safer counternarratives regarding themselves, their bodies and their expression of their sexuality.

Myths

Myth: Grooming is always sexual in nature.

Truth: Grooming may or may not be sexually motivated. Some children and young people may be groomed for other agendas, such as financial gain through stealing or other illegal acts, such as distributing drugs on county lines.

Myth: Offenders are strangers and often old men.

Truth: Offenders are often people close to the victim, particularly when grooming as part of sexual abuse; however, offenders can be of any age, gender, or sexual orientation. Whoever the offender is, they will often be caring and kind at the start to lure in the victim, or they may give them gifts or entice them by showing monetary reward.

Myth: Offenders take a long time to groom their victims.

Truth: There is no set time on how long 'grooming' someone takes as it is dependent on the offender, the victim, and the purpose of the relationship. With online contact through social media so readily and quickly available, there is also an increase in material being requested by the offender, used either for sexual gratification or blackmail purposes.

For further information, see the work being done by the Upstream Project, Scotland:

https://www.theupstreamproject.org.uk/know/myths

References

Child Exploitation and Online Protection Centre (CEOP). (2022). *What is sexual grooming?* Available at: https://www.thinkuknow.co.uk/parents/articles/what-is-sexual-grooming/#:~:text=Grooming%20is%20a%20process%20offenders,do%20if%20you%20have%20concerns

Dines, G. (2013). Grooming our girls: Hypersexualization of the culture as child sexual abuse. In *Exploiting childhood: How fast food, material obsession and porn culture are creating new forms of child abuse* (pp. 116–129). London: Jessica Kingsley.

Fixers Investigates. (2016). The trouble with . . . Sex in schools. *Sexual Harassment and Violence in Schools: In Support of the Women and Equalities Committee*. Available at: https://www.fixers.org.uk/UserFiles/Files/FixersSS.pdf [Accessed 6 Apr. 2024].

Hern, A. (2022). *Sites reported record 29.3m child abuse images in 2021.* [online] Available at: https://www.theguardian.com/technology/2022/mar/24/sites-reported-record-293m-child-abuse-images-in-2021#:~:text=A%20record%2029.3m%20items,a%2035%25%20increase%20from%202020 [Accessed 7 Apr. 2024].

Independent Inquiry into Child Sexual Abuse (IICSA). (2018). *Interim report of the independent inquiry into child sexual abuse.* [online] Apr. Available at: https://www.iicsa.org.uk/reports-recommendations/publications/inquiry/interim.html [Accessed 7 Apr. 2024].

Internet Watch Foundation (IWF). (2023). *Hotline reports 'shocking' rise in the sextortion of boys.* [online] Available at: Hotline reports 'shocking' rise in the sextortion of boys (iwf.org.uk) [Accessed 7 Apr. 2024].

Lanning, K. (2018). The evolution of grooming: Concept and term. *Journal of Interpersonal Violence,* 33(1), pp. 5–16. Available at: https://journals.sagepub.com/doi/full/10.1177/0886260517742046?casa_token=SSFYxBUkHi8AAAAA%3AJwqcVqbJCA56yaYBtn0aSvlozw3qkfxFoChYjJAPYpvCsgnvnIkM935BWhE_yHdhjOIj55t3GBM

Milgram, S. (1963). Behavioural study of obedience. *Journal of Abnormal and Social Psychology,* 67, pp. 371–378.

National Center for Missing and Exploited Children (NCMEC). (2024). *CyberTipline report, 2022.* [online] Available at: https://www.missingkids.org/cybertiplinedata [Accessed 3 Apr. 2024].

National Society for the Prevention of Cruelty to Children NSPCC. (2023). *82% rise in online grooming crimes against children in the last 5 years.* Available at: https://www.nspcc.org.uk/about-us/news-opinion/2023/2023-08-14-82-rise-in-online-grooming-crimes-against-children-in-the-last-5-years/

National Society for the Prevention of Cruelty to Children (NSPCC). (2024a). What is grooming? *What Parents Need to Know About Sexual Grooming |NSPCC.* [online] [Accessed 26 Mar. 2024].

National Society for the Prevention of Cruelty to Children NSPCC. (2024b). *Grooming: Recognising the signs.* Available at: https://learning.nspcc.org.uk/safeguarding-child-protection/grooming#:~:text=Signs%20a%20child%20is%20being,including%20when%20using%20online%20devices

Papadopoulus, L. (2010). *Sexualisation of young people review.* [online] Available at: Sexualisation of young people review (ioe.ac.uk) [Accessed 17 Mar. 2015].

Ringenberg, T.R., Seigfried-Spellar, K.C., Rayz, J.M. and Rogers, M.K. (2022). A scoping review of child grooming strategies: Pre-and post-internet. *Child Abuse & Neglect,* 123, p. 105392. Available at:

https://www.sciencedirect.com/science/article/pii/S0145213421004610?casa_token=HGSIL-I7hmIAA AAA:x_4irGgEVNPoK1u5cRsb015eiptWJXN2G5vfqzpa_nF8qPYAeLdG6W_uZFkB7I3DQ2JUSkU2

Russell, L., Alsop, R., Bradshaw, L., Clisby, S. and Smith, K. (2016). The state of girls' rights in the UK. *Plan International UK*. [online] Available at: https://plan-uk.org/file/plan-international-ukthe-state-of-girls-rights-in-the-uk-2016.pdf/download?token=upKuLdiO [Accessed 7 Apr. 2024].

Shephard, W. and Lewis, B. (2017). *Working with children who are at risk of sexual exploitation: Barnardo's Model of practice*. Barkingside, Essex: Barnardo's.

Vulnerability, Knowledge & Practice Programme (VKPP). (2024). *National analysis of police-recorded Child Sexual Abuse & Exploitation (CSAE) crimes report. January 2022 to December 2022*. [online] Available at: https://www.vkpp.org.uk/assets/Files/Publications/National-Analysis-of-police-recorded-CSAE-Crimes-Report-2022-external.pdf [Accessed 7 Apr. 2024].

WeProtect. (2021). We protect global threat assessment. *Global Threat Assessment 2021 – WeProtect Global Alliance* [Accessed 7 Apr. 2024].

Wolak, J., Finkelhor, D., Walsh, W. and Treitman, L. (2018). Sextortion of minors: Characteristics and dynamics. *Journal of Adolescent Health*, 62(1), pp. 72–79.

Wolf, M.R. and Pruitt, D.K. (2019). Grooming hurts too: The effects of types of perpetrator grooming on trauma symptoms in adult survivors of child sexual abuse. *Journal of Child Sexual Abuse,* 28(3), pp. 345–359. Available at: https://www.tandfonline.com/doi/abs/10.1080/10538712.2019.1579292

19 Addiction and stealing

Chapter introduction

How would you understand the term 'addiction'? There is a debate in the literature of 'addiction' versus 'dependence', where the term dependence has been used as a euphemism to reduce the social stigma of addicted patients; however, this resulted in confusing the necessary distinction between 'physical dependence and uncontrolled psychological craving (addiction)' (Fainsinger et al., 2006: 1). Interestingly, research into addictive disorders such as gambling, stealing, buying and Internet use shows that there are underlying phenomenological and neurobiological parallels with the addictions to substances such as drugs and alcohol (Grant and Chamberlain, 2016). There are many types of addiction, including drug and alcohol addiction, which we most commonly may think of as being 'addictions'; however, individuals can be addicted to anything, and often, for younger children, this may involve addictions such as game addiction, screen addiction, shoplifting, or eating. In this chapter, we will consider what signs and symptoms may be present in a young person with an addiction and give an overview of some substances that may be addictive for young people.

Spotting signs and symptoms of addiction

The symptoms of addiction may look different depending on what it is that the young person is addicted to, but generally, addictions are associated with serious family, school, and social problems, with many addicted individuals showing clinical functional impairment as well (Korpa and Papadopoulou, 2013). A list of some signs and symptoms are shared:

- Change in a young person's behaviour
- Mood swings
- Seeming irritable and restless
- Being late for school or attendance issues
- Drop in school work and attainment
- Loss of interest in hobbies or socialising
- Stealing money to fund an addiction

DOI: 10.4324/9781032697932-19

Strategies to support someone with addiction

A good place to start is talking to them. Listen rather than accusing them, opening up with a question such as: *'How are you feeling?'* or *'What is going on for you at the moment?'*

Listen to their answers and show that you are there to support them, regardless of what is going on. Helping a child with addictions is perhaps more complex than supporting an adult, as they may lack the skills to move forward in seeking support or intervention.

Making space for the young person to talk about what is going on may offer background information to help you understand their circumstances. If you are very concerned about a child's welfare or condition, ensure you know who to speak to at your institution, namely the safeguarding offer, who will be able to advise on the next steps, such as speaking to the parents or carers about your concerns. You should not aim to support a child single-handedly without the partnership and support of your school.

An overview of some of the substances that young people may become addicted to is given in the following section.

Drug and alcohol addiction

School curriculums and Personal Social Health Education content should cover drug use and help inform you as an educator as to what is age-appropriate to discuss with your class and when. Teaching young people about the effects of drugs can help them to make a decision for themselves and make sure that they understand the risks involved with taking drugs. Taking drugs does not just affect a young person's physical and mental well-being; however, we can see that it may leave them open to exploitation and vulnerable to further criminal activity (NSPCC, 2024). To understand more about the different drugs available, familiarise yourself by looking at the Frank website (2024).

Gaming addiction

Many people enjoy playing games on a gaming console or their phone; however, gaming addiction comes at a price when it affects functioning in other areas. A report from the NHS (2023) declared that hundreds of gamers, including children and their family members, have been treated by the NHS National Centre for Gaming Disorders, with some patients playing 14 hours a day, leading to increased violence or aggression.

Possible signs and symptoms of gaming addiction may include:

- Constantly thinking about, or wanting to play the game;
- Feeling irritable and restless (fidgety) when not playing;
- Under reporting, or lying about how much time they've spent playing, or playing in secret (such as in the middle of the night);
- Tiredness, headaches, or hand pain from too much screen time, and use of controllers;
- Not wanting to pay attention to things such as personal hygiene (e.g., washing) or eating;
- Not seeing friends as often, or doing other things they used to enjoy doing, as all their time is spent gaming/online;

- Not wanting to go to school so that they can game;
- Sleep disturbance (difficulties getting to or staying asleep, or restless sleep with or without nightmares).

(Hampshire CAHMS, 2024: 1)

It is worth stressing that showing these symptoms does not necessarily mean a young person has a gaming addiction, but these signs are a red flag that there may need to be a further conversation with them or their caregivers to investigate how best to support them moving forward.

Food addiction

Food is one thing that can be in a child's control, whether through controlling their food intake or binge eating. See Chapter 5 in this book for further discussion on eating disorders.

Hoarding

Hoarding can be part of a compulsion to keep objects and not being able to part with items due to an emotional attachment. Many young people may have 'collections' of items such as football cards, figures, or merchandise, but hoarding is where there may be less order or organisation to the items. Hoarding can sometimes have a negative impact on a young person's life if they begin hoarding items that may rot or lead to poor hygiene.

Stealing

Not all stealing is an addictive problem. Research into young people stealing shows they may have impaired problem-solving skills and may also be subject to parent-child difficulties in the home, negative peer influences and peer pressure, and poor academic attainment (Grant et al., 2011). Making the decision to steal can also be due to jealousy and wanting something they cannot afford or to prove independence and control (Gotter, 2017).

Kleptomania

Compulsive stealing is known as 'kleptomania'. Psychological trauma, especially trauma at a young age, may also contribute to the development of kleptomania (Gotter, 2017). In many cases, the individual will steal items that they do not even need or want and may have little value, which differs from 'regular' stealing, which can be due to the person not being able to afford the item. The individual may feel anxious and tense in the lead-up to the compulsive theft, the action of which then provides relief.

It is important to remember that a young person's addiction and addictive behaviours can have ripple effects throughout the whole family. A study into the experiences of parents whose teenagers are being treated for a substance abuse problem found that the parents reported a range of negative feelings, including self-blame, helplessness, anger, and guilt (Mafa and Makhubele, 2019).

To conclude, here is a short contribution from Juliet Oyadoke, who considers understanding the need for compassion to support young people who are clearly struggling.

Early intervention and prevention, by Juliet Oyadoke, BSc

Just like every other medical disorder where early intervention is paramount, stealing and addiction is no different, and early intervention has been proven to be effective against addiction and stealing. Educators are the frontline observers; they are well-positioned to identify warning signs and provide timely support. In most cases, this often involves informing the parents and collaborating with school counsellors, psychologists, and other support services to develop tailored intervention plans. These early intervention steps have only one goal – to equip the children with coping mechanisms or strategies; this is a surefire way to help the children navigate the challenges they face.

For educators, I believe their response to addiction and stealing in children should emanate from compassion and empathy; teachers should show support rather than condemnation. They should create a safe and nurturing environment where students will feel comfortable so they can share their struggles without fear of judgement. If educators embrace open communication and also build a relationship that students can trust, the barriers that prevent children from seeking help will inevitably be broken.

Furthermore, prevention is essential when it comes to preventing children's addiction and stealing. In this regard, educators have a strong role in instilling resilience and critical thinking skills in their students; this is like arming them with the right skills to make healthy choices and resist negative influences. Through proactive education and awareness campaigns, we can dismantle the allure of addictive behaviours and promote a culture of well-being within our school communities. Apart from educators and classroom efforts, there's a need for collaboration with parents and caregivers. This will greatly help children grappling with addiction and stealing.

Myth: Children steal due to economic hardship when they can't afford things.

Truth: Stealing is not always about not having the money to buy something; some people may just enjoy the adrenaline rush of stealing or to prove their independence. Compulsive stealing is known as 'kleptomania', and in this case, people often steal things they don't even want or use; they may even give the items away or dispose of them after the theft.

Myth: Using alcohol or drugs is a conscious choice, so if a young person becomes addicted to something, they must take accountability.

Truth: Sometimes, young people may take alcohol or drugs due to peer pressure or negative peer influences. They may also be subject to these substances in the home or have witnessed abuse of these from their caregivers. It is important to remember young people are vulnerable and need support to move forward with healthy behaviours.

Myth: If someone uses willpower, they should be able to stop their addiction.

Truth: Often, addictions mask an underlying need for something that is missing or not being met in a person's life. Young people with trauma, grief, or loss may be using addiction to feel control or not feel anything. It is essential that when supporting a young person with addiction, time is taken to explore what led to these behaviours in the first place and to help support the young person with kindness, compassion, and understanding.

References

Fainsinger, R.L., Thai, V., Frank, G. and Fergusson, J., (2006). What's in a word? Addiction versus dependence in DSM-V. *American Journal of Psychiatry,* 163(11), p. 2014.

Frank. (2024). *Drugs A to Z.* Available at: https://www.talktofrank.com/drugs-a-z

Gotter, A. (2017). *Stealing.* Available at: https://www.healthline.com/health/stealing

Grant, J.E. and Chamberlain, S.R. (2016). Expanding the definition of addiction: DSM-5 vs. ICD-11.*CNS Spectrums,* 21(4), pp. 300–303. https://doi.org/10.1017/S1092852916000183

Grant, J.E., Potenza, M.N., Krishnan-Sarin, S., Cavallo, D.A. and Desai, R.A. (2011). Stealing among high school students: Prevalence and clinical correlates. *The Journal of the American Academy of Psychiatry and the Law,* 39(1), p. 44. Available at: https://www.ncbi.nlm.nih.gov/pmc/articles/PMC3671850/

Hampshire CAHMS. (2024). *Gaming addiction.* Available at: https://hampshirecamhs.nhs.uk/issue/gaming-addiction/

Korpa, T.N. and Papadopoulou, P. (2013). Clinical signs and symptoms of addictive behaviors. *International Journal of Child and Adolescent Health,* 6(4), p. 369.

Mafa, P. and Makhubele, J. (2019). Raising a young addict: Parental narratives on living with a teenager with substance abuse problems. *Gender and Behaviour,* 17(4), pp. 14116–14124. Available at: https://journals.co.za/doi/abs/10.10520/EJC-1b24817aa2

NHS. (2023). *NHS treats hundreds with gaming disorders.* Available at: https://www.england.nhs.uk/2023/03/nhs-treats-hundreds-with-gaming-disorders/

NSPCC. (2024). *Children and drugs.* Available at: https://www.nspcc.org.uk/keeping-children-safe/talking-drugs-alcohol/children-and-drugs/

20 Hate crimes

Quote: 'I used to feel safe walking home from school, but now I'm scared. I don't know if today is the day someone decides to attack me just for being me. It's terrifying to live in constant fear of hate crimes simply because of who I am'.

Definitions

What exactly do we mean by 'hate' and 'hostility'? These terms lay the groundwork for comprehending hate crimes, which occur when individuals target others based on their characteristics.

Hate

Definition: Intense or passionate dislike or aversion towards a person or group.
Example: Hate speech directed towards a religious group.

Hostility

Definition: Unfriendly or antagonistic behaviour or feelings.
Example: Hostility towards immigrants in the form of discriminatory policies.

Prejudice

Definition: Preconceived opinion that is not based on reason or actual experience.
Example: Prejudice against individuals based on their race.

Discrimination

Definition: The unjust or prejudicial treatment of different categories of people, especially on the grounds of race, age, or sex.
Example: Employment discrimination based on gender.

Stigma

Definition: A mark of disgrace associated with a particular circumstance, quality, or person.
Example: Stigma against individuals with mental health conditions.

(Oxford Dictionary, 2023)

DOI: 10.4324/9781032697932-20

A hate crime is defined as

> any criminal offence which is perceived by the victim or any other person, to be moti-
> vated by hostility or prejudice based on a person's race or perceived race; religion or
> perceived religion; sexual orientation or perceived sexual orientation; disability or per-
> ceived disability and any crime motivated by hostility or prejudice against a person who
> is transgender or perceived to be transgender.
>
> (The National Police Chiefs' Council and the
> Crown Prosecution Service)
> (Allen and Zayed, 2022)

Hate crimes manifest in various forms, from intimidation and harassment to assault and property damage. Hate crime also takes place on social media. It's crucial to recognise these actions as both the means through which hostility is expressed and the impact they have on victims. 'Hate crime' and 'hate incident' are terms used to describe different types of harmful behaviours motivated by prejudice or bias against a particular group of people.

In a hate crime, the perpetrator intentionally targets the victim because of their perceived membership in a specific group. Examples of hate crimes include physical assaults, vandalism, threats, harassment, and other harmful actions. Hate crimes are not only harmful to the individual victim but also create fear and tension within the targeted community. Hate crimes carry additional penalties beyond those for the underlying criminal offense; this is called an 'uplift'.

A hate incident refers to any non-criminal behaviour or action that is motivated by prejudice or bias against a particular group but does not meet the legal criteria for a hate crime. Unlike hate crimes, hate incidents may involve offensive language, gestures, or behaviours that are hurtful or discriminatory but do not rise to the level of criminal activity. Examples of hate incidents include offensive graffiti, verbal abuse, discriminatory treatment, or expressions of prejudice in public settings. While hate incidents may not result in criminal charges, they can still cause significant harm to individuals and communities by perpetuating stereotypes, fostering division, and undermining social cohesion.

Hate crimes usually come in four main types: physical assault, verbal abuse, incitement to hatred, and criminal damage.

Physical assault

Any form of physical assault is a serious offense. If someone has been physically assaulted, it's important to report it. Depending on the severity of the attack, the perpetrator could face charges such as common assault, actual bodily harm, or grievous bodily harm.

Verbal abuse

Verbal abuse, threats, or name-calling can be distressing experiences, especially for minority groups. Victims of verbal abuse often feel unsure if a crime has occurred or think there's little they can do. However, laws are in place to protect individuals from verbal abuse. If someone has been verbally abused, they should consider speaking to the police or one of organisations listed at the end of the chapter. Even if they don't know the identity of the abuser, sharing information can help improve policing efforts in the area where the incident occurred.

Incitement to hatred

Incitement to hatred occurs when someone engages in threatening behaviour with the intention of stirring up hatred. This can take various forms, including words, images, videos, music, or content posted online. Hate content may involve messages advocating violence against a specific person or group, web pages displaying violence against individuals based on their differences, or online forums encouraging hate crimes against particular individuals or groups.

The House of Commons released 'Hate Crime statistics' in January 2024. This comprehensive report on hate crime sheds light on the prevalence, trends, and implications of such offenses within society. The report presents a detailed analysis of hate crime incidents recorded across various communities and demographics. According to police records for the year 2022/2023, there were 145,214 reported offenses where one or more of the monitored hate crime categories were identified as motivating factors. Since April 2015, there have been noticeable spikes in racially or religiously aggravated hate crimes during specific events, such as the EU referendum, the 2017 terrorist attacks, and the 2020 Black Lives Matter protests.

Home Office statistics show that in 2016-2017, of all the hate crimes reported (Wales, 2016):

- 78% were race hate crimes
- 11% were sexual orientation hate crimes
- 7% were religious hate crimes
- 7% were disability hate crimes
- 2% transgender hate crimes

* (Total is 105% because some crimes fit into more than one category)

In addition, some police forces also recognise, and record alternative subculture hate crimes. These are crimes committed against people for the way they dress or their lifestyle. The introduction of alternative subculture hate crime has been pioneered by Sylvia Lancaster, whose daughter, Sophie Lancaster, was tragically kicked to death in 2007 simply for the way she looked and her style (www.sophielancasterfoundation.com, n.d.)

> Alternative Subculture means a discernible group that is characterised by a strong sense of collective identity and a set of group-specific values and tastes that typically centre on distinctive style/clothing, make-up, body art and music preferences. Those involved usually stand out in the sense their distinctiveness is discernible both to fellow participants and to those outside the group. Groups that typically place themselves under the umbrella of 'alternative' include Goths, emos, punks, metallers and some variants of hippie and dance culture (although this list is not exhaustive).
>
> (Sylvia Lancaster OBE, Professor Jon Garland,
> Dr Paul Hodkinson March 2013)

The impact of hate

Being a victim of a hate crime can have profound emotional and psychological effects, and understanding the feelings experienced by victims is crucial in providing appropriate support and intervention. A critical aspect of the House of Commons report is the assessment of the impact of hate crime on affected communities.

Emotional impact

Hate crimes often leave victims feeling traumatised, fearful, and vulnerable. Hate crime victims may experience heightened levels of anxiety, depression, and post-traumatic stress disorder (PTSD) compared to victims of non-bias-motivated crimes. The findings (Home Office, Hate Crime, England and Wales, 2019 to 2020) show the emotional responses experienced by victims of hate crimes:

- Anger 51%
- Shock 47%
- Loss of confidence or feeling vulnerable 42%
- Fear 45%
- Difficulty sleeping 29%
- Anxiety or panic attacks 34%
- Depression 18%

Psychological impact

Hate crimes can have long-lasting psychological effects on victims, including feelings of shame, isolation, and diminished self-worth. Hate crime victims are at increased risk of developing mental health disorders, such as depression, anxiety, and suicidal ideation.

Social impact

Hate crimes erode trust and cohesion within communities, leading to increased social divisions and tensions. Hate crimes not only harm individual victims but also have ripple effects on their families, friends, and communities, contributing to feelings of insecurity and marginalisation. Hate crimes also pose significant challenges to community cohesion and social harmony, threatening the fabric of inclusive and diverse societies.

Law and legislation

Protecting people against hate crimes involves a comprehensive legal framework comprising various laws and legislations. Here are key pieces of legislation relevant to combating hate crimes:

Public Order Act 1986

- Sections 4, 4A, and 5 prohibit threatening, abusive, or insulting behaviour likely to cause harassment, alarm, or distress.

- Section 29A criminalises intentional harassment, alarm, or distress motivated by racial or religious hostility.
- Section 29B addresses intentional harassment, alarm, or distress based on sexual orientation or transgender identity.

Crime and Disorder Act 1998

- Introduces specific offenses of racially or religiously aggravated crimes, including assault, harassment, and criminal damage.
- Increases penalties for offenses proven to be racially or religiously aggravated compared to non-aggravated offenses.

Criminal Justice Act 2003

- Section 146 provides for increased sentences for offenses proven to be aggravated by racial or religious hostility.
- Section 146A addresses the racially or religiously aggravated offense of intentionally causing fear of violence.

Racial and Religious Hatred Act 2006

- Part 3A addresses stirring up racial or religious hatred, requiring intent to incite hatred and threatening behaviour.
- Offers protections for ethnic and religious groups against incitement to hatred.

Equality Act 2010

- Protects individuals from discrimination, harassment, and victimisation based on protected characteristics, including race, religion, sexual orientation, and transgender identity.
- Imposes duties on public authorities to promote equality and eliminate discrimination.

Malicious Communications Act 1988 (amended 2001)

- Criminalises sending grossly offensive, indecent, or threatening communications via electronic means.
- Extends to communications intended to cause distress, anxiety, or harm.

Communications Act 2003

- Section 127 prohibits sending or causing to be sent grossly offensive, indecent, obscene, or menacing communications.
- Addresses persistent communications causing annoyance, inconvenience, or anxiety.

Protection from Harassment Act 1997

- Prohibits harassment, stalking, or causing fear of violence, whether offline or online.
- Requires behaviour to occur on at least two occasions for conviction.

Age of criminal responsibility

While different countries have varying age thresholds, the following apply in the UK (Child Rights International Network, 2019).

England and Wales

Children can be held liable for criminal offences from the age of 10. [Children and Young Persons Act 1933, Section 50]

Northern Ireland

No child under the age of 10 can be found guilty of a criminal offence. [Criminal Justice (Children) (Northern Ireland) Order 1998, Article 3]

Scotland

No child under the age of eight can be found guilty of any criminal offence, but no person under the age of 12 may be prosecuted for an offence, and a person aged 12 or older may not be prosecuted for an offence committed while under the age of 12. [Criminal Procedure (Scotland) Act, Sections 41 and 41A(1)-(2)]

Hate crime and the internet

The internet has revolutionised how we communicate, and despite many positives to this, it does, unfortunately, mean hateful content can reach a wider audience rapidly, often without any oversight and hide behind anonymity.

Although encountering offensive material online is common, only a small portion of it is actually illegal. Hate material online is classified as a 'hate crime' when it involves a criminal act motivated by hate, as defined by law. If the online content is motivated by hate but doesn't meet the threshold for a criminal offense, it may still be recorded as a 'Non-crime hate incident' (LTD, 2022). This recording is crucial for monitoring community cohesion. UK laws aim to strike a balance between freedom of expression and protection from hate crime.

While agencies like the police are responsible for promoting positive relationships between different community groups, they lack the authority to control offensive thoughts or words unless they are shared illegally. Recognising that hate material can harm community cohesion and instil fear, the police have said they aim to collaborate with communities and the internet industry to mitigate the harm caused by online hate.

For guidance on staying safe online, resources such as Get Safe Online offer advice, and instances of online hate material can be reported to the police.

Illegal hate content includes incitement of hatred based on race, religion, or sexual orientation, among other factors. Additionally, threats or harassment targeting individuals or groups due to their race, religion, disability, sexual orientation, or transgender status are considered hate crimes.

While much online content may be viewed in the UK, material hosted on foreign websites may fall outside the jurisdiction of UK courts. However, individuals posting such content from within the UK remain accountable for their actions.

If you or your pupils see hateful content online, you can do the following:

Report it to the police if it's believed to originate in the UK.

Report it to website administrators or hosting companies; most platforms have mechanisms for lodging complaints about offensive content.

X offers the following advice:

- If you believe you are in physical danger, contact the local law enforcement authorities who have the tools to address the issue
- If you decide to work with law enforcement, make sure to do the following:
- Document the violent or abusive messages with print-outs or screenshots
- Be as specific as possible about why you are concerned
- Provide any context you have around who you believe might be involved, such as evidence of abusive behaviour found on other websites
- Provide any information regarding previous threats you may have received

Facebook

Send feedback on or report a conversation on Facebook.

'We won't let the person know who's reported them. Bear in mind that not everything that may be upsetting violates our Community Standards' (en-gb.facebook.com, n.d.).

Community Standards violations include:

- Bullying or harassment: Content that appears to purposefully target a person with the intention of degrading or shaming them or repeatedly contacting a person despite that person's clear desire and action to prevent contact.
- Direct threats: Serious threats of harm to public and personal safety, credible threats of physical harm, specific threats of theft, vandalism, or other financial harm.
- Sexual violence and exploitation: Content that threatens or promotes sexual violence or exploitation, including solicitation of sexual material, any sexual content involving minors, threats to share intimate things you want to keep private (such as images or videos), and offers of sexual services.

YouTube

Hate speech is not allowed on YouTube. They don't allow content that promotes violence or hatred against individuals or groups based on any of the following attributes, which indicate a protected group status under YouTube's policy:

- Age
- Caste
- Disability
- Ethnicity

- Gender Identity and Expression
- Nationality
- Race
- Immigration Status
- Religion
- Sex/Gender
- Sexual Orientation
- Victims of a major violent event and their kin
- Veteran Status

If you find content that violates this policy, report it. Instructions for reporting violations of YouTube Community Guidelines are available on the YouTube Help page. If you've found a few videos or comments that you would like to report, you can report the channel.

Reporting hate crimes

Reporting hate crimes is vital in combating their prevalence and ensuring justice for victims. Whether through emergency services, non-urgent hotlines, online platforms, or third-party reporting centres, it is important to know how to report incidents effectively. This advice can be passed on to your pupils:

To get help, start by talking to the police. They need to know what happened to you so they can take action. They can also connect you with Victim Support, who can help you after a crime.

If you've experienced a hate crime, there are different ways to report it. Call 999 if it's an emergency. Otherwise, you can call 101, the police hotline, which is open all the time. You can also report it online through your local police or on True Vision's website. Many people feel better when they share what happened.

For specialised support with hate crimes, Stop Hate UK is available in some parts of England. They work to fight all types of hate crime.

Another option is Crimestoppers, a charity where you can report crimes anonymously by phone or online at any time. They'll pass on the report to the right authorities. You can call Crimestoppers at 0800 555 111.

If you've been a victim of a hate crime, don't keep it to yourself. Call 101 or 999 if it's an emergency. You can also contact True Vision, Stop Hate UK, or Crimestoppers. Remember, you're not alone – tell someone and get the help you need.

Strategies and ideas

Teaching young people about hate crimes promotes awareness and tolerance. Here are some ideas and activities that can be employed:

Interactive discussions

Engage your pupils in discussions about what hate crimes are, why they occur, and their impact on individuals and communities. Encourage them to share their thoughts, feelings, and experiences related to prejudice and discrimination.

Case studies

Present real-life examples of hate crimes and hate incidents, ensuring that the material is age-appropriate. Discuss the motivations behind these crimes and their consequences on both victims and perpetrators.

Role-playing and drama activities

Organise role-playing activities where students can enact scenarios related to hate crimes. This allows them to empathise with different perspectives and understand the impact of their words and actions.

Guest speakers

Invite guest speakers, such as representatives from police and law, advocacy groups, or victims' support organisations, to share their insights and experiences with hate crimes. Hearing from real people can make the issue more tangible for students.

Media analysis

Analyse media sources, including news articles, videos, and social media posts, that cover hate crimes. Encourage critical thinking by discussing how these sources portray hate crimes and their implications on public perception.

Artistic expression

Provide opportunities for students to express their thoughts and feelings about hate crimes through art, poetry, or music. This allows them to explore the topic in a creative and personal way.

Community projects

Engage students in community projects aimed at combating hate and promoting inclusivity. This could involve organising awareness campaigns, volunteering with local organisations, or participating in community events focused on diversity and tolerance.

Legal education

Introduce basic concepts of law and legal rights related to hate crimes. Help students understand the legal definitions of hate crimes, the reporting process, and the role of law enforcement in addressing these offenses.

Empathy exercises: Facilitate empathy-building exercises where students put themselves in the shoes of individuals who have experienced hate crimes or discrimination. This fosters compassion and understanding towards others' experiences.

Reflection and action planning

Encourage students to reflect on what they've learned and brainstorm actionable steps they can take to combat hate crimes in their own lives and communities. This could include promoting inclusivity, standing up against discrimination, and advocating for justice.

It's important to adapt these activities to suit the developmental level and cultural background of the pupils you're working with, ensuring that the content is both engaging and relevant to their experiences. Additionally, creating a safe and supportive environment where students feel comfortable discussing sensitive topics is essential for effective learning.

Myth: Hate crimes are rare occurrences that don't happen often.

Truth: Hate crimes are more prevalent than commonly believed, with thousands of incidents reported each year across the globe. Many hate crimes also go unreported due to fear, lack of awareness, or distrust in the justice system.

Myth: Hate crimes only involve physical violence.

Truth: While physical violence is one form of hate crime, hate-motivated incidents can also manifest as verbal abuse, harassment, vandalism, or discrimination. These acts can have profound and lasting impacts on individuals and communities, regardless of whether they involve physical harm.

Myth: Hate crimes only target certain minority groups.

Truth: Hate crimes can target individuals based on various characteristics, including race, religion, ethnicity, sexual orientation, gender identity, disability, or nationality. Anyone can be a victim of a hate crime, regardless of their background or identity.

Support services and signposting

ChildLine www.childline.org.uk

- A confidential and free online and phone counselling service for those aged under 19 anywhere in the UK.

Dimensions www.dimensions-uk.org

- Charity that supports people with learning disabilities, autism, challenging behaviour, and complex needs.

Equality Advisory Support Service www.equalityadvisoryservice.com

- Helpline and legal advice for issues relating to human rights.

Galop www.galop.org.uk

- Charity that records hate incidents and violence directed against the LGBT+ community.

Kick It Out www.kickitout.org

- Football's equality and inclusion organisation that tackles racism and discrimination in the sport.

MIND www.mind.org.uk

- Provides advice and support to empower anyone experiencing a mental health problem.

Stop Hate UK www.stophateuk.org

- Charity that works to challenge all forms of hate crime and discrimination and provides confidential reporting and support.

The Monitoring Group www.tmg-uk.org.uk

- Charity that records racist hate crimes and incidents.

The Traveller Movement www.travellermovement.org.uk

- Charity that works with the Gypsy, Roma, and Traveller communities in the UK to tackle discrimination.

Victim Support www.victimsupport.org.uk

- Charity that works with all people affected by crime in England and Wales. This includes victims, witnesses, their family and friends.

References

Allen, G. and Zayed, Y. (2022). Hate crime statistics. *Parliament.uk*. [online] Available at: https://research briefings.files.parliament.uk/documents/CBP-8537/CBP-8537.pdf

Child Rights International Network. (2019). Minimum ages of criminal responsibility in Europe | CRIN. *Crin.org*. [online] Available at: https://archive.crin.org/en/home/ages/europe.html

en-gb.facebook.com. (n.d.). *Facebook*. [online] Available at: https://en-gb.facebook.com/help/1709360 766019559 [Accessed 30 Jun. 2024].

LTD, H.M.I. (2022). Internet hate crime. *www.report-it.org.uk*. [online] Available at: https://www.report-it. org.uk/reporting_internet_hate_crime

Oxford Dictionary. (2023). Oxford learner's dictionaries. *Oxfordlearnersdictionaries.com*. [online] Available at: https://www.oxfordlearnersdictionaries.com/

Wales. (2016). *Hate crime*. [online] Available at: https://assets.publishing.service.gov.uk/government/uploads/system/uploads/attachment_data/file/652136/hate-crime-1617-hosb1717.pdf

www.sophielancasterfoundation.com. (n.d.). *Home*. [online] Available at: https://www.sophielancaster foundation.com/.

21 Absence

Quote: 'Going to school feels like stepping into a big, scary jungle where I'm not sure what's around the corner. I get butterflies in my tummy, wondering if I'll find my way through all the rules and lessons. It feels too much, so I tell my mum I don't feel well'.

'He is 15 years old and nearly 6 feet tall. I can't exactly drag him in'.

Overview

'There are more than 9 million school age children in England alone. While the vast majority attend classes regularly, there is a significant and rising number who are regularly absent'.

> Persistent absenteeism – When pupils record less than a 90% attendance at school.
> Severe absenteeism – When pupils are present for less than 50% of their school days.
>
> (System, n.d.)

Absence is a significant challenge facing our education system. It goes beyond occasional missed days and refers to a situation where students consistently miss a substantial amount of school time. Recent statistics from DfE reveal alarming rates, with approximately 22% of students reported as persistently absent, a figure that escalates to 28% in secondary schools, underscoring the severity of the issue, especially in the aftermath of the pandemic (Department for Education, 2023; GOV.uk, 2024).

The causes and risks associated with persistent absence are diverse and interconnected, reflecting the complexity of the problem. Amanda Spielman, Ofsted's previous chief inspector, said the impact of the broken contract could be seen in 'lower school attendance, poorer behaviour and friction between parents and schools' and has referred to the 'fractured social contract between families and schools – where parents ensured their children were in class daily' (The Independent, 2023).

In response to the prolonged and worsening issue of school absenteeism exacerbated by the COVID-19 pandemic, an inquiry into Persistent Absence and Support for Disadvantaged Pupils was initiated in January 2023. Despite pre-pandemic efforts to reduce absenteeism, there has been no return to the declining trajectory seen since 2010. Concerns persist

DOI: 10.4324/9781032697932-21

regarding the efficacy of fines as a deterrent for absenteeism, especially for families facing barriers like poverty. While interventions such as attendance mentors and enrichment programs show promise, their expansion and sustainability need improvement.

In The Big Ask survey by the Children's Commissioner's Attendance Audit in March 2022, nearly 5,000 children were reported as home-educated, and nearly 2,000 children were not in school at all (Children's Commissioner for England, n.d.). Many children spoke of the challenges they had faced in school, such as bullying, struggling with anxiety and other mental health needs, or having special educational needs which weren't being identified or supported. There are also hundreds of children who have never interacted with the education system, including children who have never been on a school roll, have gone missing from care, or have been trafficked into the country.

Factors contributing to absence

School absence can stem from various complex factors, spanning medical issues, mental health challenges, socioeconomic disparities, transportation limitations, the impact of the COVID-19 pandemic, special educational needs and disabilities (SEND), school factors, and safeguarding concerns. For instance, research indicates that 'children in receipt of Free School Meals [are] three times more likely to be severely absent than their more affluent classmates' (The Centre for Social Justice, 2024), highlighting the impact of socioeconomic disparities on attendance rates.

Medical and health issues

Medical conditions such as chronic illness, physical disabilities, or severe allergies may mean a pupil unable to attend school regularly, often requiring ongoing medical treatment or frequent hospitalisations. Mental health struggles such as anxiety disorders, depression, or trauma-related conditions can also significantly impact a pupil's ability to attend school regularly, with symptoms like panic attacks, anxiety, or difficulty concentrating interfering with their ability to engage in classroom activities.

Socioeconomic factors

Poverty can affect attendance in various ways. Families experiencing financial hardship may struggle to afford transport to school, leading to irregular attendance. Inadequate nutrition due to poverty can result in poor sleep quality and attention spans, impacting a pupil's ability to focus and engage in learning activities. Additionally, pupils from low-income households may lack access to proper school uniforms, which can contribute to feelings of embarrassment or low self-esteem, further deterring them from attending school regularly.

COVID-19 impact

The global COVID-19 pandemic has contributed to a surge in school absenteeism attributed to sickness. A significant shift in parental attitudes towards their children's attendance has emerged, largely stemming from the upheaval experienced during lockdown learning periods.

These disruptions not only led to a widespread disengagement with traditional educational routines but also underscored challenges in accessing essential digital learning resources for many students. Consequently, academic setbacks incurred during this period have had lasting implications, causing some pupils ongoing struggles to maintain consistent attendance now.

SEND

Pupils with diagnosed and undiagnosed SEND may struggle in traditional school settings without appropriate support. Learning disabilities or developmental disorders may make it difficult for these pupils to engage in classroom activities or social interactions, leading to increased absenteeism.

For some children, attending school can be a challenging experience due to sensory issues. Sensory processing refers to how the nervous system receives and responds to sensory information from the environment. Children with sensory processing difficulties may have heightened or reduced sensitivity to sensory stimuli, such as sights, sounds, textures, tastes, and smells. These sensitivities can significantly impact their ability to participate in school activities and maintain attendance.

Children with sensory issues may experience discomfort or distress in certain environments or situations within the school setting. For example:

- Overstimulation: Busy classrooms with bright lights, loud noises, and crowded spaces can overwhelm children with sensory sensitivities. They may struggle to filter out background noise or focus on tasks due to sensory overload.
- Sensory aversions: Some children may have aversions to certain sensory experiences, such as specific textures of clothing or food. These aversions can make it challenging for them to participate in activities that involve these stimuli, leading to avoidance behaviours and school refusal.
- Sensory-seeking behaviours: On the other hand, some children may seek out sensory input to regulate their arousal levels. They may engage in repetitive behaviours, such as rocking or spinning, or seek tactile input by touching objects excessively. These behaviours can be disruptive in the classroom and interfere with learning.
- Anxiety and meltdowns: Sensory challenges can trigger anxiety and emotional dysregulation in children, leading to meltdowns or withdrawal. They may exhibit behaviours such as crying, screaming, or withdrawing from social interactions as a way to cope with sensory overload or discomfort.

Bullying

Bullying, whether in-person or online, can lead to avoidance of school environments out of fear. Pupils who experience harassment, teasing, or social exclusion may develop anxiety or depression related to attending school, leading to chronic absenteeism.

Home factors

Parental and familial influences play a significant role in shaping a child's attitude towards education. While many parents actively support their child's schooling, some may harbour negative perceptions stemming from their own past experiences. Additionally, familial responsibilities and priorities can sometimes overshadow the importance of regular school attendance. For instance, children may be required to assist with household chores or provide care for sick or elderly family members, diverting their attention away from their academic commitments.

Being a young carer can significantly impact school attendance in several ways. Firstly, the responsibilities and duties associated with caring for a family member can consume a considerable amount of time and energy, leaving little room for attending school regularly. Young carers may have to juggle their caregiving responsibilities with schoolwork, leading to missed classes, assignments, and exams.

The emotional and psychological toll of being a young carer can also affect attendance. The stress, anxiety, and fatigue resulting from caregiving responsibilities can make it challenging for young carers to maintain consistent attendance at school. They may experience feelings of overwhelm or burnout, which can lead to increased absenteeism. Additionally, young carers may face practical barriers to attendance, such as difficulty arranging transportation to school or managing their caregiving duties alongside school schedules. These logistical challenges can further contribute to irregular attendance patterns.

The impact of absence

Absenteeism among students has far-reaching consequences that extend beyond just missing classes. Research by Akkuş and Çinkir (2022) highlights the multifaceted impact of absence on various aspects of pupils' academic and social development, as well as their relationships within the school community.

Academically, frequent absence can lead to gaps in learning and lower academic achievement. When pupils miss classes, they miss out on vital instruction, classroom discussions, and interactive learning experiences. Over time, these missed opportunities can hinder their ability to grasp key concepts and keep up with their peers, ultimately affecting their academic progress and performance in assessments. This can become a vicious cycle; they know they are behind, which affects their self-esteem and becomes overwhelming, leading to further absence.

Socially, absence from school can isolate pupils from their peers and impede their ability to develop social skills and peer relationships. School serves as a crucial socialisation environment where children interact, collaborate, and form friendships. Persistent or chronic absence may prevent pupils from participating in group activities, extracurriculars, and school events, limiting their opportunities for social engagement and connection with their peers.

Absence can strain the relationships between pupils, teachers, and parents/carers. Teachers may become frustrated or concerned about the academic progress and well-being of pupils, leading to strained relationships. Additionally, parents and carers may face challenges in supporting their child's education and maintaining communication with the school regarding their child's attendance and academic performance.

The negative effects of school absences have also been shown to persist beyond schooling into adulthood. Absences in late childhood are associated with lower educational attainment and a greater likelihood of non-employment at age 42 (Dräger et al., 2023).

There are also well-being risks that can impact their overall development and mental health:

School provides a structured daily routine for students, including set schedules, activities, and expectations. When pupils are out of school, they may lose this routine, leading to disruptions in sleep patterns, meal times, and overall lifestyle habits. This lack of structure can contribute to feelings of anxiety, uncertainty, and difficulty in managing daily tasks.

They also have reduced access to support services. Schools often serve as a hub for accessing various support services, including counselling, mental health resources, and special education accommodations. When pupils are absent from school, they may miss out on vital support services that address their unique needs and challenges, potentially exacerbating mental health issues or academic struggles.

Extended absence from school can also have implications for pupils' physical health. Without access to physical education classes, sports activities, and nutritious meals provided at school, pupils may experience a decline in physical fitness, poor dietary habits, and increased sedentary behaviour, which can negatively affect their overall health and well-being.

Addressing the well-being risks associated with students being out of school requires a coordinated approach involving educators, families, mental health professionals, and community organisations. Efforts to promote regular attendance, provide targeted support services, and create a supportive and inclusive school environment can help mitigate the negative impact of extended absences on students' overall well-being and academic success.

When pupils are out of school, they may be exposed to various safeguarding risks that compromise their safety and well-being:

With the growing reliance on digital technologies for remote learning and social interaction, pupils who are out of school may spend more time online, increasing their exposure to online risks such as cyberbullying, grooming, and inappropriate content. Without the supervision and guidance provided by teachers and school staff, pupils may be more susceptible to online exploitation and harm.

Lack of regular contact with teachers and school staff can make it more challenging to detect signs of abuse or neglect in pupils who are out of school. Pupils may be at increased risk of experiencing physical, emotional, or sexual abuse, especially if they are isolated from supportive adults and trusted peers who could identify and report concerns.

Pupils who are disconnected from school may be more susceptible to peer pressure, involvement in anti-social behaviour or crime, or recruitment into harmful activities such as county lines, gang involvement, or substance abuse.

Absence from school can exacerbate underlying mental health issues or contribute to the development of new psychological difficulties. Pupils who are socially isolated or experiencing stressors outside of school may be at increased risk of experiencing anxiety, depression, self-harm, or suicidal ideation without access to school-based support services or interventions.

Extended absence from school may also exacerbate existing family stressors or dynamics, such as domestic violence, substance abuse, or parental mental health issues. Pupils who are out of school may be more vulnerable to experiencing or witnessing family conflict, instability, or neglect, which can impact their emotional well-being and overall safety.

Relationships

The role of relationships is essential in tackling persistent absence. Building strong, nurturing relationships among students, teachers, parents, and carers is pivotal, as it fosters a sense of trust and collaboration within the school community. Parents and carers must feel confident in entrusting their children's education to the school, knowing that their well-being and academic success are prioritised.

The power of influence, as demonstrated by Dr David M. Cullen's 25-year-long Harvard study, underscores the profound impact of one's reference group on their success and future. Surrounding students with positive, motivated individuals who prioritise personal growth and success can significantly shape their trajectory. Conversely, negative influences can hinder progress and perpetuate patterns of disengagement and absence. Recognising the importance of positive peer influence and fostering a supportive social environment within schools can mitigate the risk of persistent absence.

Strategies

There is no one solution to 'attendance'. Addressing persistent and severe absence requires a holistic approach that encompasses understanding its root causes, acknowledging associated risks and barriers, and implementing strategies that prioritise relationships, health, and positive influences. By working collaboratively to create a supportive environment where every child feels valued and empowered, we can improve attendance rates and ensure that all students have the opportunity to thrive academically and personally.

Trust

Parents and carers have to believe that sending their child in every day is for the best. Pupils need to believe being in school is the best place for them or that they will learn and be kept safe. In my experience, so much of this is down to trust. Invest significant time and energy in building relationships between children and teachers and between the school and parents and carers. Be present, find opportunities to invite parents and carers in and engage with them, take the time to seek out parents/carers, and share something wonderful their child has done that day. Build relationships based on kindness, compassion, and a genuine investment in their health, happiness, and success. Prioritise this in conversations, interactions, and decisions.

Mental health

Children's mental health is just as important as physical health, and designing a curriculum and approaches that enable children to understand their own emotions and provide them with strategies to manage these effectively is essential. By providing children with strategies for understanding and effectively managing their emotions, we see positive impacts on their attendance (Tapscott Learning Trust, 2023).

Developing feelings of safety and belonging

Having a sense of belonging is crucial. Belonging fulfils a fundamental human need for connection and social interaction. When people feel like they belong, they experience greater emotional stability, mental health, and overall well-being. Belonging to a group, community, or school provides people with a sense of identity and purpose. It helps them understand who they are, where they come from, and how they fit into the world, contributing to a positive self-concept and self-esteem. Belonging fosters supportive relationships and social connections, which serve us as sources of emotional support, encouragement, and validation. These relationships help us to navigate challenges, cope with stress, and celebrate successes together. When people feel like they belong, they are more motivated to participate actively, contribute their skills and talents, and pursue shared goals and objectives. It fuels intrinsic motivation and engagement in meaningful activities. Belonging to a supportive community also provides a buffer against adversity and enhances resilience in the face of challenges. Knowing that we are part of a network of caring individuals who have our backs helps us cope with stress, overcome setbacks, and bounce back from difficult experiences. Belonging creates a sense of safety and security, allowing us to express ourselves authentically, take risks, and explore new opportunities without fear of rejection or judgment. It provides a psychological safety net that enables personal growth and development.

The Harvard Study of Adult Development, over 80 years, has proved that embracing community helps us live longer and be happier. Close relationships, more than money or fame, are what keep people happy throughout their lives, the study revealed (Solan, 2017).

Your approach with your pupil:

- Listen without prejudice or bias.
- Ensure they understand they have your unwavering support.
- Do not claim something as a priority if it does not genuinely hold importance. Do not label a space as safe if it fails to provide the safety it promises.
- Avoid empty statements such as 'We want you here' without backing them up with consistent actions.
- Acknowledge any disparities between intentions, words, and actions.
- Establish trust explicitly, conveying messages like 'I'm here for you, but honesty is crucial for our relationship', and outline the support you can provide.
- Persistence in support eventually leads to the realisation: 'They truly have my back'.
- Emphasise a collaborative approach that caters to individual learning needs.
- Emphasise honesty and transparency as pivotal elements in building trust and fostering engagement.
- Recognise that the adolescent brain may struggle to perceive care from teachers; assist them in finding ways to reconnect.
- Consider various communication methods, including expressing thoughts and motivations and understanding others' perspectives.
- Utilise walking and talking to reduce emotional pressure and regulate emotions through movement.
- Incorporate technology as a communication tool.

- Learn to discern cues through careful observations to determine when to push and when to hold back.
- Plan and communicate effectively to ensure clarity and understanding.
- Be mindful of the privilege from which we operate and approach situations with sensitivity.
- Develop a progression plan that facilitates the transfer of new skills and confidence, recognising the necessity of pushing for growth.

In building belonging and safety

Building a sense of safety in a school involves creating an environment where pupils and staff feel physically, emotionally, and psychologically secure. Several strategies contribute to fostering this sense of safety:

Establish clear and transparent policies and procedures for safety, behaviour, and attendance. Ensure that everyone in the school community understands these protocols and knows how to follow them.

Promote a positive and inclusive school climate characterised by respect, empathy, and cooperation. Encourage open communication, celebrate diversity, and address conflicts promptly and constructively.

Foster supportive relationships between everyone. Provide opportunities for meaningful connections through mentoring programs, peer support groups, and extracurricular activities.

Offer pupils access to mental health resources and support services. Train teachers and staff to recognise signs of mental health issues and provide appropriate support.

Implement comprehensive bullying prevention programs that educate pupils about respectful behaviour, bystander intervention, and conflict resolution skills. Create a culture of zero tolerance for bullying and harassment.

Empower student voices by involving them in decision-making processes related to school and encourage them to share their concerns and ideas for improvement. Empowering student voices fosters a sense of ownership and accountability among the student body.

Continuously assess the effectiveness through surveys, feedback mechanisms, and data analysis. Use this information to make informed decisions and implement improvements as needed.

Addressing sensory issues

Addressing sensory issues in the school environment requires a multidisciplinary approach involving educators, parents, and healthcare professionals. Strategies to support children with sensory sensitivities may include:

Creating a sensory-friendly environment, adjusting classroom lighting, reducing noise levels, and providing sensory breaks or quiet spaces where children can retreat when feeling overwhelmed.

Implementing sensory accommodations. Allowing children to use sensory tools or accommodations, such as noise-cancelling headphones, fidget toys, or weighted blankets helps regulate their sensory experiences and maintain focus.

Incorporating sensory activities into the curriculum, such as sensory bins, movement breaks, or calming exercises helps children regulate their sensory systems and improve attention and engagement.

Increasing awareness and understanding of sensory processing difficulties among pupils and staff to promote empathy, acceptance, and inclusive practices within the school community.

Myth: Persistent absence is solely a result of academic disinterest or laziness.

Truth: Persistent absence can stem from various complex factors, including health issues, family circumstances, mental health challenges, bullying, or socioeconomic disadvantages. It's essential to understand and address the underlying causes rather than attributing them solely to disinterest or laziness.

Myth: Punitive measures like fines or prosecution effectively reduce persistent absence.

Truth: While punitive measures may temporarily address attendance issues, they often fail to address the root causes of persistent absence and can exacerbate underlying problems. Effective strategies for addressing persistent absence involve a holistic approach that considers the individual needs and circumstances of pupils and provides targeted support and interventions.

Myth: Parents and carers are always fully aware of and responsible for their child's attendance at school.

Truth: While parents/carers play a significant role in supporting their children's education, there are various factors that can affect their ability to ensure regular attendance. These factors may include work schedules, transportation challenges, health issues within the family, or lack of awareness of absence. Additionally, some may face their own socioeconomic or mental health challenges, which can impact their capacity to prioritise their child's attendance. Recognising and addressing these underlying factors through supportive interventions and partnerships can help improve attendance outcomes for pupils.

Resources

Department for Education (DfE) – England: The DfE website provides guidance and resources for schools, parents, and local authorities to improve attendance and address related issues.

Website: https://www.gov.uk/government/organisations/department-for-education

Education Endowment Foundation (EEF): EEF offers evidence-based guidance and resources to support schools in addressing attendance challenges and improving student outcomes.

Website: https://educationendowmentfoundation.org.uk/

National Association of Head Teachers (NAHT): NAHT provides resources and support for school leaders, including guidance on addressing attendance issues and promoting positive school culture.

Website: https://www.naht.org.uk/

School Attendance and Absence Support (SAS): SAS offers resources, training, and consultancy services to support schools in improving attendance and reducing absence rates.

Website: https://school-attendance.org.uk/

Association of Education Welfare Management (AEWM): AEWM provides resources and professional development opportunities for education welfare practitioners working to improve attendance and support vulnerable pupils.

Website: https://www.aewm.org.uk/

Local Authority Websites: Many local authorities have dedicated sections on their websites providing guidance and support for schools, parents, and students regarding attendance issues. You can find your local authority's website by searching online for '[Your Local Authority] education attendance support'.

Resources and support for parents/carers dealing with school attendance issues:

Family Lives:

Website: https://www.familylives.org.uk/

Family Lives offers a range of resources and support for parents, including guidance on school attendance issues, managing behaviour, and building positive relationships within the family.

Website: https://contact.org.uk/

Description: Contact provides information and support for families with disabled children, including advice on navigating educational challenges such as school attendance issues.

YoungMinds:

Website: https://youngminds.org.uk/

YoungMinds offers resources and support for children and young people's mental health, including articles and guides for parents dealing with school refusal and other attendance-related issues.

Citizens Advice: https://www.citizensadvice.org.uk/

Website: Citizens Advice offers free, confidential advice on a wide range of issues, including legal rights and responsibilities related to education and school attendance.

Gov.uk – Education and childcare: The UK government's education and childcare section provides information on school attendance regulations, parental rights, and support available for families dealing with attendance issues.

NHS – Child and Adolescent Mental Health Services (CAMHS):

Website: https://www.nhs.uk/service-search/other-health-services

CAMHS offers assessment and treatment for children and young people with mental health difficulties, including support for issues affecting school attendance.

References

Akkuş, M. and Çinkir, Ş. (2022). International journal of psychology and educational studies the problem of student absenteeism, its impact on educational environments, and the evaluation of current policies. *International Journal of Psychology and Educational Studies.* [online] 2022(4), pp. 1-21. https://doi.org/10.52380/ijpes.2022.9.4.957

The Centre for Social Justice. (2024). *The missing link: Restoring the bond between schools and families.* [online] Available at: https://www.centreforsocialjustice.org.uk/library/the-missing-link

Children's Commissioner for England. (n.d.). *Where are England's children? Interim findings from the children's commissioner's attendance audit.* [online] Available at: https://www.childrenscommissioner.gov.uk/resource/where-are-englands-children-interim-findings-from-the-childrens-commissioners-attendance-audit/

Department for Education. (2023). *Why is school attendance so important and what are the risks of missing a day? – The education hub.* [online] educationhub.blog.gov.uk. Available at: https://educationhub.blog.gov.uk/2023/05/18/school-attendance-important-risks-missing-day/

Dräger, J., Klein, M. and Sosu, E. (2023). *The long-term consequences of early school absences for educational attainment and labour market outcomes.* Strathprints: The University of Strathclyde institutional repository (University of Strathclyde). https://doi.org/10.35542/osf.io/7z2bx

explore-education-statistics.service.gov.uk. (2024). *Pupil attendance in schools, Week 41 2022.* [online] Available at: https://explore-education-statistics.service.gov.uk/find-statistics/pupil-attendance-in-schools

The Independent. (2023). *Restoring 'fractured' contract between parents and schools likely to take years.* [online] Available at: https://www.independent.co.uk/news/uk/amanda-spielman-geoff-barton-england-government-department-for-education-b2452283.html [Accessed 11 Apr. 2024].

Solan, M. (2017). *The secret to happiness? Here's some advice from the longest-running study on happiness.* [online] Harvard Health Blog. Available at: https://www.health.harvard.edu/blog/the-secret-to-happiness-heres-some-advice-from-the-longest-running-study-on-happiness-2017100512543.

System, C. (n.d.). *Absences from schools in the UK – The key statistics for 2023.* [online] Available at: https://www.systemc.com/knowledge-hub/blogs/absences-from-schools-in-the-uk-the-key-statistics-for-2023/?page=1#changesettings

Tapscott Learning Trust. (2023). *Improving attendance through a focus on health and happiness.* [online] Available at: https://www.ttlt.academy/blog/?pid=247&nid=6&storyid=461 [Accessed 23 Feb. 2024].

22 Suspensions and detentions

Chapter introduction

Our education system aims to provide education for all. 'Every Child Matters', the UK Government's initiative for England in Wales that was launched in 2003 (DfE, 2004), highlighted the need for schools and agencies to work together to ensure all children could be given the opportunities to be Safe, Healthy, Enjoy/Achieve, Economic, and Positive Contribution. Many schools use sanctions as a part of their behaviour management toolkit, and these sanctions may include *demerits*, which are a reverse of traditional 'house points', or *suspensions*, which is where a child breaks school rules and needs to be suspended from attending school for a fixed period of time to ensure they are not harming their education or welfare, or the welfare and education of their peers. An initial suspension is normally up to five days, and a pupil's total of fixed suspensions cannot exceed 45 days in an academic year.

Sometimes, however, a school cannot continue to meet the needs of a pupil, and the headteacher may issue an *exclusion*, which is the most severe type of punishment (Demie, 2022). Research into school exclusions shows that these actions may put young people at greater risk of exploitation, serious violence, and criminal activity (Arnez and Condry, 2021). Pervasive and repeated exclusions throughout a child's life-can be highly damaging for all involved. Exclusions not only criminalise children but also disconnect vital threads of nurture, visibility, support and protection (Gibson and Tragheim, 2022). Inherent within its very definition, an exclusion causes an explicit and immediate termination of a pathway. It could be argued that exclusions are a necessary evil. After all, all institutions must have systems of redress to signal unacceptable behaviour. An often cited rationale for invoking such restitution is for the safety of peers, practitioners or the wider community (Adams, 2022). However, such rationale implies that the removal of an immediate threat successfully punishes and protects simultaneously. Although there may be an argument for temporary alleviation, such archaic restorative justice benefits neither the victim nor perpetuator. All parties involved need support, care and inclusion (Gibson and Tragheim, 2022).

This chapter contains an insightful guest contribution from Dr Suzie Dick and Stephen Scholes, Queen Margaret University, which sheds insight into understanding exclusions, and the research behind behaviour management and the potential effects of exclusions on young people. Following this is a valuable guest contribution from David McBride, Head of Education

DOI: 10.4324/9781032697932-22

at HMP Isis, who explores how education can still be offered to some learners as part of rehabilitation if they become incarcerated.

***

Understanding exclusion, by Dr Suzie Dick and Stephen Scholes, Queen Margaret University

Introduction

Despite aspirational visions for universal inclusion, exclusions remain a controversial feature
of contemporary schooling. Broadly, exclusion can be understood as the act of not allowing
a child or young person to access a school and their education for a period of time. An exclusion is a formal sanction issued by a school, and it is expected that they are officially recorded
and reported to education authorities. Indeed, governments across the United Kingdom and
Northern Ireland publish regular updates on exclusion statistics.

Exclusions are generally considered to be a last-resort response to dealing with the
behaviour and conduct of pupils. Most exclusions that occur last for only a few days and are
usually called temporary exclusions or, in England, suspensions. Beyond this, there are exclusions that are permanent, and these see individual pupils removed from a school's register
(McCluskey et al., 2019).

The most recent comparable national statistics for England and Scotland on school exclusion are presented in Table 22.1 (Scottish Government, 2023b; DfE, Online). There is an obvious disparity in raw numbers as a result of the size of the school population in each country.
However, when considered as a percentage of the base population, the use of exclusions in
England is higher than that in Scotland (ibid.) (see Table 22.1).

One explanation offered for the disparity in the use of exclusion is that the policy landscape in Scotland has favoured approaches to dealing with pupil behaviour that is proactive and non-punitive and carried out, in more complex cases, via joined-up working that
is centred around meeting the child's developmental needs. As Cole et al. (2019: 376) have
summarised from the available research, success in coping with disruptive behaviour and
minimising levels of exclusion relates to values, policy, and collaborative, multi-agency, ade-
quately funded practice at a range of levels: national, local and school (whole-school, targeted group, and individual child).

Beyond the formal and official exclusion practices, there are sanctions that schools apply
that can also be considered forms of exclusion. For example, some schools informally exclude
pupils. This usually involves negotiated arrangements with parents/carers around a pupil not

Table 22.1 Overview of exclusion numbers in Scotland and England

Exclusion in numbers		2020/2021
Temporary exclusions	Scotland	8,322
	England	352, 454
Permanent exclusions	Scotland	1
(removal from register)	England	3928

attending school or perhaps not attending a particular class for a period of time. Such informal exclusions are not necessarily recorded or reported. A similar practice of internal exclusions sees pupils removed from classes for, usually, a day and left to work in another area of the school under supervision. In such circumstances, classwork is usually provided by the class teachers but may not always be. Both informal and internal exclusions are considered problematic practices and even labelled 'illegal' by some commentators (ibid.: 1141).

In the rest of this chapter, we consider the issue of exclusion from the perspective of different individuals and groups and how they may be impacted. We look first at the individual child experiencing the exclusion, then consider the other children in the class. Thereafter, we consider the impact on parents and carers, teachers, and the wider community. The common theme that we highlight from considering each of these groups is that any one stance on exclusion can be challenged. Those against exclusion in all instances need to contend with the detrimental realities of disrupted learning environments, and those who view exclusion more favourably must address the negative impacts on all the individuals and groups concerned.

The Child

It is accepted that exclusion is disruptive to a child's school-based education, potentially leading to gaps in learning and academic setbacks, and if the situation is not rectified, the child may struggle to catch up with their peers. The right of the child (Harris, 2009) is to have an education, and legislation across the UK is with the right to access education; the onus is on the local authority to provide an alternative place to learn if a child is excluded, whether temporarily or permanently. This may also include making an alternative arrangement to provide a number of learning hours, though this may be a reduced level of provision (Education Wales, 2019; Scottish Government, 2017; Government, UK, 2023)

There are a number of potential impacts that need to be considered, both short and long term, all with the potential to disrupt the rights of the child, not only to an education but to live without fear of discrimination, have their views heard, to belong to a group, the right of privacy and support for recovery and integration (UNICEF, 2019).

These include:

- Strained relationships within the family leading to stress as the family may struggle to find appropriate solutions and support (Gust, 2012).
- Legal implications if the exclusion leads to a legal challenge, which can further exacerbate stress for the child and their family.
- Exclusion may not address the underlying issues that led to the disciplinary problems. Without proper intervention, the child may continue to exhibit problematic behaviour in future educational and social settings (Harris, 2009).
- The child's exclusion may impact how they are perceived within their community. Negative perceptions can affect the child's relationships and sense of belonging.

This sense of belonging is perhaps the most important if we refer back to Maslow's Hierarchy of Needs with Wade's (n.d.) adaptation. Without belonging, affiliation, and esteem with others, a child is not motivated to learn (Wade, n.d.).

In the long term, the social and emotional impact of exclusion can lead to feelings of shame, rejection, and alienation from peers, leading to emotional distress. Exclusion can have a significant impact on a child's mental health, potentially leading to increased stress, anxiety, and depression. The emotional toll may persist even after the child has left the school. Expelled pupils may be at a higher risk of engaging in harmful behaviours (Michail, 2011) or falling into negative peer groups if they lack appropriate guidance and supervision. The school environment often provides support systems, including teachers, school counsellors, and other professionals who may identify and address the child's needs. Excluding a child also potentially removes the child from these support structures leading to longer-term consequences that go beyond academic progress (Michail, 2011).

Ultimately, it is important for schools and those responsible for education to consider alternative disciplinary measures (Education Wales, 2019) over exclusion that prioritise rehabilitation and support. Addressing the root causes of the behaviour, providing counselling, and involving the child, parents, and caregivers in the process can contribute to more positive outcomes for the child, working to create an environment that fosters understanding and addresses behavioural issues early to prevent the need for exclusion (McCluskey et al., 2016). There is also a discussion about the right of the child not to attend that educational establishment (Byrne, 2022). What if they feel it is not the right place for them? As outlined previously, the rights of the child are paramount at the centre of decisions being made, but dare we ask, the rights of which child?

The other children

Disruptive behaviour in the classroom can have various impacts on the other children, affecting both their academic and socio-emotional well-being (Power and Taylor, 2020). Disruptive behaviour in the class can create a distracting environment, making it challenging for other pupils to focus, may cause distress to others whose learning needs require a calm, and predictable environment, and may lead to a decline in progress for other pupils (Byrne, 2022).

The current guidance in Scotland considers the rights of others in saying that the local authority will exclude a pupil if: 'consider that in all the circumstances to allow the pupil to continue his attendance at the school would be likely to be seriously detrimental to order and discipline in the school or the educational well-being of the pupils there' (Scottish Government, 2017).

In England, the current documentation is less explicit with regards to the effect on others in the classroom but does state in their guidance that: 'Your child's school should be a calm, safe and supportive environment which your child wants to attend, free from disruption and fear of bullying' (Government, UK, 2023).

In addition to the loss of learning time, if teachers are spending additional time managing disruptive behaviour, leading to an impact on the pace and depth of the curriculum (Frenzel et al., 2021) and potential long-term consequences for their academic progress, there is also the social impact to be considered.

This includes:

- Those engaging in disruptive behaviour may face social isolation or peer rejection. This can create a divide within the class and affect the overall sense of community. The social dynamics in the classroom, leading to tensions and potentially affecting their ability to collaborate and engage in group activities.
- Disruptive behaviour can negatively influence other students, leading to a decline in their own behaviour and contributing to the normalisation of such behaviour.
- Other children in the class may feel anxious or fearful due to unpredictable and disruptive behaviour. A tense classroom environment can create stress and impact the emotional well-being of students (Power & Taylor, 2020).

Finally, disruptive behaviour, regardless of the reasons behind it, can create an environment where pupils feel less safe and secure (Power and Taylor, 2020). This can have implications for their overall well-being and willingness to actively participate in classroom activities. This safety and security extends to the teacher, and other classroom staff. With the teacher's attention disproportionately focused on managing disruptive behaviour, it is potentially straining the teacher-student relationship with other pupils who may feel neglected or under supported. Constantly managing disruptive behaviour can contribute to teacher burnout (Frenzel et al., 2021), affecting their ability to provide quality education and support to all pupils in the class. The impact on the teacher will be considered later in this chapter.

The parents

Often, the parents and caregivers are in an undesired situation, needing to balance the needs of their child, potentially other children, family dynamics, and wider relationships (Jacobsen, 2020). Often parents are quite practical and know what their child can be like, so if they are known to engage in certain behaviours, exclusion may not be, ultimately, unexpected. What is rarely considered is the rights of parents as people. At the heart of this is a debate about the role of parents – their rights versus their responsibility as parents (Roskam et al., 2021). There is a tension here between the rights of the parents to have a flourishing life for themselves, the right to health, work, and financial security versus the rights of others to be able to have those in the future. Bringing the two together, a parent has the right to understand what has occurred, but also the responsibility to prevent their child from acting on their rights in some contexts. There is a contract between the parent, child, and the education provider, and as stated by the government: 'Parents have an important role in helping schools develop and maintain good behaviour. As a parent, you should get to know the school's behaviour policy so that you can support your child to follow the school rules' (Government, UK, 2023).

It's important for schools to engage with parents in a supportive manner, providing clear communication about the reasons for exclusion and offering guidance on potential next steps (Hong, 2021). Collaborative efforts between parents, school officials, and other relevant stakeholders can contribute to a more constructive and rehabilitative approach to addressing behavioural issues in children (Scottish Government, 2023a).

However, part of a parent's role may be to advocate for their child's needs, both within the school system and potentially with other educational institutions. This can be a time-consuming and challenging process. There are a number of potential impacts for parents, including:

- The emotional stress and the range of emotions, including shock, disappointment, guilt, and frustration. The news of their child's exclusion can be emotionally distressing for parents. Parents may feel a sense of failure and become disheartened about their ability to effectively support their child's educational and behavioural needs (Jacobsen, 2020).
- Stress within the family, particularly if there are disagreements about the circumstances surrounding the exclusion or how to handle the situation going forward.
- Financial strain and work impact – dealing with the aftermath of a child's exclusion may require parents to take time off from work or attend meetings and appointments with education officials. This can affect their professional responsibilities and career, potentially leading to greater financial strain (Brooks et al., 2020).

Parents are likely to worry about the long-term consequences of exclusion on their child's education, social development, and future opportunities. Generally, support for the parent in navigating the situation and their needs as people is subsumed by their responsibilities as a parent and are limited in availability.

The teacher

In the policies and professional guidance on the role of the teacher in relation to pupil behaviour, there are implicit and explicit statements that position the teacher as a professional who can always, or nearly always, respond to challenging behaviour in ways that prioritise the well-being of all their pupils, even those pupils engaging in challenging behaviour.

For example, in England's Initial Teacher Training and Early Career Framework (2024: 24–25), Standard 7 mandates the range of things teachers should learn and learn how to do to 'manage behaviour effectively'. The General Teaching Council for Scotland's (2021: 10) Standards for Full Registration do not mention pupil behaviour explicitly but expect teachers to be able to 'utilise and evaluate a variety of strategies to nurture caring and supportive and purposeful relationships with learners and celebrate success'.

In step with the policy guidance on exclusion, Included Engaged and Involved Part 2: A Positive Approach to Preventing and Managing School Exclusions, teachers in Scotland are positioned as the relationship builders who can 'reach out and influence the lives of the children and young people in their classrooms' (Scottish Government, 2017: 3). However, with respect to the more serious incidents that may result in exclusion, this positioning of the teacher in policy is challenged by the realities of the classroom.

A recent Scottish Government (2023a: 6–7) survey of school staff's perceptions and recollections of pupil behaviour in Scottish schools has highlighted that, compared to previous surveys on the topic,

> There has been a perceived decline in pupil behaviour since 2016. . . . Staff reported increases in most of the classroom disengagement behaviours and low level disruptive

behaviours in the classroom and around the school since 2016. . . . Reports of pupils
being under the influence of drugs or alcohol and using digital technology/mobile phones
abusively have also risen since 2016. . . . Likewise, reported incidence of serious disruptive behaviours has increased since 2016, including sexist abuse towards staff, general
verbal abuse, physical aggression and violence towards staff and pupils in the classroom
and around the school.

Whether or not the perceived causes of such changes noted in the report, including 'a
perceived lack of consequences for pupils who engage in serious disruptive behaviours'
(ibid.: 8), are explanatory, there is no doubt that such behaviour makes classroom management more demanding. If exclusion is considered as a taboo resort in all cases, it, in
turn, demands more of teachers if they are to continue to meet the policy expectations of
their role. Teachers may find themselves having to devote more time and energy to managing behaviour rather than focusing on learning and attainment. Moreover, as ever more
diverse pupil needs are present in classrooms, this will also demand constant upskilling,
personalisation of strategies, and yet further time taken away from the core business of
learning and teaching.

The impact of negating exclusions on a teacher's professional time and priorities is further compounded by considering the impact on teachers' well-being. With concerns about
retention, workload, and burnout evident across jurisdictions, stages of education, and types
of schools, it is important to consider how a lack of strong sanctions on challenging behaviour can contribute to this. In short, the policy-derived picture of a strategic and detached
relationship builder must be tempered by the fact that teachers are human beings and will
experience the emotional drain, even trauma, of serious and/or repeated negative behaviours, carrying it with them into their personal lives too.

The extent of the tension between challenging behaviours, limitations in terms of sanctions and teachers' well-being can be highlighted by noting that, in some cases, individual
teachers have approached unions or the police for further action and redress. Few teachers
would advocate criminalising children, but the lack of sufficient sanctions and support for
both pupil and teacher has such potentially extreme consequences. Schools and the authorities that oversee them surely, then, must consider the needs of the teacher in exploring how
exclusion is used. In addition, schools themselves must support teachers by making time and
space for developing strong support cultures around the behaviour and providing practical
support mechanisms ranging from professional learning to counselling and a consistently
applied escalation procedure for behaviour management that removes the toll of burdens of
disruptive behaviour from the classroom practitioner.

The community

A school that deploys exclusion as a sanction for disruptive behaviour must be aware of the
consequences for the wider community. A school community can be understood broadly but
certainly includes the school's catchment area, its families, and the school's wider partnerships. Exclusion can certainly be seen as a step that protects other members of the school
community, such as the other learners and children, as discussed previously. However, there

are challenges with respect to managing the impact of exclusion on wider social issues, employability and reputational damage that need to be considered.

The statistics on exclusion from Scotland highlight that excluded young people will more likely be those from a lower socio-economic background, with 25.3 in every 1,000 pupils from the most deprived areas excluded, compared to 7.2 in every 1,000 pupils from the least deprived areas excluded in session 2022–2023 (Scottish Government, 2023b). The impact of exclusion, therefore, falls hardest on the families impacted by poverty and its associated challenges (McCluskey et al., 2019). Moreover, exclusion itself may further exacerbate the challenges being faced by parents and carers as they need to find additional childcare, lose time from work to deal with school meetings and communications, and potentially tackle inter-family dynamics without the time or support needed to do it well. While professionals highlight that some of the reasons behind challenging behaviour can be explained by parenting, in well-off and less-off situations, to expect parents/carers to address such behaviour via exclusion could be expecting too much of families unable, unskilled, or unwilling to do so (Scottish Government, 2023a). Resulting in exclusions being an ineffective sanction for resolving behavioural issues in school if the hope is to motivate parental engagement.

Exclusion has also been considered as one step on the road to social exclusions for individuals that impact wider society. Skiba et al. (2014), alongside many others, have, for example, explored the idea that exclusion can be the start of a process that sees young people more likely to become engaged in anti-social and, ultimately, criminal behaviour that leads them to encounter legal punishments and, potentially, time in prison. This 'pipeline' idea suggests that avoiding exclusion might be more beneficial given the challenges of reformation and recidivism. Closely connected to this is the point that exclusion from education can, in turn, limit individuals' employability, and such unemployment places increased demand on social welfare systems. Therefore, exclusion is not inconsequential to broader society.

To conclude

Addressing disruptive behaviour promptly through appropriate disciplinary measures, intervention strategies, and support systems is crucial to creating a positive and conducive learning environment for all those involved. Collaborative efforts involving teachers, local authorities, parents, support staff, and the pupils can contribute to a more inclusive and supportive educational experience for everyone in the classroom. There is no answer to whether exclusion is right or wrong, but a change in emphasis on the responsibility of all involved in education today for communities to work together, moving forward together.

Next, David McBride, Local Education Manager (Novus) at HMP Isis, a south London prison, helps us understand how those young people who do not have the opportunity to finish their education in schools due to adverse situations and who may find themselves admitted into a Young Offenders Institute or prison later in life, may return to education and qualifications as a means of rehabilitation to re-find their ambition and employment.

'What is the purpose of education in prison?', by David McBride

'I didn't even know that happened!' is the response I usually get when I tell people about my job.

After 26 years of teaching in primary and special schools, I made the choice to have a change of direction in April 2023. I still wanted to stay in education: it is, after all, what I studied at university and what I had been doing since then. So I applied for and was offered the job of Education Manager within HMP Isis, a prison for 18-25-year-old men, heading up Novus' team, who are contracted to deliver prison education within London and other regions of England and Wales.

The Chief Inspector of Prisons recently said that 'Education, training and rehabilitation need to be the primary focus of jail'. Coming from an education background, I can totally get on board with this. I know that this is something that is demonstrated day-by-day by my team here at HMP Isis but also by my colleagues in Novus in all of the prisons where we provide education. It is also something that the staff, led by the inspirational Governor Emily Thomas and the SMT, totally believe in at Isis, where providing education and training to find employment on release is paramount. In turn, this reduces the risk of re-offending and the cost to society.

Most curriculums are designed with a particular emphasis on the settings' needs, vision, and/or circumstances, and the curriculum for each prison will, therefore, differ depending on each prison's situation. The needs analysis, carried out by each prison, will speak to the offenders, look into the employment needs in the release area, and come up with an evidence-based document with which to plan the curriculum.

In HMP Isis, we focus on courses which provide the skills for the learners to use to get employment when released. The main focus is on functional skills in English and Maths. These provide the learners with real-life problems and situations and the skills to meet these. There is also a big focus on vocational subjects, which would give qualifications relevant to the local employment situation. For example, barbering, painting and decorating, food safety, radio, and catering all provide accredited qualifications which can be used to help secure jobs.

It goes without saying that being in prison isn't an easy experience. The punishment that someone has their liberty taken away for a period of time has knock-on effects. One of these effects is that the offenders have time and are supported to self-reflect and take advantage of support so that they do not re-offend. Some of our courses are designed to help that reflection and develop the learners' thinking skills and empathy skills. Level 3 courses in Mentoring and distance learning courses, such as Open University modules, are options for those learners. Higher Education courses are self-funded like they are for any other HE student, following a rigorous application process.

The great thing about being in prison education is that there are so many partners that work together to improve outcomes for learners. We run courses on ICT and Employability, but Isis' excellent Employability Lead also works to provide workshops, job fairs, and opportunities to get jobs on release. Some of the learners enrolled in the Catering course are linked to an organisation called Kerb, which provides training, work experience, and job opportunities to those learners interested in running a street food stall.

Is it worthwhile? The pass rates for our exams are really good. In our vocational qualifications, more than 90% of our learners regularly get their qualification. In the functional skills of English and Maths, over 75% pass their exams. For some of these learners, who struggled through school or who didn't attend that often, this is often the first educational achievement they have had. The teachers here say that is the best part of their job – giving the learners their certificates when they have passed. It really does make it worthwhile.

I'm going to finish with two case studies. A learner who is currently on our catering course is desperate to complete it so that he can cook with his children on release. He finds it hard to write but is absolutely flying through this course. His cakes are absolutely amazing and he is so looking forward to baking them when he gets out. Another learner has been released now. He was very reluctant to do his Maths Level 1. He hated Maths at school and didn't see the point of doing it. His teachers were so patient with him and were so determined he would get through. He worked in the family landscaping firm, so a big part of this was demonstrating how the maths would really help with this. He tried, and he carried on . . . and he passed the first time! His perseverance and his teachers' dedication really carried him through.

I am a proud advocate of prison education. It really has the power to transform lives, and the learners here have so many opportunities through different agencies and partners working together. So from the original statement of 'I didn't even know that happened', hopefully, more people will consider this as an education career and think, 'Prison education – why not?'

For more information on prison education careers and the roles that are available, visit novus.ac.uk/careers

***

Myth: Exclusions are an effective way to encourage a child to change their behaviours.

Truth: Often, exclusions won't change a child's behaviour, especially if it doesn't address underlying problems such as mental health conditions, undiagnosed Special Educational Needs, bullying, bereavements, and grief, or issues in the home environment that may have triggered the behaviour in school.

Myth: An exclusion from a school is final and means a child can never return to that school.

Truth: If the parent or carer disagrees with the exclusion, they can ask the school's governing board to overturn the exclusion. The Government website adds:

'If the governors do not overturn the exclusion, you can ask for an independent review by your local council (or Academy Trust if the school's an academy). The governors must tell you how to do this.

'You can ask for a special educational needs (SEN) expert to attend if your child has SEN or you suspect they have SEN.

'*If your child is still excluded you can ask the Local Government Ombudsman (or the Department for Education if the school's an academy or free school) to look at whether your case was handled properly. They cannot overturn the exclusion*' (Gov.uk, 2024: 1).

Myth: If a young person is permanently excluded from school, that is the end of their education journey.

Truth: No, this is not true. Many students may go on to be homeschooled and sit their exams at a local test centre or school site, or another school may be applied for. Education can even be delivered if, in the worst-case scenario, the young person is sent to prison, where many courses and subjects are on offer to provide opportunities for employment upon release.

References

Adams, R. (2022). Ban permanent exclusions from English primaries, says ex-children's tsar. *The Guardian*. Available at: https://www.theguardian.com/education/2022/apr/29/ban-permanent-exclusions-from-english-primaries-says-ex-childrens-tsar [Accessed 14 Jun. 2022].

Arnez, J. and Condry, R. (2021). Criminological perspectives on school exclusion and youth offending. *Emotional and Behavioural Difficulties*, pp. 87–100. Available at: https://www.tandfonline.com/doi/full/10.1080/13632752.2021.1905233 [Accessed 14 Jun. 2022].

Brooks, S.K., Smith, L.E., Webster, R.K., Weston, D., Woodland, L., Hall, I. and Rubin, G.J. (2020). The impact of unplanned school closure on children's social contact: Rapid evidence review. *Eurosurveillance*, 25(13), p. 2000188.

Byrne, B. (2022). How inclusive is the right to inclusive education? An assessment of the UN convention on the rights of persons with disabilities' concluding observations. *International Journal of Inclusive Education*, 26(3), pp. 301–318.

Cole, T., McCluskey, G., Daniels, H., Thompson, I. and Tawell, A. (2019). Factors associated with high and low levels of school exclusions: Comparing the English and wider UK experience. *Emotional and Behavioural Difficulties*, 24(4), pp. 374–390.

Demie, F. (2022). *Understanding the causes and consequences of school exclusions: Teachers, parents and schools' perspectives*. Milton Park, Oxfordshire: Taylor & Francis.

Department for Education. (2024). *Initial teacher training and early career framework*. Available at: https://assets.publishing.service.gov.uk/media/65b8fa60e9e10a00130310b2/Initial_teacher_training_and_early_career_framework_30_Jan_2024.pdf

Department for Education. [online]. *Statistics: Exclusions*. Available at: https://www.gov.uk/government/collections/statistics-exclusions

Education Wales. (2019). *Exclusions from schools and pupil referral units*. [online] Available at: https://www.gov.wales/sites/default/files/publications/2019-11/exclusion-from-schools-pupil-referral-units.pdf [Accessed 15 Jan. 2024].

Frenzel, A.C., Daniels, L. and Burić, I. (2021). Teacher emotions in the classroom and their implications for students. *Educational Psychologist*, 56(4), pp. 250–264.

General Teaching Council for Scotland. (2021). The standard for full Registration. *Mandatory Requirements for Registration with the General Teaching Council for Scotland*. Available at: https://www.gtcs.org.uk/wp-content/uploads/2021/09/standard-for-full-registration.pdf

Gibson, P. and Tragheim, M. (2022). *Black with no way back*. Available at: https://nexus-education.com/blog-posts/black-with-no-way-back/

Government, UK. (2023). *School exclusions guide for parents*. [online] Available at: https://www.gov.uk/government/publications/school-exclusions-guide-for-parents/a-guide-for-parents-on-school-behaviour-and-exclusion [Accessed 15 Jan. 2024].

Gov.UK. (2024). *Behaviour in schools*. Available at: https://www.gov.uk/school-behaviour-exclusions/challenging-exclusion#:~:text=You%20can%20ask%20the%20school's,exam%20or%20national%20curriculum%20test

Gust, L.V. (2012). Can policy reduce the collateral damage caused by the criminal justice system? Strengthening social capital in families and communities. *American Journal of Orthopsychiatry*, 82(2), pp. 174–180.

Harris, N. (2009). Playing catch-up in the schoolyard? children and young people's 'voice'and education rights in the UK. *International Journal of Law, Policy and the Family*, 23(3), pp. 331–366.

Hong, S. (2021). *A cord of three strands: A new approach to parent engagement in schools*. London, England: Harvard Education Press.

Jacobsen, W.C. (2020). School punishment and interpersonal exclusion: Rejection, withdrawal, and separation from friends. *Criminology*, 58(1), pp. 35–69.

McCluskey, G., Cole, T., Daniels, H., Thompson, I. and Tawell, A. (2019). Exclusion from school in Scotland and across the UK: Contrasts and questions. *British Educational Research Journal*, 45(6): 1140–1159.

Michail, S. (2011). Understanding school responses to students' challenging behaviour: A review of literature. *Improving Schools*, 14(2), pp. 156–171.

Power, S. and Taylor, C. (2020). Not in the classroom, but still on the register: Hidden forms of school exclusion. *International Journal of Inclusive Education*, 24(8), pp. 867–881.

Roskam, I., Aguiar, J., Akgun, E., Arikan, G., Artavia, M., Avalosse, H., Aunola, K., Bader, M., Bahati, C., Barham, E.J. and Besson, E. (2021). Parental burnout around the globe: A 42-country study. *Affective Science*, 2(1), pp. 58–79.

Scottish Government. (2017). *Included, engaged and involved part 2: A positive approach to managing school exclusions*. Available at: https://www.gov.scot/publications/included-engaged-involved-part-2-positive-approach-preventing-managing-school/documents/

Scottish Government. (2023a). *Behaviour in Scottish schools 2023*. Available at: https://www.gov.scot/publications/behaviour-scottish-schools-research-report-2023/documents/

Scottish Government. (2023b). Summary statistics for schools in Scotland. *Exclusions*. Available at: https://www.gov.scot/publications/summary-statistics-for-schools-in-scotland-2023/pages/exclusions/#:~:text=Cases%20of%20exclusion%20have%20fallen,downward%20trend%20(Figure%2035)

Skiba, R.J., Arredondo, M.I. and Williams, N.T. (2014). More than a metaphor: The contribution of exclusionary discipline to a school-to-prison pipeline. *Equity and Excellence in Education*, 47(4): 546–564.

UNICEF. (2019). *For every child, every right: The convention on the rights of the child at a crossroads*. UNICEF.

Wade, D. (n.d.). *Rehabilitation matters – Maslow's hierachy of needs*. [online] Available at: https://rehabilitationmatters.com/maslows-needs/ [Accessed 15 Jan. 2024].

23 Your own welfare

Quote: 'I just feel like I am running from one thing to the next and not getting anything done properly. I am so stressed'.

The adage is true. You can't pour from an empty cup. As educators, we tend to give everything to our pupils; that's why we get into teaching, right? On top of that, we often feel a lot of pressure and guilt. Are we giving enough to our own families? Housework, cooking healthy meals, life admin, financial worries . . . It is very easy to put yourself right at the bottom of the pile.

The Teacher Wellbeing Index 2023 report reveals teacher well-being is at its lowest in five years and lower than the national average. Over 77% of education professionals have reported psychological symptoms due to their work. Factors include excessive work hours, overwhelming workload, and the emotional demands of teaching. This crisis affects not only educators but also has an impact on students. 84% of teachers report being unable to unwind, plagued by persistent intrusive thoughts about work. This level of ongoing stress is unsustainable and poses a serious threat to both teacher retention and student success.

When teachers are supported and content, their ability to engage and inspire students increases exponentially. A positive and relaxed teacher fosters a conducive learning environment, leading to greater student success.

Stress and stressors

'Being under stress' and 'suffering from stress' are two different ways of expressing the experience and impact of stress on an individual. Let's explore the differences:

Being Under Stress: When someone is described as 'being under stress', it generally refers to a situation where a person is experiencing pressure, demands, or challenges that require them to adapt or respond. This could be due to external factors such as work deadlines, academic responsibilities, personal obligations, or any situation that demands more from a person than they feel comfortable handling. Being under stress is a natural and common aspect of life, and it doesn't necessarily imply negative emotional or psychological effects.

Suffering from Stress: 'Suffering from stress' implies that the individual is experiencing negative emotional, psychological, and potentially even physical effects as a result of being

DOI: 10.4324/9781032697932-23

under stress. This can manifest as feelings of overwhelm, anxiety, irritability, difficulty concentrating, changes in sleep patterns, and even physical symptoms like headaches or muscle tension. Suffering from stress suggests that stress is having a detrimental impact on the person's well-being and functioning.

In summary, 'being under stress' describes having external demands or pressures, while 'suffering from stress' emphasises the negative impact and the emotional and physical toll that stress is taking on an individual's health and overall quality of life. It's important to recognise the signs of suffering from excessive stress and to seek appropriate coping mechanisms, support, and stress management strategies to mitigate its negative effects.

What is burnout?

Burnout is becoming increasingly spoken about. In 2021, a YouGov TeacherTrack survey found that one in two (50%) reported having suffered at least one characteristic associated with work-related burnout 'all the time' since the beginning of the school year.

Burnout is a state of chronic physical and emotional exhaustion, often accompanied by feelings of cynicism and detachment from work. It is a response to prolonged periods of chronic stress, particularly work-related stress, and can affect various aspects of an individual's life. Burnout is not simply a result of working long hours; it is more about the nature of the work and your ability to cope with the demands.

The three components of burnout syndrome, according to www.sciencedirect.com, n.d., are emotional exhaustion, depersonalisation, and reduced personal achievement.

- Emotional Exhaustion: This is the core element of burnout and involves feeling drained of emotional resources. Individuals experiencing emotional exhaustion often find themselves depleted, both mentally and physically.
- Depersonalisation (Cynicism): This dimension involves developing negative, cynical attitudes and feelings about students, colleagues, or work in general. People experiencing depersonalisation may become detached and indifferent, viewing others as objects rather than individuals.
- Reduced Personal Accomplishment: Feelings of inefficiency and a decline in your sense of achievement at work. It involves a sense of incompetence and a lack of successful achievement in your work with people.

Several factors contribute to burnout, including:

- Workload: High demands, excessive workload, and pressure can contribute to burnout.
- Lack of Control: Feeling powerless or lacking control over one's work environment can be a significant stressor.
- Lack of Recognition: Not receiving adequate acknowledgment or rewards for your efforts can contribute to burnout.
- Lack of Social Support: A lack of support from colleagues or leaders can make it more difficult to cope with stress.
- Mismatched Values: If your values and goals are not aligned with the school or organisations, or work you are doing, it can contribute to burnout

Burnout can have severe consequences on both physical and mental health. It can lead to fatigue, insomnia, irritability, and a weakened immune system. In terms of mental health, it may contribute to depression and anxiety disorders.

Common causes and events detrimental to your well-being

I made my own list, consulted with my team, and then sent a survey out on Twitter. There were many common themes. This list is not exhaustive but includes:

- Deadlines
- Targets/results
- Lack of communication
- Change
- Individual students
- Safeguarding
- Work-life balance
- Personal issues
- Conflict
- Money
- Exams and assessments
- Ofsted

Pupil's needs are also becoming more complex, there is less funding, and there are increased pressures.

Strategies

First, and I cannot emphasise this enough, sometimes you have to put yourself first. Call it self-care, self-preservation, well-being, filling your cup, hygge, call it what you will – but you need to do it. You might not feel ready to say, 'I am prioritising myself'. If it helps your mind-set, think of it for the greater good. No one can replace you, so don't get to that point.

Let's start with self-care. How are you currently taking care of yourself? What activities or practices do you engage in that promote your physical, mental, and emotional well-being?

1. Physical exercise: Engage in regular physical activity that you enjoy, such as walking, jogging, yoga, or dancing. It can help reduce stress, increase energy levels, and improve overall health.
2. Mindfulness and meditation: Set aside time each day for mindfulness or meditation practices. This can help you cultivate present-moment awareness, reduce stress, and improve focus and clarity.
3. Time in nature: A government survey last year found that a quarter of people hadn't visited a green or natural space once in the previous 14 days. Spend time outdoors, whether it's going for a walk in a park, gardening, or simply sitting in a peaceful natural setting. Green and blue environments are associated with a reduction in stress, improved

mood, more positive emotions, and decreases in anxiety and rumination. Connecting with nature can have a calming and rejuvenating effect on your mind and body. In fact, exposure to nature activates the parasympathetic nervous system – the branch of the nervous system related to a 'resting' state. Research suggests that oxytocin, often called the 'bonding' hormone, might be the key player in this process. It seems to unleash its strong stress-relieving and rejuvenating effects when we're in natural surroundings that we find safe, enjoyable, peaceful, and familiar. Spend time outdoors, whether it's going for a walk in a park, gardening, or simply sitting in a peaceful natural setting, and aim for about 30 minutes to really feel the effects (Grahn, Ottosson and Uvnäs-Moberg, 2021).

4. In 2022, A review of 26 studies conducted across several countries, including Australia, the UK, and the US, has found that music may provide a clinically significant boost to mental health. The findings, presented in the Journal of the American Medical Association Network Open, affirm that 'music interventions are associated with significant enhancements in wellbeing', as assessed through quality-of-life surveys. These positive effects were consistent across various activities, including singing, playing instruments, or simply listening to music. According to the authors of the meta-analysis, the impact of music on mental quality of life was comparable to the improvements seen in mental health resulting from exercise and weight loss (Lu, 2022).

5. Hobbies and creative outlets: Engage in activities that bring you joy and allow you to express your creativity, such as painting, playing a musical instrument, writing, or cooking. These activities can provide a sense of fulfilment and help you relax and recharge.

6. Social connections: Nurture your relationships with family, friends, and colleagues. Make time for social activities, whether it's having a coffee date, joining a club or group, or simply connecting with loved ones through phone calls or video chats.

7. Rest and relaxation: Prioritise getting enough sleep and create a bedtime routine that promotes restful sleep. Set boundaries around work and allow yourself downtime to relax and recharge.

Remember, self-care is a personal journey, so it's important to find activities that resonate with you and bring you joy. What works for others may not work for you and vice versa.

Time mastery

'You can't actually manage time!' says David McLaughlin, CMI's ChMC assessment manager. 'It will come and go and happen whether you do anything or not . . . so we have to think about how we can use time best to achieve what we want to achieve' (CMI, 2020).

I highly recommend time mastery over time management. While it's easy to feel overwhelmed by competing demands, mastering your time is essential. Time mastery refers to the extent to which you control your own time.

This approach recognises the importance of efficiency and productivity. It involves using time effectively to achieve tasks and meet deadlines, leading to tangible results in both personal and professional areas. Mastering your time is particularly beneficial for achieving short-term goals and reducing stress by ensuring appropriate time allocation for various tasks and activities.

Furthermore, time mastery emphasises taking responsibility and ownership of your time. This sense of accountability promotes a proactive and empowered mindset when making time-related decisions. It encourages individuals to align their time choices with their values and priorities, fostering a more meaningful and purpose-driven life.

Personal effectiveness

Personal effectiveness 'enhances performance, supports us to achieve desired results, and to work towards personal goals' (www.ualberta.ca, n.d.). It involves making the most of your capabilities, managing time efficiently, setting and achieving objectives, and maintaining a balance between personal and professional life (Rayes, 2022).

Here are some key aspects of personal effectiveness:

- Self-awareness: Understanding yourself is fundamental to personal effectiveness. This includes recognising your strengths, weaknesses, values, and motivations. Self-awareness allows you to leverage your strengths, address weaknesses, and align your actions with your values.
- Goal setting: Personal effectiveness involves setting clear and achievable goals. These goals can be short-term or long-term and may encompass various areas of life, such as career, health, relationships, and personal development.
- Adaptability: Being adaptable and open to change is an important aspect of personal effectiveness. Life is dynamic, and if you can adjust to new situations, learn from experiences, and embrace change, you are better positioned for success.
- Communication skills: Strong communication skills contribute significantly to personal effectiveness. This includes the ability to express ideas clearly, listen actively, and collaborate with others. Effective communication is essential in personal and professional relationships.
- Emotional Intelligence (EI): Understanding and managing your emotions, as well as being attuned to the emotions of others, is a key aspect of personal effectiveness. Emotional intelligence helps to navigate social situations, build positive relationships, and handle stress effectively.
- Continuous learning: Personal effectiveness is enhanced by a commitment to continuous learning and self-improvement. This involves seeking new knowledge, acquiring new skills, and staying updated on relevant trends and developments.
- Resilience: Resilience is the ability to bounce back from setbacks and challenges. Building resilience is important for maintaining a positive outlook, managing stress, and persevering through difficulties.
- Networking and relationship building: Building and maintaining positive relationships with others is a critical element of personal effectiveness. Networking provides opportunities for collaboration, support, and access to valuable resources.
- Balancing priorities: Personal effectiveness involves finding a balance between various life priorities, such as work, family, health, and personal interests. Striking this balance is essential for overall well-being and life satisfaction.

Developing personal effectiveness is an ongoing process that requires self-reflection, a commitment to growth, and a willingness to adapt to changing circumstances. It involves cultivating a range of skills and habits that contribute to achieving personal and professional goals while maintaining a sense of fulfilment and balance.

Here is something to try. Identify the times of day when you work most efficiently and effectively, and practice 'eating the frog' by tackling the most challenging task during your peak productivity hours. You can start by setting up a time-tracking system to monitor your daily activities. This can be done using a planner, spreadsheet, or time-tracking app. Record the start and end times of each task or activity throughout the day, including work-related tasks, breaks, meals, exercise, and leisure activities. Now, use this to identify patterns or trends in your productivity levels throughout the day. Note the times when you feel most alert, focused, and energised as well as times when you experience dips in productivity. Obviously, there are limitations to this if you are working in an education setting and bound by the school day and a timetable, but even working out if you are better at dealing with emails first thing in the morning or at lunchtime can help.

Adapting to stressors

The ability to flexibly adapt stress responses to changing environments is critical for the capacity to recover from challenges or stressors, often referred to as resilience. There is significant variation in the way individuals react and respond to extreme stress and adversity (Osório et al., 2016).

Adapting to stressors is crucial for maintaining mental and physical well-being. (Cameron and Schoenfeld, 2018) Here are several strategies to help you adapt to stressors effectively:

Positive thinking

- Challenge negative thoughts and cultivate a positive mindset.
- Practice gratitude by focusing on things you are thankful for, fostering a more optimistic outlook.

Problem-solving

- Analyse stressors and identify actionable steps to address them.
- Break larger problems into smaller, more manageable components and address them systematically.

Boundaries and saying 'No'

- Establish clear boundaries to manage workload and prevent burnout.
- Learn to say 'no' when necessary to avoid taking on too many commitments.

Adaptability and flexibility

- Embrace a flexible mindset and be open to adjusting expectations and plans.
- Develop resilience by viewing challenges as opportunities for growth and learning.

Self-compassion

- Be kind to yourself during challenging times.
- Avoid self-criticism and practice self-compassion by treating yourself with the same kindness you would offer to a friend.

Seeking professional help

- If stress becomes overwhelming or persistent, consider seeking the assistance of a mental health professional for guidance and support.

Remember that adapting to stress is an ongoing process, and different strategies work for different individuals. Experiment with various techniques to find what works best for you, and don't hesitate to seek support when needed.

Self-regulation of emotions

The amygdala's fight-or-flight response is a basic survival mechanism rooted in the brain's limbic system, specifically within the amygdala, which governs emotions like fear and aggression (Holland, 2019).

When we encounter a perceived threat, whether it's real or just in our minds, the amygdala swiftly evaluates the situation and sets off a physiological reaction. This readies the body to either confront the threat head-on (fight) or get away from it as quickly as possible (flight). This reaction happens automatically and happens within milliseconds of sensing the threat.

Physiologically, the fight-or-flight response involves the release of stress hormones such as adrenaline and cortisol. These hormones ramp up heart rate, blood pressure, and breathing rate, providing a surge of energy and sharpened awareness. Meanwhile, functions like digestion and the immune system take a temporary back seat to conserve energy for dealing with the threat.

This primal response evolved to help our early ancestors react swiftly to physical dangers, like predators or immediate threats to their safety. While it was crucial for survival back then, in modern times, it can sometimes kick in even when there's no actual physical danger around. This can lead to heightened stress or anxiety in situations where it's not warranted.

Emotional regulation stands as a skill that can be developed and entails creating a deliberate pause, a buffer between experiencing an emotion and reacting to it, for instance, taking a moment to gather your thoughts before responding.

It may also involve waiting until you find yourself in a supportive environment to process challenging emotions.

Emotional regulation proves to be a valuable tool for overall mental well-being and for nurturing and establishing healthy relationships.

When you refine this skill, it empowers you to:

- Achieve a sense of balance and control over your emotional reactions
- Stay composed in the face of challenging situations
- Effectively manage stress

- Safeguard significant connections
- Actively listen to the needs of others
- Express your needs in constructive ways
- Maintain professionalism in work-related scenarios
- Avoid taking things personally

(Psych Central, 2022)

Ways to self-regulate

Breathing

Controlled breathing practices informed by ancient spiritual traditions such as yoga and Tai Chi have been used to rebalance emotions and reduce stress in the long term. There are also short-term benefits of controlled breathing, as in Lamaze breathing for childbirth, which enhances relaxation and decreases pain perception, or in acute amelioration of panic attacks (Ashhad et al., 2022). A single deep breath can relieve everyday anxiety.

Moving

Theories of emotion say that our feelings come from how our body reacts. Darwin and James first talked about this idea in the 1800s. Damasio, a neuroscientist, later explained it using brain and body signals. He said that emotions happen when our body tells our brain what's happening inside, like how we feel physically and what our muscles and joints are doing. This creates patterns in our brain that show our emotions, even if we're not aware of them. When you move more, like when you exercise harder or longer, it affects your body in many ways. It makes your heartbeat faster and changes how your body uses energy. This causes physical changes, such as alterations in the levels of hormones, neurotransmitters, trophic factors, endocannabinoids, and immune system function. These changes help improve your mood and make you feel less stressed, anxious, and sad (Shafir, 2016).

Reframing

Reframing your thoughts and focusing on positives involves changing the way you view situations and intentionally directing your attention towards the good aspects of life. It's about shifting your perspective from negative to positive, which can have a powerful impact on your mental well-being and overall outlook on life.

Instead of dwelling on the negatives or what's going wrong, reframing encourages you to look for silver linings, opportunities for growth, and reasons to be grateful. It doesn't mean ignoring or denying the challenges you face but rather choosing to approach them with a more optimistic mindset.

One way to reframe your thoughts is by practicing gratitude. This involves consciously acknowledging and appreciating the positive aspects of your life, no matter how small they may seem. Keeping a gratitude journal, where you write down things that you're thankful for each day, can help cultivate a more positive outlook.

Another strategy is to challenge negative thoughts and replace them with more positive and realistic ones. This involves questioning the validity of your negative beliefs and actively replacing them with more balanced and empowering thoughts. For example, instead of thinking, 'I'll never be able to do this', you can reframe it as 'I may face challenges, but I have the skills and resources to overcome them'.

Overall, reframing your thoughts and focusing on positives can help improve your mood, reduce stress, and build resilience in the face of life's challenges. It's a skill that can be developed with practice and can have a transformative effect on your overall well-being.

Workplace culture

The Teacher Wellbeing Index reports that 42% of staff feel that their organisation's culture is having a negative impact on their well-being.

School culture is defined as the values, attitudes, and behavioural norms that are created and shared by school members, including students, teachers, and other staff (Fu et al., 2022).

There is no doubt that the culture where you work can have a huge impact on your well-being. But how do you know if the culture is negative or even toxic, and what can you do about it?

Red flags

Identifying a toxic workplace culture can involve recognising various signs and patterns that indicate unhealthy dynamics and behaviours. Here are some common indicators that a workplace may have a toxic culture:

Lack of open communication: In a toxic culture, there may be a lack of open communication channels, with employees feeling hesitant or unable to voice their concerns, opinions, or ideas without fear of repercussions. Communication may be one-sided or dominated by a select few individuals.

High staff turnover: Constant turnover of staff can be a red flag indicating dissatisfaction and instability within the workplace. If staff frequently leave the organisation, it may suggest underlying issues with leadership, management, or the overall work environment.

Micromanagement: Excessive micromanagement and a lack of trust in staff's abilities to perform their tasks can create a stressful and demoralising work environment. Staff may feel disempowered and undervalued, leading to decreased morale and productivity.

Lack of transparency: A toxic workplace culture may lack transparency in decision-making processes, promotions, performance evaluations, and other important aspects of management. This lack of transparency can lead to feelings of distrust and resentment among the staff.

Negative gossip and rumours: A toxic workplace often fosters an environment of gossip, rumours, and negativity. Staff may engage in backstabbing, spreading false information, or forming cliques, creating a divisive and unhealthy atmosphere.

Bullying or harassment: Instances of bullying, harassment, or discrimination in the workplace are clear signs of a toxic culture. This behaviour creates a hostile and unsafe environment for staff and is often indicative of deeper systemic issues within the school or organisation.

Lack of work-life balance: A toxic culture may prioritise work over staff's well-being, leading to a lack of work-life balance. This can manifest in long hours, unrealistic expectations, and pressure to constantly be available, resulting in burnout and decreased job satisfaction.

Resistance to change: A toxic workplace culture may be resistant to change and innovation, with staff and management clinging to outdated practices and resisting new ideas. This stagnation can hinder growth and development within the school or organisation.

Blame-shifting and lack of accountability: In a toxic culture, there may be a pervasive culture of blame-shifting, with staff and management unwilling to take responsibility for mistakes or failures. This lack of accountability can lead to a culture of fear and avoidance of risk-taking.

It's important to note that negative and toxic workplace cultures can vary and may not include all of these signs.

Ways to improve workplace culture

Improving the culture in your school or organisation is not a quick fix, particularly if you are not in a leadership position. However, there are steps you can take to improve things for yourself and others around you:

Lead by example: Demonstrate positive behaviours and attitudes in your interactions with colleagues. Treat others with respect, kindness, and empathy, and strive to maintain a positive attitude even in challenging situations.

Build relationships: Take the initiative to build positive relationships with your coworkers. Get to know them on a personal level, show genuine interest in their well-being, and offer support when needed. Building strong relationships fosters a sense of community and camaraderie in the workplace.

Communicate effectively: Practice open and honest communication with your colleagues. Be proactive in sharing information, listening actively to others, and providing constructive feedback. Clear and transparent communication promotes trust and collaboration among team members.

Support your team: Offer support and assistance to your colleagues whenever possible. Be willing to lend a helping hand, share knowledge and expertise, and collaborate on projects. Supporting your colleagues fosters a sense of teamwork and camaraderie, leading to a more positive work environment.

Promote positivity: Foster a positive atmosphere by focusing on solutions rather than problems. Avoid participating in gossip or negative conversations, and instead, highlight achievements, express gratitude, and celebrate successes. Positivity is contagious and can uplift the mood of the entire workplace.

Be inclusive: Promote inclusivity and diversity in the workplace by respecting and valuing the perspectives and experiences of all colleagues. Foster an environment where everyone feels welcome, included, and valued for their unique contributions.

Seek opportunities for growth: Take advantage of opportunities for learning and development to enhance your skills and knowledge. Pursue professional development opportunities, attend training sessions, and seek feedback to improve yourself continuously and contribute more effectively to the workplace.

Participate in workplace initiatives: Get involved in workplace initiatives, events, and activities that promote a positive culture. Volunteer for committees, participate in team-building exercises, and contribute ideas for improving workplace morale and engagement.

No matter what your position, you can make a positive impact on workplace culture. Your actions and attitudes not only support your own well-being but can influence those around you and contribute to creating a more positive and supportive work environment for everyone.

Myth: Personal well-being is the absence of negative emotions or stress.

Truth: Personal well-being does not mean being happy all the time or never experiencing stress. It involves acknowledging and accepting a range of emotions, including negative ones, and developing coping strategies to manage stress effectively.

Myth: Personal well-being is only about physical health.

Truth: Personal well-being encompasses physical, mental, emotional, and social aspects of health. It involves finding a balance across these dimensions and taking care of oneself holistically.

Myth: If someone is smiling and seems happy, they are okay.

Truth: While a smile and outward appearance of happiness can be indicators of well-being, they do not always reflect a person's true emotional state or mental health. Many individuals may smile or put on a happy facade even when they are struggling with internal challenges, such as stress, anxiety, or depression. It's important to look beyond surface-level appearances and engage in genuine conversations to understand how someone is truly feeling and offer support if needed.

Resources

Employee Assistance Programs (EAPs): Many schools and educational institutions offer EAPs, which provide confidential counselling and support services to employees, including teachers. EAPs typically offer a range of resources, such as counselling sessions, mental health assessments, and referrals to additional services if needed.

Occupational Health Services: Occupational health services are available in many workplaces, including schools, to support employees in managing their health and well-being. These services may include health assessments, advice on managing work-related stress, and access to mental health support services.

Trade Unions: Trade unions representing teachers, such as the National Education Union (NEU) and the Association of Teachers and Lecturers (ATL), often provide support and advice on workplace issues, including well-being and mental health. They may offer resources, guidance, and advocacy for teachers experiencing difficulties in the workplace.

Professional Development Programs: Some professional development programs for teachers include components focused on well-being and mental health. These programs may provide training and resources to help teachers develop strategies for managing stress, maintaining work-life balance, and promoting their own well-being.

Online resources and helplines: Various online resources and helplines are available to provide support and information to teachers experiencing mental health difficulties or seeking advice on well-being. Organisations such as Mind and the Samaritans offer helplines, online resources, and information on mental health support services.

Local Authority Support: Local authorities may offer support services for teachers working in schools within their area. This support may include access to counselling services, well-being workshops, and guidance on managing work-related stress.

Peer Support Networks: Peer support networks, such as staff well-being groups or mentorship programs within schools, can provide teachers with opportunities to connect with colleagues, share experiences, and offer mutual support. Peer support can be an important source of emotional support and encouragement for teachers.

GP and NHS Services: Teachers can also access support for their mental health and well-being through their local General Practitioner (GP) or National Health Service (NHS) services. GPs can provide assessments, referrals to specialist services, and access to psychological therapies such as counselling or cognitive behavioural therapy (CBT).

References

Ashhad, S., Kam, K., Del Negro, C.A. and Feldman, J.L. (2022). Breathing rhythm and pattern and their influence on emotion. *Annual Review of Neuroscience*, 45(1), pp. 223–247.

Cameron, H.A. and Schoenfeld, T.J. (2018). Behavioral and structural adaptations to stress. *Frontiers in Neuroendocrinology*, 49, pp. 106–113. https://doi.org/10.1016/j.yfrne.2018.02.002

CMI. (2020). *The difference between mastering and managing time*. [online] Available at: https://www.managers.org.uk/knowledge-and-insights/blog/difference-between-mastering-and-managing-time/

Fu, C., Zhao, Z., Wang, H., Ouyang, M., Mao, X., Cai, X. and Tan, X. (2022). How perceived school culture relates to work engagement among primary and secondary school teachers? Roles of affective empathy and job tenure. *Frontiers in Psychology*, 11 Aug. 13, p. 878894. https://doi.org/10.3389/fpsyg.2022.878894. PMID: 36033005; PMCID: PMC9407979.

Grahn, P., Ottosson, J. and Uvnäs-Moberg, K. (2021). The oxytocinergic system as a mediator of anti-stress and instorative effects induced by nature: The calm and connection theory. *Frontiers in Psychology*, 12. https://doi.org/10.3389/fpsyg.2021.617814

Holland, K. (2019). Amygdala hijack: When emotion takes over. *Healthline*. [online] Available at: https://www.healthline.com/health/stress/amygdala-hijack

Lu, D. (2022). Music improves wellbeing and quality of life, research suggests. *The Guardian*. [online] Available at: https://www.theguardian.com/australia-news/2022/mar/24/music-improves-wellbeing-and-quality-of-life-research-suggests

McEwen, B.S., Gray, J. and Nasca, C. (2015). Recognizing resilience: Learning from the effects of stress on the brain. *Neurobiol Stress*, 1, pp. 1–11. https://doi.org/10.1016/j.ynstr.2014.09.00

Osório, C., Probert, T., Jones, E., Young, A.H. and Robbins, I. (2016). Adapting to stress: Understanding the neurobiology of resilience. *Behavioral Medicine*. https://doi.org/10.1080/08964289.2016.1170661

Psych Central. (2022). *Emotional regulation skills: Learn how to manage your emotions*. [online] Available at: https://psychcentral.com/health/emotional-regulation

Rayes, A. (2022). *13 personal effectiveness skills you need to master*. [online] One Education. Available at: https://www.oneeducation.org.uk/personal-effectiveness/

Shafir, T. (2016). Using movement to regulate emotion: Neurophysiological findings and their application in psychotherapy. *Frontiers Psychology*. 23 Sep. 7, p. 1451. https://doi.org/10.3389/fpsyg.2016.01451. PMID: 27721801; PMCID: PMC5033979.

The Teacher Wellbeing Index 2023. (n.d.). *Education support*. [online] Available at: https://www.education support.org.uk

www.sciencedirect.com. (n.d.). *Burnout – an overview | ScienceDirect Topics*. [online] Available at: https://www.sciencedirect.com/topics/social-sciences/burnout.

www.ualberta.ca. (n.d.). *Personal effectiveness | Human resources, health, safety and environment*. [online] Available at: https://www.ualberta.ca/human-resources-health-safety-environment/learning-and-development/workplace-skills/personal-effectiveness.html#:~:text=Personal%20effectiveness%20enhances%20performance%2C%20supports

24 The importance of a mentor or coach

Chapter introduction

What is mentoring? What is coaching? What do these terms mean, and what do they look like in terms of education and teaching? This final chapter encourages you to consider how you can either benefit from the support of a mentor or coach on your own career journey or perhaps whether you may wish to upskill into being a mentor or coach for others within your school or setting and the benefits that this role may bring to you also. This chapter also discusses Action Learning as a way for all educators to support themselves and others in problem-solving when we are faced with difficult situations through posing reflective questions that help us dig deeper to find pathways and solutions to move forward. Contributions from Sam Crome and Jocelyn Pryce offer further thought on coaching and kind leadership within this final chapter.

Communication and reflection

Hopefully, the one thing that is clear from reading this book is that often, the best solution to work out problems, support our students, and achieve more is through being open to communicating our thoughts and feelings with each other. Talking to others around us can help us find strategies we may not have thought of and encourages us to develop empathy and compassion as we consider things from another person's perspective. The most purposeful part of communication, however, can be that the process of reflection is encouraged in ourselves when we put thoughts into words. Reflection can be defined as a thinking journey that allows us to find clarity in an initially cloudy situation (Clarà, 2015).

Because reflection is often best without the input of advice and suggestions from others, we can see that finding a coach or mentor who understands the role of listener as their key appointment can be incredibly valuable in our education careers as these conversations will facilitate space for both communication and reflection, but without cloudiness from someone else's thoughts and feelings. Such spaces can also be created through Action Learning Sets, based on Reg Revans' (2017) concept of 'action learning'.

Action learning and action learning sets

Mumford (1996) advocates that one of the key bonuses of action learning is that it promotes the reframing of a problem through the challenging, reflective questions asked on the quest

DOI: 10.4324/9781032697932-24

for a solution. The additional benefit is that the problems brought to action learning sets are real-world problems, not fictional case studies; the discussions and reflections that take place may truly lead to purposeful action and transformational results. An action learning set involves a group composed of a range of people, usually around six or seven people per group, where one person (the speaker) talks for five minutes about a problem or dilemma they are having. After they have spoken without interruption for five minutes, the rest of the group can ask any clarification questions if needed for extra detail and information. Once any clarification questions have been asked, each member of the action learning set asks a question to the speaker in turn. The speaker can then choose to either respond to the question or pass on the question. This repeats until no members of the set have any further questions to ask or when the speaker feels satisfied that they have reflected sufficiently on their problem and the next steps they will take.

When action learning sets are not available, finding a person to be a coach or mentor is another positive way to make space for reflection.

Coaching and mentoring

How would you define these two terms? Do you think they mean the same thing or different things? Have you ever been a coach or mentor yourself, or been on the receiving end of coaching or mentoring as a 'coachee' or 'mentee'?

In the following contribution by Sam Crome, Director of Education and Deputy Head-teacher, we consider the similarities and differences between these concepts and what good coaching should look like.

Coaching, by Sam Crome

Teaching is a multi-faceted, layered profession, one which you will hopefully be part of for many years. It can even be described as vocation; a noble calling to apply your knowledge, skills, and desire to do good. But if we are going to provide years of service for children, we must be part of a systematic approach to help teachers discuss, think, grow, and evaluate. They must be given the time and resources to nourish their own professional development and well-being.

Coaching and mentoring are two wonderful tools to fulfil the needs of teachers. Working with a colleague 1:1 to help their development and thinking is a wonderful gift. Sir John Whitmore describes it perfectly: 'Coaching is unlocking people's potential to maximise their own performance' (2017).

Coaching throws up all sorts of problems through its name alone, though, which can make it confusing. Across sports, the corporate world, and education, to name just a few, coaching is defined in different ways. Let's try to understand what it can look like.

MylesDowney (2003) describes how coaching and mentoring can sit on a continuum. On the right side, we have a non-directive approach, which might include asking questions, listening, summarising, and giving space for the coachee to think. The line moves along to the left side, which includes more directive approaches, for example, giving advice, suggesting, instructing, etc., which might be more aligned with what we often think of as mentoring.

At various times in your career, you may be coached or mentored or, indeed, may coach or mentor others somewhere along this continuum. For novices, we often find that the directive side of the continuum can be useful, whereby less experienced or knowledgeable staff may be advised and guided while they are coached. For those looking to develop professionally or a skilled teacher looking to improve their craft, we may move further to the left of the continuum with fewer bits of advice and more questions.

It's important for us to understand the range of this continuum so that we can coach and be coached appropriately for what we need in that conversation. There is no one way to coach or mentor. This is no right or wrong way. Every conversation has a different require-ment; our job is to make sure that every experience and conversation unlock their potential as effectively as possible.

Here's why I think coaching is so important for us as teachers:

Time and space: our busy work lives mean that we rarely stop to reflect and think. Coach-ing is dedicated time to do just that. With a trained, trusted colleague, you can start to con-sider and evaluate, with no emails or marking to distract you!

Solution-focused: most coaches use a conversation structure, or coaching model, which identifies challenges and works through options until viable solutions are put forward. This structure allows the coachee to work through an issue and come out of the conversation with strategies and ideas to move forward with.

New perspective: the best coaches ask carefully crafted questions and summarise or paraphrase to reflect the coachee's words back to them; whichever tools the coach uses, it's likely they will help you consider things in a new light.

Growth: the benefit of someone regularly thinking and discussing things is that they make huge progress with their experience and expertise. There is growing research to show the impact that coaching can have on staff to improve their well-being, performance, and growth.

While coaching is a nuanced practice that takes years to craft, there are core coaching skills that are invaluable in coaching conversations, as well as in helping your colleagues grow in other contexts. The basics of coaching can be applied to any professional conversa-tion, and according to Christian van Nieuwerburgh's *An Introduction to Coaching Skills* (2017), these include:

- Listening well to encourage thinking
- Asking powerful questions
- Paraphrasing and summarising
- Giving and receiving feedback

Explore each of these skills in depth will help you both understand how to be coached and how to coach others.

Michael Bungay Stanier (2016) helps us with our questions in his fantastic book, The Coaching Habit. He outlines seven key coaching questions that you could try in a coaching conversation, with a colleague more informally, or when you are doing some self coaching. These are:

1.   What is on your mind?
2.   And what else?

3.   What is the real challenge here for you?
4.   What do you want?
5.   If you're saying 'yes' to this, what must you say 'no' to?
6.   How can I help? (I prefer 'How can coaching help?')
7.   What is most useful or valuable here for you?

What you'll notice about these questions, and indeed any other good coaching question, is that they are open questions. They encourage deep thinking. They push you to think critically about your own practice.

So, what next? If you're a new teacher, you'll likely experience coaching during your ECF programme, to help you make great strides forward with your teaching and professional development. If your school has a further coaching programme, I urge you to sign up and continue your coaching journey further. Beyond that, the best CPD I ever did was learning how to coaching; it has helped me and others. Find a good coaching course and immerse yourself in the world of coaching!

***

In this second contribution, Jocelyn Pryce, Deputy Head of School, reminds us of the value of leading with kindness.

What costs nothing but can be priceless?, by Jocelyn Pryce

Reflecting on my career, there are several insights I wish I had early on, the most powerful one being the value of kindness. Having experienced a less than direct path into educational leadership I have already been exposed to the transformative power of kindness in other settings, including healthcare, and I have been able to draw on that to inform my various roles in education. I have been incredibly lucky in that I have been mentored by some of the kindest people I know, and I have invested a great deal of time in modelling the behaviours I have seen them exhibit. Conversely, I have experienced behaviours from some for whom kindness is not a priority and, always keen to reflect and learn from every experience, I distance myself from modelling those.

Traditional leadership training, and educational leadership in particular, is often based on strategic planning, management, and academic proficiency, with the value of kindness in leadership frequently overlooked. It is often considered a soft skill, not always recognised and rarely prioritised, but it should be considered a fundamental attribute of effective leadership in any setting. It extends beyond individual interactions and is able to create a culture that fosters growth, resilience, and success.

At its core, kindness embodies empathy, compassion, and concern for the well-being of others, regardless of whether they are pupils, colleagues, or direct reports. We can exhibit kindness by being active listeners and making concerted efforts to understand the perspectives, concerns, and aspirations of others by generating genuine dialogue and showing empathy.

In pupil-teacher relationships, kindness takes on a multi-faceted influencing role, building personal resilience as well as academic performance. Teachers who model kindness create classrooms that are safe spaces, allowing freedom of expression, exploration, and learning and acknowledging the diverse needs of their pupils. Compassionate educators tailor their teaching approach to provide the right amount of support and encouragement when and where it is most needed. They are finely tuned to the needs of their pupils and are flexible in accommodating them. The benefits of creating an environment of this kind are pupils who demonstrate higher levels of academic engagement, attainment, motivation, and well-being. Immersion in an environment of this kind encourages pupils to become empathetic and inspires growth into socially responsible adults who are committed to contributing in a positive way to society. In this context, kindness becomes a catalyst for meaningful change and the development of future leaders.

In managerial roles, kindness can manifest itself in transparent communication, inclusive decision-making processes, and a safe and supportive approach to problem-solving. Kind leaders recognise the strengths of their team members and are supportive during times of challenge, initiating constructive responses to enable the team to handle it with empathy and cooperation. The relationship they foster is one of trust and collaboration. Relationships of this kind can be invaluable in combatting the effects of bullying or harassment, and the kind leader is able to take advantage of early intervention points to prevent escalation or relationship breakdown, resulting in higher job satisfaction, strong morale, and high retention rates.

Kindness between colleagues can foster environments in which educators report greater job fulfilment, increased resilience, and lower stress levels. We see evidence of mutual respect and a collegiate and collaborative approach to challenges in an environment where personal development, self-reflection, and respect for others are paramount. One of the most profound lessons I have learned is that it serves as a catalyst for building a culture of support and empowerment, a place of safety. Compassionate leaders are attuned to the needs of others, and small acts of kindness can build a culture of empathy. Recognition and celebration of achievements, providing constructive feedback, and offering mentorship opportunities are all indicative of leadership with kindness at its heart.

Kindness should not be considered a sign of weakness, especially in leadership; it should, conversely, be viewed as a source of strength and a skill which should be nurtured. I have come to realise that embracing my vulnerability is a sign of authentic leadership and the embodiment of kindness. Leaders who are gracious in acknowledging their limitations and seeking support from others foster an environment where openness and authenticity are valued. By modelling vulnerability, leaders inspire trust and build deeper connections with their colleagues. Kind leaders can foster a culture of trust, collaboration, safety, and belonging, and these traits lay the foundation for both academic excellence and individual personal growth. Leaders who prioritise kindness advocate for equity, diversity, and inclusivity across the board, fostering an environment where every individual feels valued and empowered to succeed.

As I reflect on my own journey, I recognise the profound impact that kindness has had on my leadership style and the transformative potential it holds in shaping the future. I strive to embody its principles in all aspects of my work, and I look for opportunities to model the behaviours and support the growth and development of others. As I continue to navigate the complexities of educational leadership, I aspire to lead with kindness, empathy, and commitment to embracing and nurturing the potential of others. Kindness costs nothing; its impact can be priceless.

Myth 1: People only need the help of a coach or mentor if they are struggling.

Truth: No, coaches and mentors can be useful for anyone at any point in their career, regardless of their competency or role. Coaching can help us reflect on goals we want to set, and mentoring can help guide us on how to move forward and upward. Even managers and leaders can benefit from coaching or mentoring.

Myth: Coaching and mentoring are the same thing.

Truth: Coaching and mentoring can sit on a continuum. On the right side, we have a non-directive approach, which might include asking questions, listening, summarising, and giving space for the coachee to think. The line moves along to the left side, which includes more directive approaches, for example, giving advice, suggesting, instructing, etc., which might be more aligned with what we often think of as mentoring.

Myth: Good leaders need to prioritise strategic planning.

Truth: Whilst planning and the bigger picture are essential for leaders, we must not forget the human element and the transformational power of those in leadership positions. Leaders also need to promote kindness, compassion, and empathy.

References

Bungay Stanier, M. (2016). *The coaching habit: Say less, ask more, and change the way you lead forever.* Toronto: Box of Crayons Press.

Clarà, M. (2015). What is reflection? Looking for clarity in an ambiguous notion. *Journal of Teacher Education*, 66(3), pp. 261–271. Available at: https://journals.sagepub.com/doi/full/10.1177/0022487114552028?casa_token=v-ern4URPuQAAAAA%3AUOdaE6QcGvcrYeTOMTVAROyfScLBcQzOa8OlanJ15LNsTwrPZ5miZlBvdMQcUSL29pLGlgkBep4l

Downey, M. (2003). *Effective coaching: Lessons from the coach's coach.* New York: Texere.

Mumford, A. (1996). Effective learners in action learning sets. *Employee Councelling Today*, 8(6), pp. 3–10. Available at: https://www.emerald.com/insight/content/doi/10.1108/13665629610150126/full/html?casa_token=qFOCCT6_2LYAAAAA:Et_cx1cR6ODhkJYA1Wu1kPZmTeJ9VW7i6KyrYg8LvdRHeThPfgvAYoGCQUo-ZoBqbdxjRMZ-rdnnUPKLmgFMVsy8lLAZczYcOjMfCbQwcKvSr_1_Lyg

Revans, R. (2017). *ABC of action learning.* Abingdon, UK: Routledge.

Van Nieuwerburgh, C. (2017). *An introduction to coaching skills, a practical guide.* London: Sage.

Whitmore, J. (2017). *Coaching for performance.* Boston: Nicholas Brealey.

Index

Printed in the United States
by Baker & Taylor Publisher Services